Well THAT Was Funny

Chicken Soup for the Soul: Well That Was Funny
101 Feel Good Stories
Amy Newmark

Published by Chicken Soup for the Soul, LLC www.chickensoup.com
Copyright ©2023 by Chicken Soup for the Soul, LLC. All Rights Reserved.

The publisher gratefully acknowledges the many publishers and individuals who granted Chicken Soup for the Soul permission to reprint the cited material.

Front cover photo courtesy of iStockphoto.com (©Linas Toleikis)
Back cover and interior photo courtesy of iStockphoto.com (©Dgwildlife)
Photo of Amy Newmark courtesy of Susan Morrow at SwickPix

Cover and Interior by Daniel Zaccari

Publisher's Cataloging-in-Publication data

Names: Newmark, Amy, editor.
Title: Chicken soup for the soul : well that was funny , 101 feel good stories /
    Amy Newmark.
Description: Cos Cob, CT: Chicken Soup for the Soul, LLC, 2023.
Identifiers: LCCN: 2023930652 | ISBN: 978-1-61159-101-9 (print) |
    978-1-61159-338-9 (ebook)
Subjects: LCSH American wit and humor. | Humor. | Anecdotes. | BISAC HUMOR /
General | HUMOR / Form / Anecdotes & Quotations | HUMOR / Form / Essays
Classification: LCC PN6165 .C47 2023 | DDC 817.6--dc23

Library of Congress Control Number: 2023930652

PRINTED IN THE UNITED STATES OF AMERICA
on acid∞free paper

30 29 28 27 26 25 24 23   01 02 03 04 05 06 07 08 09

Well THAT Was Funny

101 Feel Good Stories

Amy Newmark

Chicken Soup for the Soul, LLC
Cos Cob, CT

Changing your life one story at a time®
www.chickensoup.com

Table of Contents

❶

~I Can't Believe I Did That!~

❷

~Wild Kingdom~

❸
~Domestic Disasters~

❹
~Family Fun?~

❺
~Marital Mishaps~

❻

~Adventures in Living~

❼

~Mistaken Identity~

9

~That Was Embarrassing~

10

~Pawsitive Thinking~

⑪

~Senior Moments~

Chapter 1

I Can't Believe I Did That!

The Envelope, Please!

To make mistakes is human; to stumble is
commonplace; to be able to laugh
at yourself is maturity.
~William Arthur Ward

A co-worker invited my husband and me to his son's wedding reception. We'd worked in the same office with the gentleman for several years. Although neither of us had met his son, we felt like we knew him from listening to his dad talk about him so often.

We arrived at the banquet center and walked into a gorgeously decorated ballroom. I glanced around for fellow co-workers, hoping they'd saved us a seat, but didn't recognize a soul.

Scanning the room again, I zeroed in on the gift table, its beautifully wrapped boxes, and a miniature antique white trunk for wedding cards. I walked over and stuffed my envelope into the slot before joining my husband at the open bar. We enjoyed cocktails and helped ourselves to mouth-watering appetizers: prosciutto-wrapped asparagus, caprese skewers with balsamic dipping sauce, and crab-stuffed mushrooms.

The wedding party waltzed in, and the beaming couple greeted guests as they made their way to the head table filled with fragrant floral arrangements. The groom shook hands with us, cracked a corny joke, and thanked us both for sharing their special day.

My husband remarked, "You sure look like your dad."

I nodded in agreement and added, "Same personality, too."

The bride smiled knowingly. "That's what they all say."

We found two seats at an empty table and then joined the long buffet line that stretched past an open doorway. I looked up just as a woman from our office and her significant other walked by. Stepping out of line, I craned my neck and watched them enter the ballroom down the hall.

In a slight panic, I tugged on my husband's sleeve. "Honey," I whispered, "we're at the wrong reception!"

He shook his head and grinned. "I never thought of you as a wedding crasher."

"How was I supposed to know there were two banquet rooms? Follow me."

As we slunk toward the exit, he asked, "What about the card?"

"Shhh! Someone might hear you," I warned before sheepishly making my way to the gift table. My eyes flicked left and right, waiting for the coast to clear. Hands shaking and looking as guilty as Eve after she'd taken a bite of the apple, I tried to lift the metal clasp on the vintage trunk. It wouldn't budge. I leaned in closer and bumped a tall, thin box covered with sparkling silver paper, causing it to topple forward. From out of nowhere, a sawed-off shotgun of a man with a salt-and-pepper crew cut and sporting a tuxedo appeared by my side and caught the present before it hit the floor.

Raising an eyebrow, he asked in a gruff voice, "Is there something I can help you with?"

Busted! When all else fails, tell the truth. Faster than a magician whipping a rabbit out of a hat, I pulled the invitation from my purse. By the time I finished explaining that I'd already placed my card in the trunk before I realized we were at the wrong reception, Buzz Cut's icy stare had slowly melted.

He unlatched the lid and chuckled. "My son and his new wife will get a kick out of this."

Heat crept from my neck to my cheeks as I dug through the pile looking for the one with the wrong "Mr. & Mrs." scrawled across the top. After what seemed like forever, I found the envelope and held it up for inspection. Then I rushed over to join my partner-in-crime who'd conveniently hidden his six-foot-five frame behind a pseudo-marble column. I grabbed his hand and said, "Come on, Clyde. Let's make our getaway."

"Right behind you, Bonnie. I just hope we make it in time for the main course."

— Alice Muschany —

Might as Well Jump

Why must this be so mortifying?
Oh, that's right. Because it's my life.
~Tessa Dare, Romancing the Duke

My parents followed an unwavering routine, probably because the alternative was killing each other. When my father retired after forty years as a fireman, he had no idea he would be venturing behind enemy lines as he had as a teenager in World War II. But to my mother, his retirement was an invasion, and an invasion by a barbarian at that.

She had a point.

I was still living at home and had begun my first job just months before my father retired. It wasn't long before the calls from my mother commenced to my office.

"Mary, will you tell your father I am NOT going to raise chickens in our house?"

"Mary, tell your father I will NOT cook squirrels."

"Mary, your father gave me a black eye chasing away blackbirds."

Yes, fed up with the bird poop continually coating his parked car, my father had thrown a broomstick at the birds roosting in the tree above. But instead of warning his wife to "look out," he yelled, "Look up!"

In the background of these phone calls, I would hear my father muttering, "Aw, hell, I'm going to Ace Hardware." This would give my mother a brief respite, but I was convinced that I would eventually see my parents on *Unsolved Mysteries* — one disappeared and the other claiming no knowledge.

Fortunately, during this time, my first nephew — their first grandchild — made his triumphant entrance into the world, followed quickly by five siblings. My parents began babysitting six days a week, and the energy that had been focused on throttling each other was now directed toward caring for children.

But while kids bring unpredictability to most families, my nieces and nephews reached out their tiny hands and led my adoring parents into a hypnotic routine: Mondays, Kids' Club; Tuesdays, the zoo; Wednesdays, violin lessons; Thursdays, story hour; Fridays, the Lodge; Saturdays, the Y. All peppered with Cheerios, grilled cheese, and *Barney*. My parents would arrive at my brother's house punctually at 7:10 A.M., but they would begin their day with robotic precision long before.

My father would rise each morning by 3:00, trudge down to the basement, and walk back and forth the length of our short house for three miles a day. His only diversion was the battered, yellow transistor radio that he would hold close to his deafened ear and from which he would derive a unique interpretation of the news that could only come from hearing every third word.

While pacing for three miles in a tight space might be unnerving to most, it came naturally to my father. As a child, his mother would tie him to a table leg to keep him from wandering off. Walking in circles brought back warm memories of home.

My mother would be up by 4:50 a.m., fixing the breakfast they would consume well before 5:30 so they could take Communion at 6:30 Mass. With three cups of black coffee to fuel her 5'8", 115-pound frame, she would hand-wash the dishes, mix bread, and be ready to leave the house with my father at 6:18. By the time my alarm rang at 6:45, I would have the lone bathroom to myself and could hurriedly get dressed for work.

But, one morning, I was startled awake by a ferocious slam that rattled my bed and dresser. From the living room came the sound of drawers being wrested from the breakfront, riffled through, and shoved back in place. *Dammit, Dad,* I thought. *The rest of us don't want to get up at 3:00 A.M.* I punched my pillow and flipped over to squint at my alarm clock, which was still quivering from the aftershocks. 6:38 A.M. 6:38! That wasn't Dad! It was someone who knew my parents would be gone!

I scrambled to my knees, clutching the sheets to my chest, and cringed as the bed creaked loudly. Heavy footsteps fell in the hallway, followed by one closet door squeaking open, then another. My eyes desperately combed the room for a weapon and settled on the bottle of hair spray. I slid out of bed, grabbed the bottle, and slipped behind my closed door. But as I raised the hair spray into firing position, it occurred to me that it was a pump. Great, when the intruder entered my room, I'd spritz him with a gentle, welcoming mist.

The footsteps drew closer but mercifully turned into my parents' bedroom across the hall, where again I heard drawers yanked open, change jingling, and papers rustling. I knew my room was next. I had only one option left. I sprinted on tiptoe to my eternally stuck window, unlocked it, and heaved it open with herculean strength. Easing up the storm window, I slid my rear end onto the sill and swung my bent legs through the opening with all the grace of an elephant being born. As the metal window frame cut into my derriere, I leapt the four feet to the front lawn and let the storm window fall back down behind me.

I quickly stepped out of sight of the window and stood there, bare toes digging into the cool, dewy grass. *Now what?* I scanned my neighbors' homes but saw no signs of life. *Where do I run? Is the intruder alone, or does he have an accomplice waiting to shoot me as I run past the corner of my house?* Summoning all the stealth tactics I'd learned from *Starsky and Hutch*, I crept along the cold brick wall and peeked tremulously around the corner. No one was there. With a burst of bravery, I decided to continue circling the house to "case the joint." Okay, truth be told, it wasn't bravery. I was just less afraid of getting shot than of showing up on my neighbor's doorstep in my "pajamas" — circa 1980, butt-hugging gym shorts and a faded Han Solo T-shirt.

Crouching well below the windows, I advanced to the back corner of the house with a strut that resembled a headless chicken. Around the corner, fifteen feet from my hiding place, protruded the windowed porch that my parents had added before I was born. If anyone was inside, they would see my approach. Perceiving no movement, I lunged across the yard and dove against the cold, concrete base of the porch. I lay there, covering my mouth to keep my heart from popping out. Finally, I crawled on my elbows, peeked around the corner... and spied my parents' car in the driveway.

"Aw, hell." I lumbered to my feet, sauntered around the porch and up the concrete steps, and flung open the back door. My mother, seated at the porch table writing checks, swung around in surprise. "Where have *you* been?" she asked.

I countered with exasperation, "Why aren't you at Mass?!"

"Grandparents' Mass is at 8:00 A.M. We're going then," she explained.

"Who's been rummaging through the drawers?" I whimpered.

"I was trying to find my checkbook."

— Mary Kay —

Going to Pot

Never say never! I'm open to trying new things.
~Miranda Kerr

Feeling like someone parked a refrigerator on your head is no way to start the day. But when I got out of bed yesterday, I recognized the onset of seasonal allergies. My sinuses were throbbing, and it hurt to breathe. When my mom called, the first thing she said was, "You sound like you have a cold. Better take some vitamin C."

I sniffled. "Definitely allergies. Other than a pressure headache, I feel fine."

"Do you have a neti pot?" she asked. "A whatti pot?"

"A neti pot. To flush your sinuses."

As she talked, I did a quick Internet search. Phrases like "nasal irrigation" and "sinus washing" popped up on the screen, along with several images. It looked harmless enough, like a tiny teapot from a child's toy box. When I clicked a how-to-use link, I was grossed out by the gallery of visual instructions. Basically, you pour the contents of the teapot up your nose. The solution runs in one nostril and out the other, like a demented garden fountain.

"I'm looking at pictures online," I told Mom. "Ick! Why would anyone do that to themselves?"

"Because it works. I have a couple extras if you want one."

"Eww!"

"They're not used." She laughed. "New, in the box. I can drop one off tomorrow."

"Sure," I said, not saying aloud what I was thinking. *Why do you have multiple pots? For gift-giving purposes? In case you're invited to a tea party?* But I didn't question her generous offer. Instead, I told myself it's just what moms do. They buy extras of essential items — just in case. You never know when a loved one will need to have their nose irrigated.

This morning, when she dropped off the neti pot, I thanked her but declined her offer to show me how to use it. "I draw the line at live demonstrations," I told her. She was still giggling when she disappeared out the front door.

I took "Ned" from its package and turned it over in my hands. Then I reboxed it, not feeling brave enough to attempt the disgustingly impossible. But, by 2:00, I was desperate for relief and decided it was time to stop being such a baby.

I filled the little teapot with warm, distilled water and stirred in a packet of the enclosed powder. Then, I stood at the bathroom sink with Ned in one hand and printed directions in the other. The pamphlet said to lean over the sink, look toward the drain, and then tilt my head to forty-five degrees. Open mouth slightly to allow airflow and prevent solution from backwashing into the throat and mouth. I remembered what a lousy multi-tasker I was and almost chickened out.

I took a deep breath, leaned forward and tilted my head. As the little blue pot came close to my face, my peripheral vision noticed something. I straightened and examined the spout. What sicko designed this thing!? It looked like a… well, let's just say it was anatomically correct. I felt a surge of giggles bubbling inside and again told myself to grow up, for heaven's sake! If you start laughing while pouring water up your nose from a tiny, obscene teapot, you could drown! "I can't believe I'm going to do this," I said to the face in the mirror.

Again, I leaned over the sink, pressed the spout to my nostril, opened my mouth and started to pour. My brain screamed at me, "OMG! This is awful! It's exactly like the time your cousin pushed you off the dock, and you didn't have time to hold your nose." The memory was crystal-clear. Lake water had blasted my sinuses, making my nose and eyes burn.

As I poured into the right nostril, liquid dribbled from the left and into the sink. When a droplet hit my lip, I instinctively shut my mouth and immediately regretted my decision. The salty solution filled the back of my throat and made me gag. My brain screamed again, "Abort mission! This is the dumbest thing you've ever done."

My eyes watered, my mascara ran, and I had to blow my nose about sixteen times. I couldn't help but wonder who had invented this tiny torture device. Did they walk into the kitchen one afternoon and say, "I'm feeling a bit stuffy today. I think I'll forego the cup and just pour the tea directly into my nose."?

Once the initial trauma dissipated, I did feel better. The sinus pressure was tolerable, and I could actually breathe. But, since then, I've had an old song playing in my head on a loop. I finally had to turn on the radio and crank the volume to drown out the classic lyrics. A girl can only take so much of "I'm a little teapot, short and stout. Here is my handle. Here is my spout."

— Ann Cunningham —

A Remote Conversation

I love technology, and I love new gadgets.
I can no longer figure out how to use any of them,
but I love them.
~Jerry Zucker

Mark's cellphone rang. "It's Emily!" he yelled. I put down my book. We both looked forward to our daughter's calls on Saturdays. Emily had stayed in Oregon when we'd moved to Florida. She visited once a year, if we were lucky, so this was our only way to be close the rest of the time.

Mark sat on the couch and I in my rocker with his phone on the end table between us. He put his phone on speaker, and Emily's cheerful voice came through loud and clear. It was almost like having her sitting in the room with us. "What's new in Oregon?" I asked.

She told us about her job, boyfriend, and cat. "What's new there?" she asked.

"A rabbit ran across the back lawn this morning," I said. "And we saw two sandhill cranes near the pond." Our lives probably seemed boring. The weather here was often the main topic, especially during hurricane season. But at the moment there were no tropical storms in the Atlantic.

Mark mentioned the cabinets that were installed in our garage earlier in the week. "Like kitchen cabinets?" Emily asked.

"I'll take a picture and send it to you," he said, and left the room. While waiting, I told Emily about her cousins' lives. "Rachel's planning her wedding. It sounds as if it's going to be a big affair. And I saw photos of Jennifer's baby on Facebook. She's so cute. I can't believe how fast she's growing."

Emily was quiet. *Oh, no. Maybe she took what I'd said the wrong way.* "I'm not hinting for you to get married or have kids," I added, and then tried to fill the awkward silence by switching the subject to the weather.

Mark returned. "Who are you talking to?" he asked.

"Who else? Emily."

He laughed and held up his cellphone. "I took my phone with me to the garage and texted her a picture of the cabinets. She's been talking to me."

In disbelief, I stared at the tabletop beside my rocker. "But—but—the phone was right there!" I said, pointing. Yet it wasn't. The whole time I'd been rambling on and on to the TV remote.

—Mary Elizabeth Laufer—

An Alarming Situation

To succeed in life, you need three things: a wishbone,
a backbone, and a funny bone.
~Reba McEntire

I sat down to watch a recorded TV show after my husband left for his night-shift job. Not ten minutes into my favorite medical drama, I was alerted to the unmistakable beeping of the smoke alarm indicating a low battery. Sighing, I paused my program and got up from the couch.

I need a stepladder to reach our ten-foot ceiling. Unfortunately, that ladder was in the closet of the spare bedroom where our cockatiel, Bob, slept at night. I didn't want to wake him and have to listen to him talking, screeching, and whistling, but I had no choice.

Sure enough, the second I flipped the switch, Bob went into action, beginning with a whistling, off-key version of a theme from a program I'd watched as a child and stupidly taught him. Since I'm tone deaf, it sounded very little like the TV version. I both winced and smiled at his heroic attempt.

Bob followed his melody with a raucous "Hello, Bob," "Gimme a kiss, Bob," "Bob, go to sleep," "Bob's a silly bird," "Bob's a scary bird," and every single other phrase he was ever successful at mimicking—including a stern command of "Go lie down" to our poor dog, Mack, who'd followed me into the room. Surprisingly, the dog obeyed.

I quickly grabbed the ladder, turned off the light, and shut the door to instant quiet—well, except for a more urgent beep warning me that battery life was quickly expiring.

I climbed up the ladder to reach a box of spare batteries on the highest shelf in our kitchen where my husband kept them — "on the moon," as I often accused him. Dragging the ladder to the hallway, I scrambled up and quickly replaced the battery. Rather than fully waking the cockatiel again, I decided to leave the stepladder in the kitchen overnight. I folded it shut and leaned it safely against the counter after putting back the other batteries.

The second I sat down and started watching my show, the beeping started again. Evidently, the replacement battery was dead, too, so I went through all the motions again.

I'd barely picked up the remote and pressed Play a third time when the alarm went off yet again. I muttered some unladylike comments — under my breath so Bob couldn't pick up an undesirable phrase — and tried again. This time, I was one rung down when the same thing happened.

By then, I was out of nine-volt batteries. I had to scour the entire house for some electronic gadget that housed the same kind. I finally found one in an old clock. I crossed my fingers, hoping the battery still had some juice, and popped it in.

No luck! That round, plastic contraption that was designed to save lives was about to make me have a nervous breakdown! Frustrated, I yanked the entire thing out of its "nest" and actually yelled at it to shut up before I ripped out its useless innards. Clutching it, I climbed back down and almost killed myself by practically falling over the dog and two cats who always investigated every move I made and every breath I took — like homicidal, little stalkers. Shooing my entourage out of the way, I dumped the alarm on the table and made a mental note to sleep fully clothed in case I smelled smoke. Carbon-monoxide detection would be taken care of by our backup alarm downstairs.

I glared at the offending item once more before stalking off to plop myself on the couch again. My program was already forty-five minutes into the drama because I'd forgotten to pause it. Within seconds, that inexorable sound hit my ears again!

"That's not possible!" I bellowed to the empty room. "It's discon-
nected!" I informed the uninterested dog now lying at my feet. "How
can that be?" I asked his prone form. Of course, there was no reply.

I've always been nervous when I'm alone at night, but now I
was completely spooked. Though the acoustics in our home can be
deceiving at times, I knew the sound was not coming from our second
alarm in the basement because its warning sounded totally different
from the one upstairs. I even rewound the medical show on TV to
make sure the sound wasn't coming from some life-support device in
the background. The beep continued even when I muted the volume
completely on the television.

I stood up and walked toward the hall. On the way, I had to
pass by our other bird — a canary. I stopped in my tracks when the
beep sounded again. This time, the sound clearly came from his cage,
making me realize that I had never turned off the lamp next to him.
It was shining into his cage, making him think it was daytime. The
poor, tired creature couldn't sleep. He'd been protesting against the
intruding light that filtered through a small opening of his cloth cover
that I hadn't adjusted correctly.

I expelled a loud sigh of relief, turned off the light, replaced the
battery, and slipped the alarm back into its port, grateful no one could
witness my embarrassment. I finally sat down to enjoy my show — from
the beginning — thankful that my birds never learned to mimic the
sounds of dynamite or gunshots!

— Marya Morin —

My Adventure with Skinny Jeans

It is bad to suppress laughter. It goes back down
and spreads to your hips.
~Fred Allen

I was shopping at a women's clothing store in search of a birth-day gift for a friend. For a few moments, I got sidetracked and forgot about the gift when I spied a display of ripped, pencil-legged, skinny jeans.

I'd flirted with the idea of purchasing a pair of the jeans in the past, but l always put that thought on the back burner since most gals that I saw wearing them were much younger than me. This day, though, the temptation to try on a pair was stronger than my uncertainty.

I grabbed jeans in my size and moseyed over to the dressing room where I was greeted by a young, perky girl who had been chatting with a co-worker. She turned to me and said in a loud voice, "Oh, these will look adorable on you." She then turned to her co-worker and asked, "Wouldn't she look adorable in these jeans?" Her co-worker nodded in agreement and echoed, "Yes, absolutely adorable." So much for trying to be inconspicuous!

Once in the dressing room, I held up the jeans in front of me and looked in the full-length mirror. I could visualize myself in them, but would I be brave enough to wear them? I had been living most of my days in stretchy leggings. I rarely wore jeans, let alone pencil-legged, skinny jeans with fashionable rips from thigh to ankle.

I slipped the jeans over my calves. They were already tight, but I had gone this far, so I proceeded to pull them up my thighs and then up to my waist. There was no way I was able to zipper those jeans. They were way too tight. It was obvious that, during my legging-wearing years, I must have gone up a size, or perhaps two.

I tried to sit down on the bench in the dressing room to take off the jeans, but my knees literally wouldn't bend because the jeans were so tight on my legs. I waddled over to the wall and leaned on it for support to tug off the jeans. In the process, my foot got stuck in one of the jeans' rips, and I fell to the floor with a loud thud.

The employee called out, "Is everything okay?" I looked under the dressing-room door that was raised about a foot from the ground, and I could see her walking toward my stall. Clearly, if I could see her, she could see me in a crumpled ball on the dressing-room floor!

"Oh, I'm okay," I yelled out to her. "I just need a larger size." I called out a size, and she made a U-turn to get me another pair. I hoped that would give me time to untangle myself from the floor.

I figured if I could bend my right leg slightly, I'd be able to pull my left foot out of the rip on the leg. Twisting and tugging, I had to laugh. This was so reminiscent of my favorite childhood game, *Twister*.

Laughing at myself and the predicament I had gotten myself into made unfurling my legs from the wrath of the skinny jeans more difficult. I surrendered and ceased the battle. The skinny jeans won.

My laughter was halted by a soft voice beyond the dressing-room door. "Ma'am?" the sales employee inquired quizzically. I tried to answer but couldn't get the words out of my mouth without laughing. "I have your jeans," the salesgirl continued. She tried to hand me the jeans through the bottom of the door.

I managed to speak a few words without laughing. "Hold on, I'm coming," I assured her as I tried to maneuver my way closer to the door so I could grab the jeans. It was hopeless. I imagined I must have looked like a crab trying to scurry on a windswept beach.

I couldn't hold my laughter any longer. I had one of those uncontrollable episodes where you can't stop, no matter how hard you try. "Come in," I said with a snort. So, there I was, on the floor, tangled in the jeans with half my leg protruding out of the ripped jean leg. Right on cue, the salesgirl started tugging on the legs in an attempt to free me. Now, we were both roaring with laughter.

Finally, in what seemed liked forever, the tug of war was over. The skinny jeans were finally off, and I was free, but the laughter continued as I stood up. The salesgirl handed me the new, larger-sized jeans to try on. "No, thank you. I think I'll stick with my safe leggings!"

"Oh, you are so adorable," she said once again.

It wasn't until I got home that I realized I had forgotten to get my friend her birthday present. I also learned two things that day. One, I'm "so adorable." And, two, skinny jeans will forever remain on the back burner for me. Also, my grandmother was right when she said, "We should always wear clean, pretty underwear out because we never know what could happen!"

— Dorann Weber —

The Iris Caper

Blessed are we who can laugh at ourselves
for we shall never cease to be amused.
~Louisa Thomsen Brits

I n the spring of 2021, we had been in our new home for three years. The yard was landscaped with shrubs, trees, and a lawn that looked like a beautiful green carpet. But there was something missing: color. We needed color!

Our neighbor had lovely irises, and he told me, "We have plenty of volunteers in our side yard. They're yours if you're willing to dig them up!" I was beyond excited. I went home and told my husband, who was less than thrilled about having to dig in the hard South Carolina clay soil.

He said, "I like the yard just the way it is. It's easy to maintain, and I don't want to weed around more plants. I say no!"

Shortly thereafter, he headed out for his daily walk around our neighborhood. I knew that I had about an hour before he returned home, so I quickly put my plan into action. I grabbed my bucket, shovel and a pair of gloves, loaded up the golf cart, and went on my way. It only took me a minute to arrive at my destination where a colorful array of irises was nestled between the loblolly pines and the oaks. I could hardly wait to dig up these beauties and transplant them to their new home.

Then, it happened…

I took one step, and then another, only to discover that I had sunk into a mud bog up to my knees. The more that I tried to extricate myself, the deeper I went into the gooey mire. I was in a pickle, and it wasn't getting any better.

Then, out of nowhere, a voice yelled, "Are you okay? Can I help you?" It was our neighbor, Christine, who lived down the street. She had been out for a walk and happened to pass by when I took the plunge into the mud bog.

I said, "Christine, you're an angel that the Lord sent my way! Did you see me fall, or was it the expletive that I yelled out that caught your attention?"

She laughed and said, "Actually, it was both!"

Now, Christine weighs all of about ninety pounds dripping wet. I, on the other hand, well, let's just say that I weigh twice that amount and leave it at that. Logistically speaking, it was going to be impossible for this little lady to rescue me from the pond of mud in which I was entrapped. We pulled and pushed for almost an hour. Those who know me can attest that, when I get in a jam, I tend to laugh. The more Christine pushed and pulled, the more I laughed. Soon, we were both laughing hysterically as we realized that I was doomed to spend the rest of the afternoon in the bog or until someone with more muscle came along.

In the chaos, I'm not sure exactly when I looked up into the loblolly pine in front of me, but I had the feeling I was being watched. And there it was... my neighbors' home-security camera perched amongst the tree limbs, recording my every attempt to escape unnoticed. I could only imagine how many times they would play the video to the delight of their friends and family. It would be a real showstopper.

It also occurred to me that my husband was surely almost done with his walk and on his way home. Out of sheer desperation, I told Christine to run up the hill and get my golf cart. I thought that if I could reach up high enough to grab the seat handles, then with a short tap on the accelerator, I could be pulled free. So, without hesitation, Christine retrieved the golf cart, stopping just short of the mud bog, and yet close enough for me to reach the cart handle. The plan worked perfectly, and with a sound reminiscent of the pop when opening a bottle of champagne, I was free!

I was covered with red clay mud from head to toe, looking much like a gingerbread doll. I knew that I had just minutes to make it home, get showered and change into clean clothes before my husband discovered what I had been up to while he was on his walk. Several of the neighbors had gathered around to see the spectacle when I looked up and saw my husband rounding the corner. He approached the scene ever so slowly, not quite believing the vision of his wife that was unfolding before his eyes. Very calmly, he said, "What in the world?" After forty-one years, this was yet another one of Sharon's adventures that he would add to his many memories of my past antics.

He thanked Christine profusely for rescuing me and wanted to know how we could repay her for her kindness. I blurted out as she was walking away, "Christine, do you drink wine?"

She looked back and replied with a chuckle, "I do now!"

— Sharon E. Albritton —

Window Dressing

Imperfection is beauty, madness is genius and it's better
to be absolutely ridiculous than absolutely boring.
~Marilyn Monroe

ary leaned down close to me, with a serious look in her eye. "Lauren and Ned have decided to get married next month," she announced. "They insist on inviting only immediate family members. Since Mike and you are like our family, they want to include you as well." She leaned back in her chair, took a sip of her morning coffee at our annual yard sale, and let her words sink in.

I was surprised, but the unbelievable part was yet to come. She looked around to make sure no yard-sale customers were near us. "Before they send you the wedding invitation, I need to know if Mike and you can climb through a window."

"Climb through a window?" I asked. Now, that was the unbelievable part! I tried to visualize Mike and me heaving ourselves up to a window ledge and pushing ourselves over to the other side. "Well, I think we can, but exactly how high and how large is this window?"

Mary chuckled. "Let me tell you the details. Lauren and Ned want to do a pop-up wedding. It's when the bride and groom find a special location. Then, the wedding party just 'pops up' and holds the wedding." She added, "Lauren has always been fascinated with Marilyn Monroe. There is a mural of her face painted in Washington, D.C. on an outside wall of the third floor of a building. She wants to get married on the roof of that building in front of the forty-foot mural of Marilyn Monroe! Ned has agreed. The only thing is that you both will have to climb through a window in the beauty salon located next to the building to get to the roof area. And I am not sure of the size of the window."

I nervously replied, "Before I answer, I need to check with Mike and see if he thinks he can climb through a window." I turned and walked quickly toward our house. "I can't believe it! I will have to double up on my Fit for Life class and take Mike with me," I mumbled as I opened the back door and went into the kitchen.

Mike was sitting at the table checking his e-mail, ignoring the fact that there was a yard sale in our driveway. Picking up one of the few remaining doughnuts from the box on the counter to share with him, I turned and gave him a big smile. I asked, "I was wondering, if you needed to, could you climb through a window?"

He looked up from the computer, gave a nervous chuckle, and said, "Okay, what happened at the yard sale? Did the garage door get stuck again, and I have to crawl through the side window?"

I quickly explained all the wedding details, what an honor it was to have been invited, and finished with, "So, do you think you can climb through a window to get to the wedding site?"

With a look of disbelief, Mike replied, "What? I can't believe Lauren! Does she think her parents can climb through a window?" Thinking it over for a few moments, he agreed. "We can't let Mary and Joe down. We'll try, if they can do it and want us there. The only question is, what will we wear to a wedding where you climb through a window to get to it?"

I looked at him and shrugged my shoulders. "Sweatsuits and sneakers, I guess!" We both laughed at the image of four gray-haired, slightly chubby people wearing sweatsuits and sneakers climbing through a window along with the bride and groom. What an adventure this was going to be!

Mike and I began having second thoughts as the wedding day drew closer. *What should we wear? Is it too dangerous at our age? Are we both crazy?* Each night, I would dream of falling over the edge of a roof. I could feel myself falling down, down, down, to the bottom of...? Thank goodness, I always jerked awake before I found out.

Mike and I met Mary and Joe at the subway station in our best "athletic but dressy" outfits on the wedding day. We would meet Lauren and Ned at the entrance to the Salon Roi. This hair salon is dedicated to Marilyn Monroe. The owner paid for her mural to be painted forty years ago and has continued to maintain it.

Arriving at the salon, Joe opened the door to the reception area, and we found ourselves in a fantasy world. The walls were a bright peppermint pink, gold crystal chandeliers twinkled from the ceiling, and portraits of Marilyn filled every available nook and cranny. Young women were sitting on soft, puffy couches with flutes of champagne in their hands and feather boas around their shoulders, waiting for their hair stylists. Everyone was busily chatting. No one seemed to notice we were there.

One of the pop-up wedding officiants met us and suggested we follow him to the wedding site. We nervously climbed up the three winding flights of tiger-fur steps—each step leading us closer to a large, mesmerizing picture of Marilyn putting on her bright red lipstick. Stopping at a small wooden door, he gave a quick knock. I whispered to Mary, "Do you think this door leads to the window we must climb through?"

Just as I was about to ask how the rehearsal went the night before, the officiant opened the door. We could only see one tiny white sink and toilet with a square window beside it. He looked at me and said, "Now, I need you to climb onto this toilet seat and step through the window to the other side."

I looked at him in shock! Everyone, including the bride and groom, was as surprised as I was. I don't know what I had been thinking, but this was not even in my wildest dreams. Then, I realized that there had been no rehearsal.

I was shaking as he helped me up on top of the toilet lid. I glanced down at the hard tile floor and wondered how serious my injuries would be if I slipped and fell. I couldn't decide how to move my body through the window—feet first or head first—but the officiant just seemed to push me over and through. I found myself standing on a rickety, metal fire escape.

Next, I reached my leg over the daunting space between our building and the next. While between buildings, I looked below and noticed nothing but hard, gray concrete with a few trash cans to break my fall! I reached the next rickety fire escape on the other side. Finally, I climbed up and over a short, brick wall, scrambling to the safety of the rooftop.

Watching the others behind me, I wondered how we would get back into that bathroom window. I didn't plan on being the first one again. I would be fine if firefighters climbed down a rope from a helicopter to rescue us. I wouldn't mind being the lead story on the 6:00 P.M. news if I made it home in one piece.

We could all hear *crunch, crunch, crunch* as we tried to walk directly to the mural. There were no walls around the rooftop and the gravel had to be at least six inches thick. Gray, rusty air-conditioning units hummed along.

Once our group made it to the mural wall, we all paused for a moment and looked up at the massive face of Marilyn looking out toward Washington. We were so thankful to have made it. It was thrilling to be up on the rooftop with no one down below knowing we were even there. Taking a deep breath, I realized how happy I was to share this special day with Lauren and Ned.

With the vows exchanged, the bride and groom kissed, and everyone's attention turned to one thought: *Who would be the first to go over the brick wall, to the rickety fire escapes, through the window, and onto the bathroom toilet?*

I quickly placed myself in the middle of the group this time. Following close in a line, we retraced our earlier path. Shouting encouraging words and helping each other, we successfully passed each obstacle. No one in the hair salon seemed to notice as eight people of varying ages walked out of the tiny bathroom, one right after the other, heading down the tiger-fur steps. It was just a typical day at the Salon Roi.

But four gray-haired, slightly chubby people had all been to a "pop-up wedding" on a rooftop with Marilyn Monroe and lived to tell about it.

— Valli Cowan —

A Perfect Fit

*Just keep it simple. When you over-think
what you're wearing, that's when wardrobe
malfunctions tend to happen.*
~Guy Berryman

I hate to shop for myself. I can spend hours in stores trying to find the perfect gift. I'll even gladly trail after my girlfriends or my incredibly gorgeous "everything-in-size-six-off-the-rack-fits-me-and-looks-stunning" daughter-in-law. But when it comes to clothing myself, I'd rather walk a tightrope across Niagara Falls without a net than walk into a store and start the ordeal of finding something to wear.

To begin with, I'm only five feet tall. I used to be an inch taller, but I was robbed of that inch sometime after the age of forty. And my size—well, suffice it to say, I'm a perfect "round." If Chanel or Dior ever decided to start designing clothes for large apples or giant, misshapen pears with feet, I'd be fine. But, until that happens, I'm at the mercy of today's fashions.

Recently, I needed something to wear to a christening. This wasn't one of those christenings of yesteryear where someone dribbles water on a baby, guests coo at the little darling's howls of outraged fury, and then everyone goes to the child's home to celebrate with a potluck. No, as luck would have it, I married into a family where a hall is rented for a minimum of one hundred guests, complete with a table of honor, a deejay, a seven-course meal and dancing into the wee hours of the morning. Furthermore, dress is formal. The moment I opened the invitation, I groaned. I realized it would entail an entire week of non-stop searching for something flattering.

I began seven days before zero hour. I already owned a pair of slinky, classic black pants and just needed a nice blouse or sweater. Sadly, the gorgeous blouse I'd originally bought to go with the pants had not grown along with my body since the last baptism we had attended.

I began in earnest by selecting a mall that had no less than 200 stores. I encountered the usual problems for the first three hours. If I loved the item, it was not available in my size. If it buttoned without gaping on my ample chest, the sleeves dragged on the floor in a simian-like fashion. If it looked like it would drape beautifully, hiding flaws, it transformed into a clingy, roll-hugging monster on the journey to the dressing room. If it fit perfectly, it came in only one hideous, glow-in-the dark color that complemented no human being I'd ever met. If the sleeves and chest were right, the garment weighed seventy-three pounds and was meant to be worn without a coat in Antarctica.

Sleeveless blouses had armholes that either ended at my waist or enhanced my upper arms' jiggling, sagging skin. I didn't even try on the gauzy items. My worst enemy didn't deserve to see the glaring flaws those might expose.

After eight hours of relentless shopping, I was ready to cry. I'd bulldozed my way through every clothing shop, including those that catered to different "frames." I must have decimated thirty well-meaning salesclerks with my unflinching, "Don't even think of suggesting that was made for me" glare. All that remained was a hardware store, and I seriously considered something in burlap or canvas just to put an end to my misery.

I was exhausted. My hair had enough static to supply power to three provinces, and I dreaded the miasma that would drift up when I removed my comfortable sneakers. I also made a mental note to chastise the deodorant company for false advertising. Long-lasting, my foot! Don't even get me started on the eighteen hours of comfort the bra people touted!

The next day and the ones following it were no better. The pursuit of the perfect top was now abandoned. I was ready to settle for something that looked "okay." Even with my standards lowered, I was no closer. I considered throwing myself at the mercy of my future hostess. I was ready to pawn the contents of my home to bribe her with the "twenty big ones" she bragged about spending for the upcoming shindig. She could have it all just to allow me entry in jeans and a sweatshirt. However, I knew I would be wasting my time. She is also a perfect, off-the-rack size six, so she had no qualms about putting me through the rack to find something appropriate to wear.

On the day before the christening, my husband offered to drive me to the one section of the city that still had stores we hadn't visited. He even agreed to accompany me, since the alternative was to wash the week's supply of laundry that I'd had no time to get to. Buoyed by his unusual courage, I pounced on the offer.

I took a deep cleansing breath before entering the first store and rummaging through a marked-down rack of sweaters just inside the entrance.

After I rejected the first three garments, my shriek of joy pierced the air, almost shattering my own eardrums. I obeyed my husband's embarrassed plea to lower my voice and waved the article I'd found at him. Without another word, I tore toward the clerk, demanding directions to the dressing room. Seconds later, I heaved a sigh of relief. I had found it — the perfect sweater! It fit to a tee, flattering my figure in all the right places and hiding every new flaw I'd discovered during the last seven grueling days of torture.

I removed it carefully and exited the room with a grin of triumph, clutching it to my chest possessively in case some evil twin appeared and tried to wrench it from my arms. I took only three steps before my husband's horrified gaze reminded me that I was wearing only my jeans and a bra, while the shirt I wore to shop in was still in a heap on the dressing-room floor. Mortified, I slithered back in to get dressed.

The day of the christening was chilly, so I wore a matching jacket over the top I had bought. I planned to remove the jacket indoors.

When I got to our assigned table, another guest I'd never met sat there smiling. She stood to introduce herself, and I gasped when I saw she was wearing the very same sweater I had on.

"Nice top," I murmured after composing myself.

"Thank you," she grinned. "I was so lucky. It was the first one I tried on," she told me, preening. I gauged her to be a perfect size six!

Needless to say, I left that sweltering jacket on for the next ten hours.

— Marya Morin —

Wild Kingdom

10

Don't Feed (or Tease) the Ducks

"Well, that escalated quickly" is our family motto.
~Author Unknown

It was a park day, an opportunity to relax with my wife and son and maybe steal a moment of solitude for myself. But it didn't turn out that way.

We had not been to this park before, but it was clearly well-equipped: playground, picnic tables, ducks, bathrooms, even a park patrol. Perfect.

The gentle lap of the water lured us to the lake. A group of ducks paddled in our direction. Mika, my five-year-old son, took notice. "Dad, let's give them something to eat."

A quick once-over of our surroundings revealed numerous signs that read: Do Not Feed Ducks. "We can't, Mika. Feeding the ducks is not allowed."

"They look hungry."

"Human food can make them sick. They need duck food."

"Maybe they have some," Mika suggested, pointing.

I looked and there, across the lake, were an elderly man and woman feeding the ducks.

"They probably didn't see the signs," I hastily explained. And then, to distract him, I added, "Why don't we go see what your mother made us for lunch?"

We found a grassy spot at water's edge, and my wife began unpacking a gourmet lunch — well, for a five-year-old. Peanut butter and jelly, potato chips, apple slices, chocolate milk.

As we ate, I noticed the elderly couple we had seen feeding the ducks walking toward us. They were in their advanced years, with the woman leaning heavily on a cane and the man tightly gripping the handles of a walker.

And, over the front of his walker, hung a half-loaf of bread.

I tried not to look, hoping they'd veer off.

"Howdy do!" a deep voice hailed.

I cringed. "Hello!" I responded, trying to sound cheerful.

"My wife and I saw you with the youngin. Thought you'd like some bread to feed the ducks."

My brain quickly slipped into chess mode because, in the game of chess, you weigh each move and the ramifications of that move before you pick one.

Move 1: Tell the nice elderly man and his wife that people shouldn't be feeding the ducks and risk offending them.

Move 2: Tell the nice elderly man and his wife that you don't want his bread and risk having them think I'm biased against old people.

Move 3: Graciously accept the bread and then try to explain to Mika why I am violating the rules of the park and risk angering my wife for confusing him.

Move 4: Run away, screaming.

I was leaning in the direction of Move 4 when the elderly man spoke again, trying to coerce me into making Move 3. "It's raisin bread," he said with a wink. "They just lovvvvvve raisin bread."

"Thank you," I surrendered. "That's kind of you."

Satisfied, the elderly man and woman puttered away, finding refuge from the sun at a nearby park bench. As we finished our lunch, I noticed they kept looking our way, awaiting the moment, no doubt, when we would amble over to the lake and provide the ducks with their next raisin-bread fix.

My wife, of course, was studying me closely. "They're watching," she snickered. "What now, genius?"

"I've got this," I boldly declared, even though I knew that I didn't. "C'mon, Mika."

As the two of us approached the lake, I glanced over my shoulder. Yep, they were watching, but at a good distance. I began to formulate a plan.

"Okay, Mika," I began, stuffing the bread under my shirt. "Since we can't actually feed the ducks, we're going to pretend to feed them. Ready?"

Mika looked at me like I was crazy.

"Watch. I'll show you how to throw a fastball," I said. I wound up like a pitcher from the 1900s and hurled a ball of imaginary raisin bread into the lake.

Fortunately, the ducks were not good at discerning real raisin bread from imaginary raisin bread and began paddling en masse in our direction.

Mika enthusiastically joined me in our charade. We were having a fine time, and a quick check with our raisin-bread benefactors revealed that they were buying our performance.

Success!

Until my wife, who was not at all impressed by these hijinks, arrived.

"I see you're preparing our son for a life of crime."

"We're not technically breaking the rules, dear. We're merely pretending."

"Well, when our son pretends to rob a bank, we'll see how that goes. C'mon, Mika. Let's check out the playground."

Mika looked at me, looked at Mom and wisely chose to go with her.

I was alone and figured this was my chance to ditch the bread. After a little reconnaissance, I liberated the raisin bread into a garbage can.

Success!

"Excuse me, sir. Can I have a word?"

It was the park ranger. He did not look happy.

"What's up?"

"Well, I saw you feeding the ducks."

"Oh, no, officer. Wouldn't want to break the rules."

"Which makes me wonder why you were feeding them."

As if my predicament wasn't bad enough, I noticed that the elderly purveyors of raisin bread had seen what was transpiring and were approaching.

"I was only pretending to feed them."

The park ranger shook his head in disbelief. This was clearly a defense to which he was unaccustomed.

"Morning, sir," the elderly man called out. "What's going on?"

"This gentleman was feeding the ducks. I'm going to have to write him a citation."

"I wasn't feeding them," I protested. "I was pretending."

"What's that?" the elderly man interjected. "I saw you and your boy feeding them."

"No, we weren't. I mean, we were, but we weren't really feeding them."

"He says he was pretending to feed them," the ranger explained.

"No, I saw him and the boy," the elderly man persisted, "and they were throwing the bread to them."

"No, it's here in this garbage can."

"You threw away my raisin bread?"

"Well, not right away."

The ranger pulled out his citation book. "Sir, it clearly sounds like you were feeding the ducks."

"No, officer, we weren't. I just didn't want to offend this nice man and his wife."

"Why would you throw away my bread? The ducks love raisin bread."

"I didn't want to hurt your feelings."

"Throwing away my raisin bread hurt my feelings!"

The ranger stopped writing and stared at me. "Sir, were you teasing the ducks?"

The elderly woman looked at me and scowled. "Honey, I think you've got a screw loose."

"Sir, I'm writing you a citation for feeding the ducks and one for aggravating the wildlife."

My wife, who was watching from a safe distance and, I might add, laughing hysterically, decided to approach at this point.

Like a skilled defense lawyer, she painted a portrait of a confused father trying to keep from offending anyone but ended up offending almost everyone.

The elderly man and woman took their leave but not before retrieving their raisin bread. The park ranger gave me a stern warning against "feeding or teasing" the ducks. My wife returned to the playground, still giggling.

And I found a quiet place under a shade tree away from everyone so I could sulk. At least I had done one good thing. I had taught my son the proper way to throw a fast ball—even if it was with a piece of imaginary raisin bread.

—Dave Bachmann—

11

Bear Witness

*Adventure, yeah. I guess that's what you call it when
everybody comes back alive.*
~Merced Lackey

The month prior to our Alaskan vacation, Google began sending me grizzly (no pun intended) bear stories. These were not
warm and fuzzy anecdotes, like "Bear and Ranger Share Pot of
Honey."

It was more like: "Hiker Loses Limb after Bear Mauling."

Apparently, Google thinks I have a dark side.*

I shared my concerns with my husband Steve and friends, Lorraine
and Nick, as we began our bike ride along the Alaskan coast.

Scanning the forest adjacent to the trail, I asked, "What if we see
a bear?"

"You make yourself big," Steve said.

"You play dead," Nick said.

"If it's a brown bear, play dead," Steve elaborated. "Black bear,
be big."

"How big?" I asked, sizing up my five-foot-three-inch frame.

"Just stand tall, wave your arms and make a lot of noise," Steve
explained.

"But no high-pitched screaming," Nick said.

I'm pretty sure if I run into a bear, my voice will be high.

Also, my pants may be wet.

"Talk to the bear in calm tones," Nick added.

"What should I talk to the bear about?" I asked.

"Pretty much anything," Nick answered.

"Just not religion or politics," I said.

"Also, black bears aren't always black," Nick said. "Sometimes, they're brown."

Whoa, Whoa, WHAT?!

"So, how do I know if it's a real black bear or a black bear that's identifying as a brown bear?" I asked.

"By the hump."

"And the ears."

Steve and Nick conducted a mini bear-hump-and-ear tutorial.

In case you missed the tutorial: Brown bears have smaller ears and a hump on their back.

Also, if their ears go back, they're about to charge, and you're in a wee bit of trouble.

"And don't ever get between a mama bear and her cub," Lorraine added.

Duh.

It was a lot of information, but in summary…

Black bear, big,

Brown bear, dead,

Don't get between,

Mama and her cub.

(I think I have the makings for an adorable, albeit disturbing children's book.)

"Either way, the bear probably won't get all of us," I said.

I proceeded to share a recent story of how a grizzly had attacked four hikers.

Three got away.

I sized up my middle-aged, injury-riddled bunch.

I liked my chances.

For sixteen miles, we saw nothing but lush greenery, calm waters, and puffy clouds.

On Mile 17, Lorraine and I (who were slightly ahead of our husbands) turned a blind corner and…

Thirty feet** in front of us…

Smack dab in the middle of the trail…

Dark fur, huge paws, mammoth claws...

GRRRRRRR!

I slammed on my brakes, praying I would stop without flying over the handlebars and catapulting myself into the bear.

What's the strategy if you crash into the bear?

Thankfully, I screeched to a halt and jumped off the bike just in time.

With trembling hands, I laid my bike on the side of the trail.

Slowly, I lifted my eyes.

My mind started racing. Is it okay to look directly at the bear?

Or, like a gorilla, do I avoid eye contact?

Or should I give it a subtle wink, like, "Hey, bear, we're all good. Nothing to eat here."

My heart pounded in my ears as I stood motionless, taking in this majestic creature.

The bear sat in the middle of the trail, gnawing on greenery.

Was he a vegetarian?

Excellent!

I seemed to recall from Steve's seminar that black bears are vegetarians, but was this a black bear?

Unfortunately, I'm slightly color-blind, so I couldn't tell you the exact color.

I could, however, tell you the size…

GINORMOUS!

RUN, RUN, RUN! I screamed to myself.

"Do NOT run!" Lorraine read my mind. "And don't turn your back on it!"

The bear continued to chomp on shrubbery.

That's it, spoil your appetite. Good bear.

My heart raced. I turned to Lorraine for words of comfort.

"Do you want to take a picture?" she asked.

No, I want to live.

I edged backward, forcing myself not to bolt.

Lorraine just stood, enjoying the view.

How could she be so calm?

But then, I remembered.

Lorraine was voted "Most Cool, Calm and Collected" by the Class of 1984.

(Fellow Trojans, you voted correctly.)

"Can we get out of here?" I whimpered, turning my back on the bear.

(I should have been voted "Least Likely to Follow Directions.")

Lorraine nodded and backpedaled, keeping her eye on the bear.

"We're going to be fine," Lorraine reassured me. "But remember, if he attacks, lie on your stomach so he can't get your organs."

Goodbye, Lorraine. It's been nice knowing you!

Seconds later, Steve and Nick appeared on the path.

I planted myself in the middle of the trail and raised my hand as if I were directing traffic.

"Stop!" I commanded. "There's a bear!"

WHOOSH!

That was the sound of the two of them riding past me.

"Cool!" Nick said, as he pedaled toward the bear.

"Awesome," Steve added, as he jumped off the bike and began videotaping.

And the rest is history.

One day, a group of slightly injured, fairly misguided, bear-loving friends went on a bike ride and encountered a bear.

And lived to tell about it.

Take that, Google.

— January Gordon Ornellas —

*I do.

**In all honesty, we were probably more like fifty feet away, but a bear story is like a fish story. Ask me in a couple of weeks, and I'll tell you that the bear and I rode off into the sunset together.

12

Playing Possum

You can't deny laughter; when it comes, it plops down
in your favorite chair and stays as long as it wants.
~Stephen King

Newcomers to Tennessee, my friend Mary and I chatted as we drove to meet a group of fellow senior citizens who had invited us to their monthly Bunco game.

After everyone had arrived and introductions were made, we found spots at the table. The bell rang to start the game. I looked across the table at Mary. Her face was ashen, and her eyes were wide with panic. I followed her stare and tried not to gasp.

We saw two huge possums saunter into the room and watched as one crawled onto the back of the sofa. The animal proceeded to move from the sofa to the kitchen counter where it sniffed the food on dishes meant for the players. The other possum moseyed under the game tables. As the critter brushed up against each of our legs, Mary and I tried not to freak out because the others were playing as if this was totally normal.

Doesn't anyone else see these animals? I wondered.

Eventually, I had to use the powder room. I was relieved (please excuse the pun) to get away from these two possums. Entering the bathroom, I encountered yet a third possum using a litter box. Before the furry creature could pounce on me, I turned and dashed out.

I had had enough and wanted to leave. I gave Mary a frantic eye roll and told our hostess that I was getting a migraine. As we made our hasty exit, we noticed movement on the staircase and watched as a raccoon and two weasels came scampering down the steps. We were leaving just in the nick of time.

We raced to the car and closed the doors. I could tell that Mary was mad when she slammed her door. She screamed, "You set me up!"

I was laughing and crying at the same time. "Mary, I had no idea."

Mary's anger dissipated, and she started to laugh. We fed off each other, and I became so unglued that I couldn't even start the car.

My friend who had invited us to the Bunco game called me later that evening. "Bless your little hearts for coming tonight. I had no idea that we would be surrounded by all those critters inside the house. Please forgive me."

I apologized to her for leaving abruptly. "I just couldn't stand the possum brushing up against my legs."

With a chuckle, she said, "What gets me is that our hostess couldn't understand why no one touched the food she set out on the counter."

— Terry Hans —

13

A Misunderstanding

If Laughter cannot solve your problems, it will
definitely DISSOLVE your problems; so that
you can think clearly what to do about them.
~Dr. Madan Kataria

While stationed at Hickam Air Force Base on the island of Oahu in Hawaii, I decided I wanted a dog and scanned the advertisements in the newspaper. I found a listing for koi in the pets section. The listing stated that they had three.

The following conversation took place when I called on the telephone. A woman's voice answered, "Hello?"

"Good evening, are you the party that has the koi for sale?"

"Yes, I am."

"What can you tell me about them?"

"I'm not certain what you would like to know. There are three of them, and they're all available for sale."

"How old are they?"

"I'm not certain but about two months. They're not very big yet."

"What is the coloring like?"

"Just about like all the rest."

"What were their parents like?"

"Pretty much like all the others I've ever seen. But I'm really not sure who the parents were."

"How many are males, and how many females?"

"I don't know."

"Have you looked?"

"No."

"Why not? Aren't you curious?"

"It's not that I'm not curious; I just never thought about it."

"Could you check for me? I'd really like to know how many are male and how many are female."

"I could check, but I don't know what to look for."

"Is there any way you can describe to me what they are going to look like when they grow up?"

"Pretty much like any of them that I've ever seen. There may be some variation in color, but they all look pretty much the same to me."

By this point, I wasn't sure if I wanted to deal with this woman. She didn't seem to know anything about what she was selling. Then, I asked the key question, "Do you have any idea what kind of dog they will look like when they're fully grown?"

My question was answered with hysterical laughter. "Dog? These are koi. They are fish."

Later that day, I found out that mixed-breed dogs in Hawaii are called poi dogs — not koi dogs.

—C. Allan Butkus—

14

Discovering Fluffy

There is nothing more deceptive than an obvious fact.
~Arthur Conan Doyle

"Animal Control. How can I help you?" a deep, gruff voice bellowed through the phone receiver.

"I'd like to report a wounded animal," I replied. My voice was quiet and soft compared to the gentleman on the other end of the line. I continued to explain approximately where I saw the animal. I wasn't sure what type of critter it was since only the backside and tail were protruding from the tall grass. I was promised someone would go out that day to investigate and remove the animal if need be.

Earlier that morning, I'd been on my way to meet a friend for breakfast. Driving down a long stretch of road that connected two neighborhoods, there was nothing but tall trees and grassy areas on both sides of the road for a few miles. The morning light was bright, so I pulled down the sun visor. Then, I caught a glimpse of a fluffy brown, black and white tail swaying in the breeze on the side of the road. I took a quick peek as I got closer. I said a silent prayer for the little fluffy critter's safety as I proceeded to my destination.

Throughout breakfast, I couldn't get the animal off my mind. I named him Fluffy. Perhaps it was someone's loving cat or dog. Maybe a fox? I wasn't sure. All I knew was that I had a soft spot for animals, both domesticated and wild.

After I called Animal Control, I decided to look on social media to see if anyone was missing a dog or cat in the surrounding neighborhoods where I had spotted Fluffy. There weren't any listed missing pets that matched the description of what I saw, so I wrote a post describing Fluffy's coloring and asked if anyone was missing a pet in that area. By the end of the day, I didn't get any replies to my post, so I came to the conclusion it must have been an animal in the wild.

The next morning, I was curious to find out if Animal Control had found sweet Fluffy, so I called for an update.

The same gentleman with the distinct, deep voice answered my call again. I admit, his assertive tone was a bit intimidating. I held my breath and said in my most confident voice, "I called yesterday about a possibly wounded animal on the side of the road, and…" I was gently interrupted and reassured that he drove by the area I had indicated twice and didn't see any sign of an animal. I hung up the phone, relieved that the critter must be okay and had ventured on.

I grabbed my purse and headed out the door. I had a full day ahead of me. But, first, I wanted to stop and get my daily dose of a large iced coffee. The route I had to take was the same as where I had seen Fluffy. Feeling good, I blasted the radio and started singing along at the top of my lungs — until I saw Fluffy! There he was, farther down the road, half behind some brush with his tail sticking out and moving. Now, I was worried he would go onto the road. Maybe Animal Control could capture and relocate him to safety or bring him to a wildlife refuge if he needed help. I wasn't sure how situations like this were handled.

I got my iced coffee, eased my way into a parking space, and dialed Animal Control once again. I was hesitant to make the call and felt like an annoyance. But poor Fluffy needed help, and that was more important. By now, I had memorized the phone number and dialed. The familiar voice answered. "Good morning, Animal…"

"He's here now!" I blurted into the phone before the employee with the deep, gruff voice could finish his greeting.

There was a moment of awkward silence. "Who's there? Are you in danger, ma'am?" he asked. His voice was softer and kinder.

Without thinking, I responded, "Fluffy is there, by some brush. He moved!"

There was another moment of silence. "Fluffy? Who's Fluffy?"

He laughed. Without having to explain again, he remembered me. He asked if I was able to meet him where I last saw the animal. Giving him the location where I saw Fluffy, I drove to meet him.

I slowed down to where I last saw Fluffy. Thankfully, he was still at the same spot. Pulling onto the shoulder of the road, I put on the four-way blinkers and waited for Animal Control. About ten minutes later, I saw the township Animal Control truck pull up behind me. I got out of my car to meet the man with the gruff voice. Two men got out of the truck. One of the men had to be at least six-and-a-half-feet tall. He had a full-face beard, suspenders and a plaid shirt — a stereotypical depiction of a lumberjack. The other gentleman was younger. The bright-red polo shirt and tan, khaki trousers made him look like a college student.

The younger man came up to me first, shook my hand and introduced himself as Tom, the Senior Animal Control Officer. In his infamous, deep, assertive, gruff voice, he asked, "So, where is this mysterious animal you've been talking about?" I pointed to the brush. Both men squinted to take a better look and simultaneously walked toward Fluffy.

When they got next to the animal, they both squatted down to get a better look and then turned to look back toward me. "Looks like we have to name this one Target!" Tom yelled to me. My mind was racing. Why would they name the animal Target? Was the animal rabid, and they had to use emergency euthanasia? I turned away and got in my car. I was about to drive off when I heard the men approaching my car, both laughing hysterically.

How rude! I thought.

I turned to see Tom cradling Fluffy in his arms. I was happy to realize that Fluffy wasn't rabid or injured since the two men were smiling. I rolled down my window as Tom announced, "Meet Target, a 100-percent-cotton pompom beanie!" That's when I noticed the Target price tag dangling from Fluffy.

My face must have been as red as his polo shirt. Fluffy was a hat!

— Dorann Weber —

15

Turkey Trot

When turkeys mate, they think of swans.
~Johnny Carson

I was running late for work one morning but moving at a good pace. I thought I might even be able to arrive on time after all. Any hope for that was soon dashed, however, when I saw the long line of cars in front of me. Vehicles were stopped on both sides of the road.

I watched the clock on my dashboard as it ticked through the time. One minute... two minutes... three minutes... four minutes... five minutes. Still no movement on either side. I was starting to get irritated. Now, I was going to be *really* late!

I opened my window and stretched my head out to look ahead and try to get an idea of what was going on. Off in the distance, I saw a group of animals in the middle of the street.

Was that a flock of turkeys?

I pulled my car to the side of the road, locked it, and headed up to where the birds were. I had to walk several car lengths before I knew for certain that what I had seen was, in fact, turkeys.

In the middle of the street stood several hens and one fancy male. The tom was showing off to all the females in his presence. He strutted along the roadway as if it were a stage. His fan-shaped tail waved in the air. His chest was puffed out, and his head was held high. He pranced to the left and then to the right in a circular direction to ensure that all the girls could see him. He was making quite an impression.

Everyone remained in their vehicles watching the show. No one was doing a thing to help move the birds along.

Well, this is ridiculous! I thought to myself. *A bunch of dumb turkeys are holding all of us captive!*

I decided I would be the one to save the day.

Walking toward the back of the birds, I held out my arms at waist level and started to guide them to the sidewalk. Each one readily marched toward the area I was directing them to.

This was so easy. Why didn't anyone think of this before?

I was about to get the answer.

The last hen reached the sidewalk. I turned toward the tom that had stayed behind. As he neared the sidewalk, he suddenly lunged at me. Shocked, I jumped back to avoid getting pecked by him.

He sprang forward and tried striking me again. I had no idea what I did to deserve this attack, but I wasn't sticking around to find out.

I turned and started to run. He followed suit, pecking at me all the way. It was all I could do to keep out of his reach. I weaved back and forth like a prizefighter in a championship match. I picked up my speed, high-stepping all the way.

Meanwhile, the cars that had been stopped began to move. As they passed me, the drivers waved, honked their horns, gave me a thumbs-up or smiled. They were obviously amused at my situation.

We continued the chase down the sidewalk. Until that morning, I had thought of turkeys as slow, ambling creatures. I was very much mistaken. That bird kept up with me.

My car was finally in sight. I bolted for it, with the tom on my heels. I tried to open the door, but I had locked it. I fumbled for my keys. I finally got them in my hands, but they dropped onto the pavement. As I reached down to grab them, my attacker charged at my head. I threw my arms up to protect my face. I just missed getting struck by that sharp beak. I tried to get the keys again, but the turkey kept up the attack. In desperation, I kicked the keys toward the back of the car. It was the break I needed. I was able to outmaneuver him and race to the trunk. I bent down and picked up the keys. I hustled to the driver's side door, got into my car and started it. Before I could pull away, however, the tom and all of his female cohorts surrounded my vehicle.

I waited a minute to see if they would disperse on their own. They didn't. I tried blowing my horn. They were undeterred. I opened my door slowly to sweep them away. That only piqued their curiosity, and they started to walk toward the opening. I quickly shut the door.

As I sat contemplating how I was going to get out of there, I glanced at my rearview mirror. I had an opening. I quickly put my car in reverse and drove into a nearby driveway. I was finally free!

I headed back to work but in the opposite direction of where the birds were. I wanted to avoid any more confrontations. It was going to take me longer to get to my destination, but it didn't matter; I was already late.

I don't worry anymore when I'm stuck in traffic or even question what the reason for the delay is. I'm perfectly content to wait it out from the safety of my car.

— Kathy Diamontopoulos —

16

The Bear Facts

Camping is nature's way of promoting
the motel business.
~Dave Berry

I drove to Yosemite Valley, California, for the first time in years. Around the curve in the road stood the majestic El Capitan, 7,573 feet of sheer, golden-gray granite. Tears filled my eyes, and a collage of images of the fun-filled times our family of six spent in The Valley filled my mind. Summers when we hiked, rock-climbed, and played in the refreshing Merced River. Winters when we ice skated in the snowy forest wonderland, skied Badger Pass, and even once attended the fabulous Shakespearean Bracebridge Dinner.

This was the first time I'd traveled to The Valley by myself. The kids were grown, and my adventurous husband of many years had died recently. With his passing, I determined to somehow create a brand-new life for myself. Dan and I were outdoor people, and this became a priority for me.

I reconnected with old friends of ours and found out about Facelift, a project started by rock climber, Ken Yager. The goal was to spend a week volunteering to clean up trash in Yosemite Valley.

Thankfully, Yosemite Valley only has one or two roads, so it was impossible for the directionally challenged (me) to stay lost for long. I pulled into Yellow Pine, the campground set aside for volunteers at the event.

I felt shy and insecure as a new single. When I found the Group

C camp area, I saw eight event coordinators I'd been talking with recently but had never met. These were outdoor people. With their camping vans, Westfalia VWs and Toyota pickup trucks, these were the vehicles that *real* outdoor people drive. Suddenly, panic gripped me. *What am I doing here in my shiny, black BMW sports utility vehicle?* I felt like a phony. In fact, I felt so out of place that I drove right past them and left the campground to regroup.

Okay, Lynne, you can do this. They are just people, nothing to be afraid of. But that did not lessen the intimidation I felt. I knew I must return to set up my tent before it got dark, get my stove ready for dinner, and put all my food in the bear box. The bear box. Bears. That was a whole new, intimidating topic. I would sleep alone, every night, in my tent. Bears…

I turned around and returned to the campground. I found a campsite, parked, got out, and walked over and introduced myself. They were nice. No one mentioned my car.

The week turned into a wonderful learning experience. Meeting new people was a bonus. A few became forever friends.

But the nights were really hard! I was alone in my tent in the thick, black forest. There were absolutely no lights. I rarely slept. A ranger warned us about recent bear activity in our campground. A bear sow and her cub had been spotted prowling around during the day. The ranger explained that bears with cubs are especially dangerous. *Great information,* I thought. *What do I do with it? I know, double up on the fear quotient.*

Each night, I wrapped the elastic band of my headlamp around my wrist so I could instantly turn on its bright light. I placed a couple of metal pots by my sleeping bag to make noise if I heard anything. I lay awake most of the night staring at the tent door to see if it moved.

The week flew by. I enjoyed every part of it, except for the sleepless nights. My daughter joined me on the last day. Leah and I would drive together back to San Diego.

Sadness gripped me while packing up camp. I hugged my new best friends and exchanged cell numbers. Then, Leah and I were off with a last wave, a blast of the horn, and a blown kiss to the rock, El Cap.

The drive was fun as we caught up on each other's lives. Leah asked how I did camping alone for the first time. I said I'd remembered much from my outdoorsy past, but the nights were hard, really hard. I told her about the terror each night would bring. How I rarely slept, watching the door of the tent to see if a bear would break in. All night, I would watch that door, I said, listening for any slight sound or movement, dozing only briefly and then waking with a start at the slightest noise. I told her about the headlamp, and the pots and pans.

After I finished, Leah gave me a funny look. Then, there was dead silence for a while. I could tell she was thinking. Finally, with hesitation, she said, "Uh, you know, Mom, bears don't really know where the door in a tent is once it's closed and zipped up."

I thought for a moment, putting everything she said in place, and then started laughing hysterically. The entire week, while I was watching the door, a bear could have ripped open the thin tent wall right behind my head or the wall right next to my sleeping bag.

I felt like such a fool. Of course, a bear wouldn't know where the door was and focus his break-in there. And I'd felt semi-safe watching and listening all night long to make sure the bear didn't come in the tent's door.

We laughed out loud together all the way home.

—Lynne Leichtfuss—

17

To Bee or Not to Bee

Do something good; no one sees it. Do something
embarrassing; everyone sees it.
~Author Unknown

In 2021, I received a phone call that I had been chosen as one of three 2022 Grand Prize winners of "A Hotel Room of One's Own: The Erma Bombeck/Anna Lefler Humorist-in-Residence Program." It's a writing residency that *Forbes* magazine calls "the best in the country."

As Humorist-in-Residence at the Erma Bombeck Writers' Workshop at the University of Dayton in October 2022, I would be privileged to meet and workshop with such esteemed comedy writers as Cathy Guisewite, Laraine Newman, Annabelle Gurwitch, and Alan Zweibel. I was looking forward to finishing my book project during the two-week residency and indulging in some quiet. I knew without a doubt that the lack of distractions would lead to prolific productivity.

But, on the first Saturday of my writing residency, I discovered a bee in my hotel room.

I immediately FaceTimed my oldest son.

"Honey, there's a bee in my room."

"A bee? What floor are you on?"

"Third."

"How did a bee get into your room?"

"I left the window cracked."

"Your hotel-room window on the third floor opens?"

"No."

"No?"

"No."

"Then, how did the bee get into a window that doesn't open?"

"I opened it."

"Is this an Abbott and Costello routine?"

"I needed fresh air. I used my eyelash curler to unwedge the metal piece that prevents the window from opening."

"Can you put it back in when you leave?"

"I'm not sure. The metal kind of broke off."

"I see."

"So, what should I do about the bee?"

"Um, kill it?"

"What if it doesn't die and then seeks revenge on me while I sleep?"

"Insects don't seek revenge."

"There's an entire coterie of screenwriters who devote their lives to disproving that theory."

"So, catch it and release it."

"I can't catch it. What if it stings me?"

"Jeez. Where is it?"

"Here in the room."

"No, what part of the room?"

"Oh. On the glass part of the window."

"So, catch it in a cup. Do you have a plastic cup?"

I looked around and saw two Styrofoam coffee cups.

"Yes."

"Slide it into the coffee cup, put the lid on it, and then release it out the window."

"Okay."

I propped the phone up on a coffee mug facing the window, grabbed one of the two plastic cups, and managed to trap the bee in it. But each time I slid the cup to the open window and lifted it from the window surface, I couldn't get the lid on before the bee flew out, angrier each time.

Finally, I had the bee trapped, lid on, and released it out of the cracked window. It flew back in, and I screamed as it dive-bombed me.

In my terror, I dropped the cup out the window and ran screaming to the bathroom. I could hear raucous laughter coming from the phone.

Of course, I felt shame sitting in the bathroom. Who wouldn't? *Three days on my own, and this is what I've become?* I thought. *Hiding in the bathroom from a bee?*

No, I decided, *this is not how I'm going out.*

I marched, confidently this time, back into the room and saw that the bee had once again taken up residence on the window, oblivious to the fact that the promised land was merely six inches above him.

To the sound of my son yelling through the phone, "You got this, Mom!" I grabbed the second coffee cup and trapped the bee. Not willing to take any risks — and not really thinking it through — I threw the entire cup out the window and watched as it flew three stories down, right near the first one and at the feet of a couple who were trying to enjoy a glass of wine on the hotel patio.

"What the hell… again?!" The man jumped up and stared toward my window.

I yelled down to him.

"Look, I'm really sorry. But would you mind letting the bee out of that cup? He's been through a lot, so be careful as you release him."

They looked at me, back at the cup, and then back at me. I heard him mutter to his wife, "Is she kidding?"

Embarrassed, I drew the blinds across my window but caught my foot on the edge of the bed. I tripped and pulled the drapes halfway off their pulley. Startled, and in a very undignified manner, I fell to the ground to the sound of more laughter emanating from the phone.

Rising, I turned to see my son and his friend laughing but staring worriedly from the screen.

My son's friend turned to him. "How long is your mom writing in Dayton?"

"Two weeks," my son replied.

His friend shook his head.

"She's not gonna make it."

— Mary Oves —

18

Battle in the Night

The more disastrous the mishaps
the simpler the reviewing task.
~Donal Henahan

I hate spiders… always have and probably always will. Over the years, someone has always been around to see my irrational behavior when I spot one in the house. But one day, I was alone (except for a sleeping husband) and had to take on the battle by myself.

It happened at the end of one of those really long days when I'd finished my entire to-do list instead of pacing myself. That was a mistake. By the time I went to bed, I was spent, totally exhausted. The feathery down blanket felt like heaven as I wearily snuggled under it. Ahhh… It felt so good to just lie down!

Husband Pete was already asleep, so I was careful not to move around too much, and I was asleep within seconds.

About 2:00 in the morning, I rolled over, only to spy a long-legged, gargantuan spider crawling down the wall next to the closet about two feet away. Panic struck!

"Psst! Psst! Pete, wake up!" I'm not sure why I was so quiet since I wanted him to wake up and come to my rescue. "Psst! Psst!"

Now, you need to understand, I have this irrational fear of spiders. No matter how big or small they are, black, brown, or white… It doesn't matter. They just freak me out.

Yes, I know I'm over the top, especially for a normally rational adult. Often, I try to convince myself that, next time I see one, I'll be brave and just get rid of it. (By the way, all that self-convincing hasn't worked.)

So, Pete wasn't waking up with me quietly "Psst-ing" him, and I knew this long-legged intruder was probably still moving down the wall, coming closer. I jumped out of bed.

"Pete!" He didn't budge. I jammed my feet into my slippers and charged off to the kitchen.

There, I grabbed a flashlight and a flyswatter. I knew there was no way I could let this thing go cruising around my room and remain in there myself for the rest of the night.

With the swatter held high over my head, ready to strike, I charged back to the bedroom and skidded to a stop just far enough away not to be face-to-face with it. The flashlight clicked on, and I hoped it was loud enough to wake up Pete. No such luck.

I wasn't sure I could handle this all on my own, but I knew I couldn't wake him up just to kill a spider.

I focused the light on the wall. The spider was gone!

Systematically, I began the search up high, down low, in the closet, by the bookcase. Nope, it was well hidden or gone. GREAT! I knew I was never going to stay in the bedroom with it crawling around somewhere. What if it came up the side of the bed?

The couch in the living room was calling my name, but then I remembered a few nights earlier that a fast little bugger had run out from under it and scurried across the floor at record speed. Okay, count out that option.

With great reluctance and no alternative other than going out to the car to sleep for the night, I slipped back into bed, trusty swatter in one hand and flashlight in the other, intermittently searching the wall and floor.

It was going to be a ridiculously long night, but I was also kind of proud of myself for actually lying down in the same room. That NEVER would have happened before, so I guess I was improving somewhat.

Quietly, I waited... hoping, but not hoping, to spot it again. I wanted this to end so I could get back to sleep. I shut my eyes, hoping to drift off but still took an occasional glance at the wall just in case.

The flashlight got tangled up in the comforter, and I couldn't find it. It was just so dark, and I couldn't see anything.

Then, it dawned on me. Wait just a minute!

If I needed a flashlight to track down this spider, how could I have seen it crawling down the wall in the first place? The room was in complete darkness, and I had just woken up.

It was impossible! I must have been dreaming.... It wasn't real. There was no spider in reality, just a terrible, taunting dream!

Sheepishly, I got back out of bed and returned my weapons to the kitchen. I was thankful Pete never did wake up since I might have scared him to death wielding a swatter next to the bed, ready to strike!

Quietly, I slipped back into bed, pulled the comforter back up under my chin, and peacefully fell back to sleep for the night.

I didn't let on the next morning what I'd done, but eventually I told my family. All they could do was laugh and shake their heads while picturing me in the dark being valiant and brave.

Imagine, a dream transitioning into a real, wide-awake battle with a challenge I was willing to take on by myself. Who knows, maybe all that self-talk about not freaking out every time I saw a spider was actually beginning to take hold.

Well, maybe...

— Merry Broughal —

19

An Embarrassment of Riches

*Attitude is the difference between
an ordeal and an adventure.*
~Bob Bitchin

Sharon was missing! She was a sweet, innocent lady who had
grown up in Tulia, a small city in the Panhandle of Texas. She
could charm anyone with her "Howdy, y'all."

We had invited Sharon and her husband Bill to New York
City — the Big Apple — to celebrate their wedding anniversary. We
were staying at a luxurious hotel overlooking Central Park.

While having breakfast in the hotel dining room, Sharon excused
herself to go to the ladies' room. When she hadn't returned after thirty
minutes, I became concerned. Surely, she would have gotten a seat by
then. Bill didn't seem worried. He was busy explaining to my husband
what a terrific deal he had gotten on Sharon's life-insurance policy.

I went looking for her. She wasn't in the ladies' room or anywhere
in the hotel lobby. I asked a security guard if he had seen a pretty blond
lady. He said he had seen plenty of pretty, blond ladies. Wise guy!
He was no help.

Then, he asked, "When did you discover she was missing?"

"Sometime between the bacon and the eggs," I replied. I had been
raised in New York, so I could be just as much of a smarty as he was.

Maybe she went up to her room, I thought. I got on the house phone
and called. No answer.

At the front desk, I asked for Sharon's key. "Name?" the clerk wanted to know. I gave them Sharon's last name. They assumed that it was me since they had seen us together. Okay, maybe I didn't make myself clear, but I was worried about my friend. I took the key and went up to the tenth floor.

As I approached the room, I heard a man's voice.

What's a man doing there? I was alarmed.

When I heard a woman moaning, I quickly stuck the hotel key card into the door and pushed it open. Past a tiny hallway, I could see the bed.

Big mistake! A man and a woman were tossing around in the sheets. I didn't see much except for their expressions of shock. Escaping quickly, I yelled, chuckling, "Sorry! Wrong room. Carry on!"

Back at the breakfast table, Bill was still talking about life-insurance policies and bragging about how rich he'd be if anything ever happened to Sharon.

Sharon was still missing. She had been gone about an hour by then. Could she have walked out the front door and disappeared into Central Park across the street?

At the back of the dining room there were empty tables, and it was quiet. But I did hear something. If I listened closely, I thought I could hear a faint: "Help! Help!" Was I imagining it, or did the pleas for help have a Texas twang?

There was a door with a "No Trespassing" sign on it. I opened the door into a dimly lit hallway. At the end was another door: Powder Room. The pleas for help were more pronounced. I turned the handle and, inside the dark powder room, I heard Sharon's voice coming from behind a stall. "Help me!"

"Sharon, is that you?" I called.

"Eva! Help! The doorknob is missing. I can't open the d*** door."

It seems Sharon had stumbled into a powder room ordinarily open only at night and meant for the bar patrons. The doorknob on the inside of the stall had fallen off, and there was no space under the door for her to crawl out.

I quickly ran out to get security. They came and released poor Sharon.

Returning to our breakfast table, Sharon's face was beet-red. She was dripping in perspiration and verbally attacked her husband for not looking for her, for not rescuing her, for not giving a darn about her. My husband Larry tried to explain that Bill had gotten lost in conversation about her life-insurance policy. He only made it worse.

However, by the next morning, we had all calmed down. On Sharon's behalf, I made a complaint about the broken powder-room doorknob. Management apologized profusely and said they would compensate her for any inconvenience. They would be sending her a gift basket of fruit and flowers.

Back at the breakfast table, we began joking about the events of the previous day. I relayed my story about walking into the room I thought was Sharon and Bill's. The four of us were laughing and howling as I described barging in on the couple in bed. Maybe I exaggerated a bit about what I had seen. Or maybe not.

People at nearby tables heard us and joined in the laughter. Then the man at the next table tapped me on the shoulder and said, "Well, hello again!" It was the man I had walked in on while looking for Sharon. (Yes, I did recognize his face.)

"YOU'RE the one! You barged into our room yesterday just as we were… just as we were getting up for breakfast."

He went on to say that he had complained to the management about a stranger breaking into their room. The management compensated them as well.

"We received a free hotel stay for the weekend, dinner at the gourmet restaurant, and two tickets to a Broadway show."

We congratulated the couple, and, when they had left, Sharon uttered with some disappointment, "Life is not fair. Sounds like they got a Key to the City when I can't even get a Key to the Potty."

Maybe next time we will stay at a hotel in Brooklyn. I hear that's an up-and-coming neighborhood.

— Eva Carter —

Chapter 3

Domestic Disasters

20

Fit to Be Tied

Housework won't kill you, but then again,
why take the chance?
~Phyllis Diller

urely by accident, I came across a video on YouTube of a
woman, Kaylee, teaching others how to fold a fitted sheet. She
was perky and full of enthusiasm, and I could tell she had a
passion for her task.

What?! What foolishness is this? No one folds their fitted sheets.

Oh, you should have seen Kaylee go at it. She spread the fitted
sheet across the bed and tucked and folded and smoothed and patted.
And then she gently inserted her masterpiece into a matching pillowcase
for storage. Imagine that. She had matching pillowcases. A camera
shot into her linen closet showed adorable, papered shelves holding
several rows of neatly stacked pillowcased sheet sets. These brightly
colored parcels of bedding were lined up just so, color-coordinated,
with lighter colors on the left and deepening colors and prints to the
right. They were also complemented by a curved porcelain dish of
French soap, a lovely green plant in a hand-thrown clay pot, and a
pretty, antiqued makeup mirror.

What planet are we on? What kind of trickery is this? There are real-
world problems out there, Kaylee.

Not only are my sheets not stacked neatly, but half the time
they're on the floor in front of the open closet door. And I leave them
there. For days. French soap? Antiqued makeup mirror? I'm lucky the

shelves are still on the wall.

I decided to open my linen closet to take a peek, you know, just to examine and study the difference in our methods — if you can call what I do a method compared to Kaylee, who is obviously a mystical witch or has some kind of superpower or something. The door was barely cracked when wads of uneven lumps of material fell off the shelf and deposited themselves around my feet. Not only did my balls of sheets and other shelf jumble not come even remotely close to Kaylee's closet, but it also appeared that I had attempted a no-one-actually-lives-here look. The sheets, towels, washcloths, toilet paper, cotton balls and other assorted toiletries made it look like a terrible brawl had taken place. If I were a detective on a murder case, I'd look for a body hidden amongst the debris.

To my knowledge, there are only three ways to deal with a fitted sheet. Number 1: Wash it, dry it, and put it immediately back on the bed. Number 2: Tuck one corner into the other, fold in half, angrily roll in a ball, cry a little, have some wine, stuff in the closet. Number 3: Set the sheets on fire and bomb the sheet factory. Personally, I have always opted for #2, but I do think #1 is practical, and #3 appeals to the dark side in me.

I've struggled for years to find a trick for storing sheets. Well, not struggled. That's a stretch. Each time I did the wash, I generally gave it about ten seconds of thought before I threw my arms in the air and stuffed the offending sheets into the laundry basket where they stayed until I needed them. I used to tell my daughter that that's where sheets lived.

There was a time when I foolishly tried to manipulate the sheets on the folding table in the laundry room of my building. I liked to do it when they were nice and hot right out of the dryer, thinking they would bend to my will. But, of course, they were too big for the table. I'd inevitably bang my knuckles on the side of the wall in an attempt to get straight edges, or I'd end up dragging the whole thing on the floor. When I folded them at home, invariably one side always ended up so uneven and hung so low that I ran the risk of tripping on it. How embarrassing it would have been to have to call 911 and be taken out by stretcher for a sheet accident. I could imagine the look of disgust on the EMT's face as she lifted me off the floor and spotted my bed in a disarrayed, wrinkled sheet set that didn't match. And I just knew she would zoom in on the one pillow with no pillowcase on it.

I decided to leave it to the dryer to carry out the task. Whatever shape, ball, knot or wad my sheets end up in when the dryer has finished the cycle is exactly how they get shoved into the back of the linen closet. Doing it this way has its pitfalls. Sometimes, I don't notice that an odd sock has hidden in the sheets. Or a dryer sheet ends up inside a pillowcase in an annoying lump. But these are small prices to pay for not having to fold my sheets.

I'm almost positive that the "Macarena" is just a tutorial on how to fold a fitted sheet. Think about that for a minute. And let's hope they never make folding fitted sheets a roadside sobriety test, or some of us are going to be in big trouble.

It's not that I begrudge Kaylee's thoughtful video. Some people naturally drift to people like her. We have a lot more housekeeping help and guidance than we used to. I sort of resent that. In my day, we were lucky to have even one relative who would set us straight (probably our mother-in-law, and she likely relished the thought of setting us straight), let alone the worldwide web with all its tricks and hacks.

I watched the video a couple of times, learned nothing I could use, shut down the computer, scooped up the jumble outside my closet door, powered it back inside, and went and made some coffee. I'm quite confident that Martha Stewart is not coming to inspect my house this week.

—Jody Lebel—

21

No One Will Ever Know

Every survival kit should include a sense of humor.
~Author Unknown

I am organized and tidy, but sometimes I have to let things go. My daughter Lizzie's high-school graduation was one of those times. The day came in the middle of my end-of-the-year teaching responsibilities. Add hosting a graduation party and volunteering for the all-night grad party at her high school to my to-do list, and it was no wonder my house ended up being a mess.

On my way out the front door to the ceremony, I glanced back at bags of groceries left sitting on my kitchen counter. Dirty dishes, pots, and pans were piled up in the sink, left over from a hastily made macaroni-and-cheese dinner. Realizing that nothing needed to be refrigerated, I left the bags slumped over with a loaf of bread and several bags of chips overflowing onto the counter.

I also hadn't vacuumed all week, and our dog Cagney's hair was all over the living room. Upstairs, the outfits I had decided not to wear lay crumpled on my bedroom floor, and my make-up and hair curlers were spread out in the bathroom.

Picking up my keys and closing the front door, I gave one final look and clicked the key in the lock. A little voice assured me, "Valli, don't worry. No one will ever know. You can spend the whole day taking care of everything tomorrow."

The graduation ceremony was beautiful, with congratulatory hugs and photos all around. As the new graduates threw their caps in the air, our college-age son Adam, my husband Mike, and I gathered our programs and flowers and left for Lizzie's graduation party with her friends at our community center. It was a wonderful family celebration.

Later, while everyone at the party shared their memories of the day, Mike tapped me on the shoulder and said, "We better get going to the all-night grad party. It's getting close to the time for our shift." We quickly gathered our remaining party items and decided to make a short stop at our house. We dumped the extra sandwiches, pieces of graduation cake, and party balloons wherever we could find space. I let Cagney out the back door in the laundry room and rushed up the stairs to refresh my make-up.

Knowing Adam had a key to our house, we headed out to the all-night grad party. Once again, walking out the door, I took a moment. I looked back and noticed even more enormous mounds of items lying everywhere. I assured myself, "Valli, no one will ever know. You can take care of everything tomorrow."

At the all-night grad party, Mike enjoyed being the dealer at the "poker table" with the graduates while I passed out their goody bags full of coupons and gift cards. Finally, at 3:00 A.M., the next shift of volunteer parents came to replace us, and we headed home. Mike sighed and said, "Even though this day was so memorable, I can't wait to get home and get some sleep."

Just as we turned onto our street, a security car zipped by us. Adam was standing outside the front door as we parked in the driveway. Walking up the sidewalk, I asked, "Did you notice the security car on our street? I wonder what they were doing in our neighborhood at this time of night."

Adam explained, "Well, they just left our house."

"What happened? Are you okay?" I exclaimed. I quickly looked him over from head to toe but didn't notice any blood or bandages. Even the house looked the same as I had left it.

Adam answered, "I called them because when I came home, the place looked ransacked. I thought that maybe someone had broken in even though Cagney was still here. We all know he isn't much of a watchdog, so I called them to check on our house."

Mike asked, "How long were they here?"

"I guess for about a half-hour. The men asked me if anything was missing. I really couldn't tell. Nothing looked normal to me. So, they asked to check the entire house to make sure that no one was still here," Adam explained.

I gasped. "They checked everywhere? Surely not the upstairs, too?"

Adam said, "Yes. When they went downstairs, they noticed the laundry-room door was open, and piles of clothes were thrown all over the floor by the washing machine. They asked if I wanted them to check the downstairs and the bedrooms and bathrooms upstairs. They even checked all our closets. The entire house. I was so glad they didn't find anyone."

I turned around and saw the mess I had left. I could imagine the conversation as they drove away from our house. Security guard 1: "Man, Bob, I can't imagine living in a place like that. Food was lying out all over the kitchen counters."

Security guard 2: "Yep! It looked like they just threw everything all over the place, everywhere downstairs and upstairs. It looks like it might eventually turn into a serious hoarder problem."

1: "When I get home at night, I always tell my wife, 'You never really know how other people live.'"

Shaking my head as I walked upstairs to our bedroom for some much-needed rest, I whispered to myself, "I can't believe it! Why did I think that no one would ever know?"

— Valli Cowan —

22

Dad Lights the Furnace

Insanity runs in my family. It practically gallops.
~Cary Grant

Thanks to modern technology, the household furnace rarely elicits the fear and anxiety it once did in our home as fall rolled around. The annual lighting of the furnace was the most dangerous part of our winter preparation. Most families do not have to go through this yearly ordeal, but my father always turned off the pilot light in the spring to save on a few pennies worth of fuel with the result being The Annual Lighting of the Family Furnace. Imagine a blast of heralding trumpets to set the proper tone.

During the process of lighting, there would be an occasional, resonating "thump" accompanied by the ground briefly shaking due to Dad's efforts. One year, he shot out of the cellar doors trailing a cloud of smoke and flung himself to the ground to extinguish his smoldering sleeves.

And yet he never learned. Every fall, the same scenario would play out. We got so used to it that we didn't even look up at his hysterical exit from the basement, roaring profanities.

One fateful year, Mom had persistently reminded Dad that the house was getting colder as the days went by, and every day he promised to light the furnace after work. This went on for weeks until the first snow fell. At that point, completely exasperated, Mom reminded Dad before he left for work that if the pilot wasn't lit that night, she was going to hire someone. She was tired of wearing her coat and gloves in the house.

Well, that was throwing down the gauntlet for Dad. He would by no means allow her to hire someone for such a ridiculously simple chore. He insisted he'd do it that night.

What Dad had failed to mention was that, for the past month, he had been covertly trying to light the pilot. He had exhausted two boxes of 100-count wooden matches, their charred remains scattered about the basement floor.

Arriving home that night, he furtively crept down into the cellar, matches in hand. He had noticed upon his arrival that Mom's brother and family were upstairs. He had five children and the family pooch, which, combined with us, came to a total of ten children, four adults and two dogs in a three-room house. Dad wasn't particularly fond of these family members. They always managed to arrive precisely at mealtimes, and the children were allowed to range unsupervised, getting into everything. If they had known what he was doing, he would have quickly been inundated with questions and poking fingers, and the matches would have disappeared in seconds.

Quietly, he removed the panel that housed the pilot. Despite his past disastrous efforts, he wasn't convinced that fuel oil was flammable. Every layman he had consulted had reassured him of that fact. However, had he consulted a professional, he would have been assured that, yes, fuel oil was very flammable under the right circumstances, and if a fine enough mist was present, it could blow like gasoline.

Bending forward, he struck a match and held it close as he twisted the valve to the pilot orifice, watching in disgust as the match fluttered out. Striking another match, success eluded him once again. Muttering a curse, he went for broke.

Leaning inward, he struck a bundle of matches alight and then turned the burners on high, bypassing the pilot. He extended his blazing bouquet, and there was a sudden flash of fire and an eardrum-busting BOOM as the vapors trapped inside the boiler ignited, followed by an expulsion of air and flames, which blew all the accumulated soot loose since the furnace's installation many years before.

The furnace practically leaped into the air, discharging a belch of air and soot straight up the registers, resulting in high-pitched shrieks and screams from upstairs. The basement briefly became a vacuum as all the air was sucked up and thrust out through the registers.

Propelled backward by the explosion, Dad lay on the floor briefly dazed. But, being a man of action, he struggled to his feet after a few seconds, reeled up the cellar steps and stepped into what could have been the Twilight Zone. He had left a family of one wife and five children that morning in a spotless, little house with freshly painted walls. What now confronted him was a soot-covered family and soot covering every surface in the house. Mom later found a layer of soot inside the refrigerator. Although Dad didn't realize it, he was unrecognizable as well, wearing a layer of soot and minus his eyebrows.

Initially paralyzed by shock from the boom, Mom was uncharacteristically silent until her sister-in-law began to cackle, while ten children alternately shrieked and sobbed and the dogs barked in a frenzy, not recognizing anyone or each other.

Slowly, Mom turned her white-rimmed, cold green eyes upon Dad, who stood babbling his explanations. As the children screamed, and her sister-in-law cackled in delight, Mom exacted her revenge.

No one ate and no one left until that house was cleaned completely to her satisfaction.

And Mom was a perfectionist.

— Laurel L. Shannon —

How to Drive Like a Canadian

Life literally abounds in comedy
if you just look around you.
~Mel Brooks

One evening, a few weeks before Christmas, my husband Mike rushed into the house, stomping snow all over the floor. "Boy, it is FREEZING out there! And with ice raining on top of the snow, it was a tough drive home!"

"Well, at least it will be a white Christmas!" I smiled, turning to go upstairs for the night.

"I got a full vanload of food. It's gonna feed a lot of people!"

He had just been to a grocery-store outlet, where he bought a large skid of food for donating to many of the needy people in our community.

"The van is absolutely packed full. I even took out the back bench seat before I left so I could fit in extra food!"

"You took out the van seat?" I thought immediately of our three little kids who would need that seat to sit on.

"Don't worry. The seat is sitting in front of the garage. I'll put it back in after I deliver the food."

The next morning, as usual, Mike bounced out of bed and raced out the door.

"I've got an early coffee meeting. I'll just take the truck!" he called, heading toward our small pickup truck parked in the garage.

A cold blast hit me as he opened the door.

"Wow, it's cold! Drive carefully!" I called.

He hopped into the pickup and headed out the driveway and down the street.

It had been snowing and raining overnight, creating a thick, uneven crust on the roads. We lived in a small town on the Canadian border by Buffalo, New York, and weather was very unpredictable.

Looks like I'm too early for the snowplows! my husband thought. *But I'm Canadian — these roads are no problem for me!* He loved a challenge.

Turning the corner onto the main road, he thought again, *These roads are really rough! The ice is cracking as I drive on it!*

A car on the opposite side of the road honked and waved. He stuck his hand out the window and waved back. "Everyone is so friendly in this town!"

We'd only lived there a few years, but people had been so welcoming, and we'd made many friends.

The next car flashed its lights at him, another car honked, and a man standing on the corner waved both arms.

Boy, people are sure happy to see me today! Mike smiled, thinking how much more popular he would be when he shared all the donated food later that week. He thought, *I sure hope the snowplow gets out here soon. This ice is crazy! I can't believe how bumpy and noisy it is.*

The icy, scraping sound was getting louder the farther he drove.

Every car that passed honked or waved to him, bolstering his confidence in his morning winter drive.

"I AM CANADIAN!" he proudly chanted to himself.

A van going the opposite way slowed down, and the driver stuck his head out the window, pointing frantically at the front of our truck.

What is that all about? he wondered, pulling over to the side of the road.

When he got out of the truck, he noticed something strange. There was something in front of it.

It was the plush, tan van seat that he had removed the night before. He'd forgotten to move it out of the front of the garage and had been pushing it down the road for miles like a snowplow in front of his little truck.

It was completely covered in slush and snow, and the metal bottom was bent but miraculously still in one piece.

Sheepishly, he threw it into the back of his truck and continued on his way.

But the story of how Mike had been out snowplowing our town's streets with the back seat of his van spread through the whole town before the plows could clear any of the snow off our roads.

—Lori Zenker—

A Hairy Dilemma

*Housework is what a woman does that nobody
notices unless she hasn't done it.*
~Evan Esar

The flowers stood still in the walkway. Even the leaves on the maple tree hung motionless over the driveway on this serene Sunday afternoon. My mission: test my new handheld vacuum cleaner on our minivan, which bore evidence of four children and their beach adventures. Would the device live up to the proficiency the smooth-faced salesman promised?

An inch or so of sand and miscellaneous debris on the vehicle's floor served as mementos of our family escapades. But, for whatever reason, they seemed to drive my husband crazy. Perhaps this vacuum would restore peace to Camelot. Some sort of warning was etched on the device, but I paid no mind and went about my work.

I settled into a steady rhythm, impressed with the quiet purr and efficiency of this cleaning tool. Then, without warning, the vacuum lurched, caught a strand of my hair, and charged upward like an angry animal. "Thwap!" It affixed itself atop my head. Deep, guttural growls emitted from the menacing machine. I tried to wrestle myself from its grasp while it snapped and snarled like a wild, hungry beast and attempted to scalp me. Unable to reach the switch, I swallowed my pride and hollered for help, my cries shattering the neighborhood's sleepy silence. "Turn it off, turn it off!"

"It's off," my husband said in his deadpan voice. "I pulled the plug, so you can stop screaming now." His calm demeanor and bemused look only further agitated me.

"Oh," I said, sniffling. A small mountain arose and pulsated on my forehead where the vacuum had smacked me en route to its destination.

My husband cast a hasty glance at the scene and propelled me toward the garage. He appeared more concerned about the neighbors as audience and the demise of the vacuum than my hair. Or perhaps jealousy raised its ugly head. He hasn't much to lose as the long locks of his hippy days had long since departed and left him bald.

After several minutes of unsuccessful tries to pull my curly hair out of the beater brush, he slowly backed away. I imagined the newspaper headline: "Mr. Fix-It Fails to Free His Wife from Carnivorous Cleaner and a Dusty Demise."

"I'll be right back," my husband said. "Don't go anywhere."

My glare forbade his stifled laughter's escape.

Tell me, where did the man think I was going with a vacuum bobbing from my head?

He returned with a cordless screwdriver, and eleven screws later I scampered free, scalp intact. But, alas, the machine now lay in pieces, and all the king's horses and all the king's men could never put my brand-new vacuum cleaner together again. But perhaps it was better — at least safer — this way.

I retreated to the back yard with an ice pack on my swollen forehead. My five-year-old daughter rode up on her tricycle and, with furrowed face, demanded, "What happened to you?"

"I was cleaning the van, and the vacuum swallowed my hair and hit me on the head."

"You're weird!" she said and pedaled away.

I finally read the warning inscribed on the vacuum. It said to secure your hair. Good idea. Yup! I've found we risk getting tangled up and sucked into some pretty hairy dilemmas when we don't read and heed the maker's instructions.

— Rachael M. Colby —

What's for Dinner?

I realized very early the power of food to evoke
memory, to bring people together, to transport you to
other places, and I wanted to be a part of that.
~José Andrés Puerta

My husband and I had been friends with Steve and Becky for quite a few years. They had been to our house many times for dinner. Each time, as they were leaving, they'd say they'd had such a good time being with us and that we absolutely needed to come to their house for dinner. *Okay,* we'd think to ourselves, *but you must ask us first. We just can't drop in and expect you to have dinner ready. An invitation would be nice.* They kept making excuses for why they weren't inviting us, though: They needed to have the carpets cleaned. They needed to have the living room painted. They were having new kitchen appliances installed, and they had to learn how to use them.

Finally, the much-anticipated invitation came. A date was set for us to have dinner at their house. They asked if we had any dietary restrictions. That was considerate of them. We had none. They told us they really liked Chinese food and, if that was okay with us, that's what we would have. Sounded good to us. As long as the food isn't too spicy, we like and eat everything.

On the evening of the dinner, we arrived at their house. We had brought a bouquet of flowers and a special bottle of wine for our hosts. They seemed appreciative and thanked us profusely. We noticed that there were no food aromas to be sniffed out, but maybe the Chinese dishes they were cooking didn't give off much of a smell. We sat down and talked for a while, waiting for them to offer us some wine or bring out some appetizers. Cheese and crackers? Nuts? Anything would have been nice. They were very talkative and friendly, and our discussion was fun and interesting, but neither of them made a move toward the kitchen.

After about forty-five minutes, they told us it was time for dinner and asked us to move into the dining room. The table was set for four with only a dinner size plate and a fork at each place. We sat where they told us to. They both went into the kitchen. My husband and I looked at each other, wondering what was going on. This evening had started on such a weird note. What would the rest of the evening bring?

They both came into the dining room carrying a few white, take-out food cartons. Really? What happened to their excuse about needing to learn how to use their kitchen appliances? It seemed like the only kitchen appliance they had used was their telephone, to call the Chinese restaurant.

They put the take-out cartons on the table, opened them and put a teaspoon in each one so we could serve ourselves. Now, my husband and I both love Chinese food; all the different sauces and textures are so delicious. This take-out food? Not so much. Texture... hard to say. And everything was only room temperature, like it had been picked up earlier in the afternoon and sat in the kitchen for a few hours.

The plain white rice was clumpy and stuck together in big globs, making it difficult to chew. The chicken dish supposedly had an orange sauce on it. I guess they forgot to put the oranges in the sauce. It was just kind of tasteless and gummy. The sweet-and-sour pork... I can't even describe it. It could have been sweet-and-sour shoes for all we knew. And what was that square thing that was kind of grayish, squishy and watery? So glad we didn't know. There were no egg rolls, dumplings, hot-and-sour soup, duck, shrimp or crab. And no fortune cookies! Now, that was disgraceful. There was nothing to drink. Nothing! I finally asked for a glass of water so I could chew my food... and swallow it.

Although the conversation was easy, and there were none of those awkward and dreadful silent periods where no one says anything and the silence is deafening, my husband and I were stunned. We were astonished. We were stupefied! And needless to say we didn't — really, couldn't — eat much, so we were also starving! Why would anyone intentionally buy and want to eat that food (if you could even call it food)? And I wanted a glass of wine — that lovely wine we had brought for our hosts. Please, just give me a glass of wine!

We left as soon as we could, making excuses that we needed to get back home to let out the dog. The dog was fine; *we* had to get out of there! Not only because we were going to burst out laughing if we looked at each other one more time, but the most important thing was: We were famished! Absolutely starving. We jumped in the car and headed for the closest McDonald's, hoping it would still be open at 10:00 at night. Thank goodness, it was. We ordered our Quarter Pounders with cheese, French fries, and soft drinks. If only McDonald's served wine, everything would have been perfect. The burgers came, and we wolfed them down. Nothing had ever tasted so good.

— Barbara LoMonaco —

26

The To-Do List

A house is made of walls and beams;
a home is built with love and dreams.
~Willian Arthur Ward

After my two children finished college, I realized that my big empty nest was too big and too empty for only me. So, after a few weeks of searching, I found myself the new owner of a somewhat smaller but very nice townhome.

It was beautiful and just what I needed. There was plenty of room for me and just enough space for guests and possibly, someday, visiting grandchildren.

There are always projects that need attention when you move into a new home, so I started a to-do list. There were a few things that I thought I'd be able to fix inexpensively regarding my bedroom's walk-in closet:

1. The outdated shiny brass handle on the closet door needed to be replaced. I preferred a sleeker design in brushed nickel, not the curved style with the curlicue at the end.

2. The fluorescent light in that closet sometimes took as long as ten minutes to pop on and would have to be repaired. At the home-improvement store, surrounded by a knot of serious older men in orange aprons, I learned all about something called a ballast. I figured it must be something important because the word "ballast" was used many times during their meeting of the minds. There was head shaking and nodding going on simultaneously, but all I heard was "Hmmm,

blah blah, blah, ballast, blah, blah, hmmm, ballast." I just wanted the light to pop on.

3. And finally, the closet lacked wall hooks, so I had no place to hang my robe when getting dressed. I am not a throw-things-on-the-floor kind of girl, and this task was a snap. No need for a team of well-meaning home-improvement gentlemen. The stick-on type of hooks would work just fine. I slapped a hook on the wall and hung my oversized, terry bathrobe up by its sturdy loop. Five seconds after I walked away, I heard a soft thwump and found my robe, with the hook still attached to the loop, on the closet floor.

Okay, fine. I needed help. That weekend, my brother Tom said he would stop by and change the door handle, install a few good hooks in my closet, and deal with the ballast situation. Great. What could go wrong?

Here's what could go wrong.

I was taking a shower about a half-hour before Tom was due to arrive when I realized I had left the front and back doors wide open. It was a beautiful day, and I wanted to let the warm spring breeze come through the house, but now I was concerned that he might come in while I was in the shower. I quickly finished and put on my robe.

With my underwear in hand, I headed to my closet to pick out clothes for the day. Because of the previous day's hook failure, I tossed my robe across the room onto my bed. No way would I let it fall to the floor.

Then, steadying myself carefully against the closet door, I stepped into my underwear. With only one leg through, I realized I had wedged the fabric of my panties into the curlicue of the door handle. I pulled. I tugged. I was stuck.

I had to think fast. I was firmly affixed to the door handle by one leg hole, ninety-nine percent naked. The front door was open, my robe was hopelessly out of reach, and my brother was just minutes away. I would have to shuffle with the attached door bumping and closing behind me to grab some clothes from inside the closet. I snapped on the light, but, of course, it did not pop on because of the ballast, so I was now in complete darkness, unable to see or reach any clothes and still hopelessly jammed into the curlicue.

And then the unthinkable: The doorbell rang. Since I couldn't answer, in a few moments, I heard Tom clomping up the stairs, toolbox rattling, calling my name.

After a very confusing conversation through the closed door, I cracked it open an inch and stuck out my hand. He gave me a pair of scissors. Then, presto! The light finally popped on. I cut myself out and quickly pulled on some clothes.

I now have hooks. And a modern-looking door handle. And a functional ballast (even though I still don't know exactly what it is). But I am much more careful about locking my doors when I shower.

— Loretta Morris —

27

Our Covid Christmas Cake

Where there is cake, there is hope.
And there is always cake.
~Dean Koontz

I t was the Christmas when everyone got Covid. Well, almost everyone.

My son had a stuffy nose, which we assumed were his typical allergies from my parents' dog until he got a fever. By the time we figured out it was Covid, he had passed it to his brother and me, and I passed it to my sister's kids, who shared it with their mom, Lauren. We thought my daughter, Kate, was in the clear until she caught it at band practice.

My husband and our older daughter, Amy, dodged it. That was good news, except that it meant we couldn't spend the holiday together.

My sick kids and I were staying with my sister, so Lauren and I planned a last-minute Covid Christmas. After we had to call off the plans to visit our parents, we thought about how we could make the best of being stuck in on the holiday.

As we were discussing a new festive meal plan for five children, Lauren had a burst of inspiration. "We should get a cake that says, 'Happy birthday, Jesus. Sorry your party sucks.'"

In all the sickness and frustration, I laughed. "Oh, we're definitely doing that." I reached out to our personal Christmas elf, Amy.

Amy was seventeen and happy to utilize her new driver's license to pick up my online orders for stocking stuffers and holiday meal fixings to leave on our doorstep. I asked her to put in a special order for a cake with my sister's exact wording.

"How do I order a cake?" Amy asked, which is a fair question for a high school student.

I told her to go to the grocery store bakery and get a form to fill out, emphasizing that it was incredibly easy, and she had nothing to worry about. She found the process daunting but completed the errand, requesting to pick up the cake on Christmas Eve.

The day came, and Amy called me from the store. "Mom, this cake is really big. I think I need help getting it to my car."

"Oh, I'm sure it's fine," I said because that's what you say when your teenager orders a birthday cake for Jesus when you have Covid. Amy somehow got it out of the store and into the back of her Subaru. A little while later, she was kicking at our door because her hands were full, and she couldn't reach the doorknob. We let her in to find out that she couldn't leave the cake at the door because it was the size of the doorstep.

There were seven people isolating at my sister's house. This cake could serve a small wedding. Amy had ordered a whole sheet cake because, well, why would you order less than a whole cake? She didn't realize she had to request a specific size, and I never clarified that detail. She admitted it seemed kind of expensive, but she wasn't sure how much a custom cake ought to cost. She had no idea how much cake she bought until she picked it up.

And, there it was, enough white cake with lemon filling for fifty people, taking up more than its fair share of real estate on the countertop in my sister's small kitchen. "Happy birthday, Jesus. Sorry your party sucks" was written elegantly in red icing with red and green buttercream flowers to give it a festive touch. It was so, so, so much cake. Since we all had Covid, we couldn't share it outside the home. No one would want it.

The original plan was to serve this cake on Christmas Day, but it was still early in the day on Christmas Eve. "I guess we should have some cake," I said. There wasn't room in the fridge, and the sooner we started eating it, the less would be wasted before it went stale.

"But then we won't have dessert for Christmas!" Lauren protested.

"I think we'll have plenty."

So, we cut into Jesus's birthday cake early and then again that evening. We let the kids have some cake for Christmas breakfast, and then we had it again for Christmas dinner. We snacked on it as we played on my nephew's new foosball table, watched movies, and Lauren and her daughter roller-skated in the house. We wore pajamas or comfy Christmas sweatshirts all day, and if the kids wanted cake, they didn't have to ask permission.

As I took another piece of cake on Christmas night, I told my sister, "This party didn't suck after all." Yes, it was disheartening that our whole family couldn't be together, and we were tired and congested as we recovered from being ill, but we still enjoyed the time we had and made a memorable holiday.

And Jesus's birthday party continued as we ate His cake for the next three days.

— Rachel Ollivant —

28

The Egg Hunt

*At the height of laughter, the universe is flung
into a kaleidoscope of new possibilities.*
~Jean Houston

"Ready, set, go," Daddy yelled, as three generations of our family raced around the yard.

"I found one." Our eleven-year-old son, Joe, plucked a shiny orange egg from among the tulips, dropped it into his Easter basket, and dashed off to explore the next spot.

My older brother, Doug, grabbed a blue egg from the crook in the locust tree. With a smirk, he stepped over and turned up the frond of a sword fern to discover a purple one. At the same time, our older son, Ben, and his younger sister spotted an egg hidden in the branches of the Alberta spruce.

Bethany dove her hand toward the egg. "Hey, I was gonna get that."

Ben plunked the green egg into his basket. "Yeah, but I got it first."

We scoured the surrounding flowerbeds, grass, and shrubbery but discovered no more eggs. "Let's count off," I said.

My husband, Loren, glanced into the shopping bag he carried as a makeshift Easter basket. "I have three."

"Me, too," Bethany added.

As each person called out their number, we calculated the total. "That can't be right." I scanned the search area. "That's only twenty-three. There have to be more."

The egg hunt was the highlight of Mom and Daddy's Easter gathering.

My parents started the tradition at their home in the country when my children were little. With at least ten of us on the hunt, Mom always hid well over a hundred eggs.

Before enthusiasm waned, I sprinted to the house. The aroma of fresh-baked ham greeted me as I opened the front door. Mom buttered rolls at the counter and placed them in aluminum foil.

"Mom, where did you say you hid the eggs? We can only find twenty-three."

Drying her hands on a dishtowel, she came out into the yard. With a wave of her hand, she pointed. "Most of the eggs are hidden in the grassy area between the lawn and that row of fir trees, up toward the back of the house and halfway down the driveway to the cherry tree." As she finished instructing us, her mouth gaped open. Shock covered her face. Looking at my dad, she gasped. "Gar, you mowed the grass!"

Appearing just as confounded, Daddy sputtered, "Well, uh... it was getting overgrown. I wanted to clean things up before everyone got here."

"That explains these." I scooped up a handful of purple, orange, yellow, and blue fragments that lay scattered across the lawn, all that remained of the eggs Mom had hidden the night before.

Gathered in the yard, with some of our baskets still empty, we stood in shock until Doug broke out laughing. "Didn't you hear the plastic breaking?"

"I wore ear plugs." My dad shrugged. "I didn't hear anything."

Someone giggled. Then, like popcorn popping, laughter bounced from one of us to another. We laughed until our eyes watered, and we doubled over trying to catch our breath.

Since that memorable egg hunt, another generation has joined our Easter fun. The surprised grandkids of yesteryear are now the ones hiding the eggs. Rarely a year passes without someone saying, "Hey, remember when Grandpa Fox mowed over the eggs?" Laughter and giggles carry through the yard while great-grandchildren, who never met him, recall his Easter mishap as our family's annual egg hunt continues.

— Kathleen Kohler —

29

Quacking Up

All great deeds and all great thoughts
have a ridiculous beginning.
~Albert Camus

Oh, no, not again. It was 6:30 a.m. and I heard the psychedelic guitar playing of Jimi Hendrix in the back yard. And my wife screeching.

My wife is stubborn and determined. When she wants something she makes it happen. And that is why we opened our pool in April, even though no one with half a mind opens a pool in April in Connecticut. First of all, it is still sleeting, if not snowing, and secondly, and this is important... April is when the ducks are looking for their new homes. They've flown back up from the south and they're setting up housekeeping again, building nests, laying eggs, and starting their next batches of ducklings.

But my wife was the team mom for the high school's lacrosse team, and they were having their team dinner in April. My wife wanted to crank up the heat and give those boys a treat — a pool party in April, two months before it really gets warm enough to swim.

The first year we opened the pool that early we had an unintended consequence: two ducks — a male and a female — made our pool their home. We chased them away again and again, but they kept coming back, and they made our pool unusable for months, because their droppings are *huge*. We finally got rid of them in July and were able to use our pool for the second half of the summer.

Even though my wife is very analytical, she refused to see the light on this one. So, sure enough, she opened the pool in April again the following spring in anticipation of another lacrosse-team pool party. And the ducks returned.

This time she was a bit chastened. And she confessed that this might have been a big mistake. So she set out to conquer the ducks. The former Wall Street analyst in her emerged and she started mapping out a battle plan. She had learned that the ducks didn't care at all if she yelled at them. But she remembered a historical fact that had tickled her fancy — that when Panamanian strongman General Manuel Noriega was being deposed by U.S. troops he had holed up in the Vatican Embassy in Panama City. He wouldn't come out, even when the embassy was surrounded. So the U.S. Army engaged in psychological warfare — by blasting hard rock at Noriega. Their playlist included songs by The Clash, Guns N' Roses, The Doors, and Van Halen. After one week, Noriega, an opera lover, surrendered.

My wife, a child of the Seventies, rolled out the big guns: Jimi Hendrix. She tried various songs and learned that the ducks really hated "Purple Haze." "Purple Haze" would get them moving, and with two-acre zoning we wouldn't be bothering the neighbors. She also learned that the ducks didn't like it if she looked bigger than she really was.

So that's why our mornings began as follows: she would get up, look out the window, and start yelling, "They're back. The stupid ducks are back." She'd rush downstairs and turn on the Jimi Hendrix CD that was preloaded and ready to rock and roll. As the outdoor speakers filled the back yard with electric-guitar riffs, she would run out in her robe and blue, fuzzy dog-paw slippers, grab a pool noodle to look bigger, and start threatening the ducks with the bouncing noodle, all while screeching at them to "go somewhere else."

I'd be watching the whole thing and laughing. The ducks would flap their wings halfheartedly in response to the loud music and the menacing pool noodle and hop out of the pool and onto the lawn. My wife would wave them off a bit longer, and then come back inside and turn off the music.

And the ducks would hop back into the pool.

Thus, we spent a second spring and early summer sharing our pool with the ducks. That meant *they* got the pool and *we* got the hot tub, which was the body of water they did not sully with their droppings. And then, one day, we watched our tenants fly into the pool as we sat in the hot tub. And my analytical wife realized something: ducks take off and land like airplanes. They don't drop straight in like a helicopter. They need a long gradual flight path, and they don't want to be hemmed in once they are in a body of water.

So my wife took every single piece of outdoor furniture we had and arranged them around the pool. It was a wall of eighteen chairs and chaise lounges, all with their backs to the water, making it impossible for the ducks to glide in for a landing like an airplane.

That was the end of the ducks. But for the rest of that summer and for the next couple of springs, our pool looked rather peculiar. Every time you wanted to go swimming you had to move a chair out of the way and then put it back in place when you got out. We had to make sure that the ducks had fully committed to someone else's pool before we could go back to normal, or whatever passes for "normal" in our house.

— Bill Rouhana —

Family Fun?

30

This Is How We Do It

I have always felt that laughter in the face of reality is
probably the finest sound there is and will last until the
day when the game is called on account of darkness.
~Linda Ellerbee

I t started with a clumsy fall in an uneven crosswalk. I was mystified as to how I didn't auto-correct myself like I've done so many times before. If I caught my foot on something, it would lead to me using a quick step to regain balance or an athletic roll to the ground, which usually turned into a comedy routine while I stealthily maneuvered to my feet and finished it by raising my hands in the air while announcing, "I'm okay!" or "Nailed it!"

Embarrassment was my first thought, but that was replaced with puzzlement as I was helped up by my wife, Connie.

Weeks passed before another peculiar incident gave me a warning. As I carried out a collection of leftover pizza slices from one of our favorite eateries, the box began to shake. I switched the box to my right side in order to look at my quivering left hand. I hid the misbehaving hand in my jacket pocket as I quickened my pace to catch up with my fast-walking wife. My gait was off its normal stride. I could hear my trailing toes dragging across the sidewalk.

My sporadic shuffling feet and hand tremors continued for many months, but I refused to acknowledge them. A few years before, the boredom of becoming suburban empty nesters became a call for change. Connie and I boldly flipped the switch to embrace urban life in downtown Cincinnati. Everything we enjoyed doing together was mere steps away. Our new adventure didn't need to be slowed down because I was starting to age.

Spring opened with an unusually warm March, prompting our favorite parks, restaurants and bars to open windows, gates and outside tables to trigger what had become our favorite pastime: roaming downtown to meet up with friends. While pushing to get to a gathering on time, I caught a dragging toe on a raised corner of the sidewalk and face-planted into the concrete. My mind didn't auto-command my body to use a quick step or a roll. It proved the old joke was true: The hardest part of falling is the ground.

A concerned Connie got me upright, and we continued to our destination. We laughed about the fall as I took some heat from my good-natured friends. I politely smiled while the left hand continued shaking in my pocket. It didn't stop until a few hours after we got home.

The next day, we decided to skip our planned walk and took a trolley across the bridge to Kentucky to join visiting friends. They selected a floating restaurant on the Ohio River that features a beautiful outdoor deck with an incredible view of downtown Cincinnati. The trolley stopped short of the traffic light nearest the restaurant. Quickly exiting the trolley, since our friends had saved us a seat already, we tried to catch the crosswalk light. I tripped again. The fall was worse this time.

I couldn't shake this one off. Pain stabbed into my shoulder and ribs. Angry, I refused to be helped up to my feet. After falling two days in a row, Connie insisted something was wrong. I finally agreed to see my physician.

The doctor checked my ribs, tested my balance and observed my hands manipulate different exercises. He recommended I see a neurologist at the University of Cincinnati. I asked him to give me his opinion of what was wrong.

He was always straightforward with me. He told me it could be an inner-ear problem, but the falls, tremors and results of my coordination exams indicated it might be Parkinson's disease.

The neurologist appointments came and went. The diagnosis was

Parkinson's. The disease was not a death sentence, but we were devastated. With no cure... lots of prescriptions... a degenerative disease.

It was terrifying to think of telling our sons that I had Parkinson's. Both boys lived out of town. Kevin had moved to New York City to work, and Nate was finishing up his degree at Ohio University. We were to be together at Christmas to celebrate the holidays. Connie and I agreed that breaking the news to them in person was best.

I remember thinking, *What a gift*. "Guess what you get for Christmas, guys? Your father is sick!"

It was so uplifting when the boys came home. Behind conversations about past Christmases, friend updates and their lives outside of Cincinnati was the aura of the unspoken. I could feel they sensed something was wrong. We knew it was time to talk.

The explanation didn't take long, but it was difficult. They both knew that Parkinson's disease is serious. I only answered questions as they arose. Connie did most of the talking because I didn't want to seem too emotional about it. Soon, the room became silent as we all were lost in our thoughts. They looked so sad. It felt heavy. Dark. Foreboding.

The moment hung awkwardly until Nate lifted his eyes like an idea had just popped into his head and asked, "Okay, how long before we can start having fun with this?"

I saw a twinkle in his eye, a sheepish grin by Kevin, and a look of amazement on Connie's face. My wonderfully modern, dysfunctional, close-knit family was looking for my response. They wanted to handle this crisis as we always did: with humor! It is the way we heal relationships, settle arguments, and support each other. The answer was already on my face. I was smiling.

I gave my approving nod while replying, "Now would be good."

Nate rose out of his seat. He had always been comfortable on stage. Kevin leaned forward with anticipation. Connie was already giggling at him. I sat back and waited for my comedic assassination.

"You know," he began, "you'll still be able to work. You could be a bartender."

After a perfectly timed pause, he added, "With those tremors, you could shake the shit out of a specialty cocktail."

Kevin picked up on the vibe and added, "Think about this. With the way this Parkinson's thing progresses, you will only get better at it!"

With that, laughter broke out, and the darkness disappeared. Playful insults, snarky barbs, bad puns and dad jokes ruled. But, most of all, Parkinson's didn't win that day.

— Sherm Perkins —

31

The Ride of My Life

Courage is being scared to death...
and saddling up anyway.
~John Wayne

One summer vacation, I allowed my husband and our three
sons to talk me into going horseback riding. I'd never been on
a horse in my life. Horses scare me. They look at you funny
like they know something you don't.

"It will be fun," they said.

"What if the horse bucks, and I fall off?" (I wanted to add, "...And
I break both legs and both arms and am in a full-body cast, and you
all have to get your own meals, buy the groceries, run errands, wash
and iron clothes, and clean the house." However, I kept my mouth
shut. I was trying to be a good sport.)

When we arrived, the trail leader assured me that he would give
me his most gentle horse. He told me that he had never had a horse
buck anyone. The horse he brought out for me may have looked gentle,
but he was very big and tall... about sixteen feet tall, it looked like
to me. How on earth was I going to get on this horse using only one
little stirrup on the side? Well, it took my husband and three sons to
do it, but they got me on that horse!

I still don't understand why there is only a little knob on the
saddle to hang onto. I wanted handles or a sturdy bucket seat with
a seatbelt or even one of those big baskets they put on elephants. I
sat wondering why I was doing this in the first place. But I was too

embarrassed to say I had changed my mind.

Since the trail leader knew I had the gentlest and slowest horse, he placed me at the very end of the trail line. I was happy because then I could grumble without anyone hearing me. If I looked ridiculous sitting on this horse, everyone else would be in front of me and couldn't watch me. So, off we went, with my husband and three sons smiling with all the other people on the trail. I wasn't smiling; I was hanging on. It was bumpy and uncomfortable, and I knew I wasn't going to like it. But I'd sacrifice my feelings for my family. After all, it was just a simple horse ride, and it would be over soon.

The trail leader told me I didn't have to do much because the horse knew exactly what to do and where to go. He would follow along the trail with the other horses. It would be a gentle ride through the woods and fields and then back to the horse barn. He also said I only needed to know two things:

1. Kick my heels in the horse's side to make him go.
2. Pull on the reins to make the horse stop.

"Nothing to worry about," he said. I was hoping the horse had heard that, too.

We started out just fine, and as soon as we got into the woods, my horse became very gentle as well as slower. By the time all the other horses were out of the woods, my horse and I were still in the woods! I saw our youngest son waving to me in the distance. I waved back, faking a smile. This seemed to be the longest ride with this boring horse and me. *Are you supposed to talk to a horse?* I didn't know. Besides, I certainly didn't have anything to say. However, I didn't want to irritate him because I had heard that horses know when you're scared or don't like them, so I would just have to fake him out.

We finally got out of the woods and were in a bean field. Suddenly, my horse stopped. Then I remembered one other important thing the trail leader had told me. He said, "Don't let the horse stop to eat the beans because then the horse won't want to go back to the barn." I looked down, and the horse was eating the beans.

"Oh, my goodness!" I yelled at the horse. "Don't eat the beans."

The horse just turned his head, looked at me (I think he was scowling), and kept on eating the beans. Now I would never get back to the barn! What was I supposed to do? *Maybe I wasn't nice enough,* I thought, so I said to the horse very nicely, "Please, horse. Don't eat the beans." It didn't matter because the horse was determined to stay there. I heard the echo of our youngest son asking my husband, "Where's Mom?" They all looked back at me but just kept riding back to the barn. I saw the trail leader motioning with his hand for me to come ahead.

"Let's see," I mumbled. "In order to make the horse go, you kick the horse on the sides with your heels." So, I did that, but the horse didn't move. What's more, I don't think he liked it. He turned his head, looked at me and then nudged my toe with his mouth. I thought he might bite my foot, so I took my foot out of the stirrup. *I'll fool him,* I thought. Kicking didn't work! I tried, "Giddy-up," which didn't work. Then I just said, "Go!" That wasn't working either. He just kept right on eating those beans. I wanted to cry, but I figured that wouldn't work either, so I got angry. I said, "Giddy-up" and "Go" louder as I scowled at the horse. Nothing worked! He was at a dead stop, and he wasn't going to budge.

Finally, the trail leader must have realized I was in trouble because he left everyone back at the barn and came back to rescue me. I saw this, but so did the horse, who suddenly got the message that he was in trouble. He made the decision that it was in his best interest to immediately stop eating the beans and get back to that barn as fast as he could. I didn't have to kick. I didn't even have to say "Giddy-up" or "Go" because he just started to gallop, and he galloped faster and faster in a straight beeline for that barn!

There I was, with only one foot in the stirrups, not much to hang onto, bouncing up and down on this gentle son-of-a-gun horse that had turned into a galloping fool. The horse and I passed up the trail leader and the entire trail group. He went galloping right into the barn door and came to a dead stop. Both of us were out of breath! I must have looked pale, shaken and mad because my husband and three sons rushed to help me get off. They tried not to laugh. My only words were: "Don't you ever, I repeat, ever ask me to ride any horse again in my entire life!" They were silent. I wasn't in any mood to be reckoned with. I think, this time, they paid attention.

— Lynn Assimacopoulos —

32

Labor Pains and Sleepovers

Motherhood: Powered by love.
Fueled by coffee. Sustained by wine.
~Author Unknown

If you are a parent, there will come a time in your life when your daughter will ask sweetly, "Can I have a sleepover?" I'm using a daughter for this example because eighty-nine percent of all sleepovers are with girls. I know it's true. I Googled it. Sleepovers are just like labor pains in my book. Hour by hour, centimeter by centimeter, the pain grows.

1 cm: Your first thought may be pure delight. Your child has friends, and she wants them to stay overnight at your house. (Does that mean you are the cool mom?) You might even shed a tear. Well, wipe that tear away right now and batten down the hatches! As a mom who survived five kids and hundreds of sleepovers, I am here to offer some expert advice.

2 cm: Forget about buying healthy food. You can spend eighty dollars on granola mix, fruit, veggie dips, low-fat potato chips, and no-salt pretzels, etc. These girls only want pizza, real chips, ice cream, gummy bears, licorice, and extra-butter popcorn. Mental note for your sanity: Never buy graham crackers, marshmallows, and chocolate. They will attempt to build a campfire in your yard at 3:00 A.M. to make s'mores. If you must, buy marshmallows in a jar and let them microwave a snack. The fire marshal will thank you.

3 cm: The most important thing is to keep the number of kids

to an even number. I don't care if it's two, four, six, or eight. And, truthfully, if it's six or eight, you probably should be in a mental ward. If you have an odd number, there is an unwritten rule that, at 2:00 A.M., someone will feel left out and have hurt feelings. That child will cry loudly, very loudly, until you call her parents to take her home.

4 cm: It's always the dad who fetches the sobbing night owl. By the time he arrives at the door, the girls will be lining up like soldiers to hug, squeeze and tell Suzy they love her. For the past hour, they bickered, but now in the darkness, there is a "Kumbaya" moment. At this point, there will be an hour-long discussion about whether Suzy wants to leave. It's all very dramatic. "Please don't go! We'll miss you!" Sometimes, the other girls even cry while saying it. The mood will shift, and Suzy will decide to stay. You and Suzy's dad will bond while you apologize that you had to wake him to drive twenty minutes for nothing.

5 cm: There should be a parents' code where we swear never to tell a soul how either parent looks at the "fetching hour" of the night. This is another reason why you should be very careful about your daughter's sleepover choices. Stay away from the girls with hoity-toity parents. You don't want them gossiping about your scary self. You might remember Suzy's dad as a handsome man: clean-shaven with bright blue eyes. That's his daytime look. At the "fetching hour," he looks like Fred Flintstone. I could only hope he didn't mention to anyone that I looked as if I'd been electrocuted. I look like a mad woman when I don't get my sleep.

6 cm: You've had just about enough of the dramatic almost-farewell. As you close (slam) the door, you fall asleep climbing the stairs to go back to bed.

7 cm: The heavy-duty labor pains are coming fast!

8 cm: Just after you tuck in each child and say goodnight (morning), your daughter will remember that there is popcorn and ice cream downstairs. You will hear what sounds like a herd of centipedes running down the stairs as your head hits the pillow. Your husband will sleep through all of this, so be sure to make mental notes. He'll love to hear all about it in the morning.

9 cm: There is usually an array of talent in the sleepover group: a gymnast, a dancer, a singer, and a baton twirler, if you're lucky. After ice cream with sprinkles and whipped cream, these talents come to life at 4:00 A.M. Music will fill your house. No, really, music will FILL your house. Dance lessons will ensue as they learn new shake moves in their nighties. The gymnast is always a winner because she uses your sofa top as a balance beam while she shimmies. And let's not forget the singer who is not a singer in the darkness of the night. After eight mugs of strong coffee, and after the sun has risen, I might enjoy her rendition of "I'm Too Sexy for My Shorts."

10 cm: The girls who thought you were the sweetest of all moms will now change their minds after you swoop into the family room looking like a flying monkey from *The Wizard of Oz* and screaming, "Go the hell to SLEEP! Stop singing, balancing, and dancing, and, for the love of God, my broom is not a baton!" It is very important that you watch your language here. If you slip and use a curse word, it will go down in history. The moment their parents ask, "Did you have fun at your sleepover?" they will rat you out.

Unlike after popping out that baby and having breakfast delivered to your hospital room, you now have to get back into the kitchen. The breakfast-menu request is usually pancakes. Try to stay awake while flipping on a hot grill. They will all be wide awake and chatting about how cute Suzy's dad is and how he's so nice. They will not say that about you. The only thing they might say is, "You make good pancakes. Do you have chocolate chips?"

Within two hours, all the girls will be gone. You and your child will go back to bed and be unable to sleep. She will want to chat about how happy she is that they were all at her house. As you doze off, you might hear her ask, "Can we do it again next Saturday night?" And, if you're really tired, you might dream that you said, "Yes. It was so much fun!"

As I said, sleepovers are like labor. When you're going through it, labor is hell. When the baby arrives, you forget the pain until you have another baby. The memories will rush back with each contraction.

When it comes to sleepovers, you will weaken as you regain your lost sleep, and there will be a group of little people with sleeping bags and backpacks at your door once again, and again, and again.

And when those days are over, you won't remember the labor-like pains. You'll smile at the memory of Fred Flintstone (Suzy's dad), the broom baton, "I'm Too Sexy for My Shorts," and those little centipede legs running down the stairs in the middle of the night.

Trust me, you don't want to miss this!

— Anne Bardsley —

33

The Viewing

*Nobody will understand the craziness of your family
better than your cousins.
~Author Unknown*

"I s that legal?" I asked my cousin, Jackie.

"Oh, yes," she said. "I just have to show a copy of the death certificate that says she died of natural causes."

Jackie had confirmed this before she put my late Aunt Ruth in the back of a rental truck — the kind of truck you would use for a move across town — and hauled her from Portland to Seattle.

Aunt Ruth had moved down to Portland to live with Jackie and her family after Uncle Jack died. When Aunt Ruth herself went to her reward, Jackie started the arrangements, picking out a coffin and authorizing preparation of the body. She contacted the cemetery in Seattle, where Uncle Jack reposed in a double plot, and got a quote for opening the grave. When all the charges were totaled up, there was no money left from two small insurance policies to ship the body from Portland to Seattle, let alone to hold a traditional funeral service.

The casket would not fit in the back of the old family station wagon, so Jackie called a truck-rental company, which confirmed that a vehicle would be ready first thing Saturday morning. That gave Jackie plenty of time to pick up the casket at the funeral home, drive to Seattle, and drop off Aunt Ruth before the cemetery closed at 5:00 P.M. That was the plan, anyway. In fact, no truck was available until mid-afternoon, which meant that Jackie, her husband Buddy and their cargo did not start up I-5 until well after three o'clock.

My husband Jim and I were waiting at my mother's house in Seattle, along with my two sisters and Barbara, Aunt Ruth's other daughter. We caught up with each other while Jim played with a litter of kittens from one of several cats that seemed to live there now. Jackie called on her cellphone to say they were passing through Centralia, an hour or so away, and there was no chance they'd make it to the cemetery in time. It was nearly 7:00 when the truck finally pulled up, followed by the kids in the old station wagon. While they piled out of the car, Buddy slid open the back door of the truck, lowered the ramp, and opened the casket. He announced that the viewing could begin.

My sisters and I were glad that our own mother, whose mind was in a different world, was happily unaware of the pop-up event in her front yard. "It's disrespectful," my sister Eileen hissed.

I thought so, too, but in the end it was irresistible, and I joined the line of hesitant mourners. Jim, rolling his eyes, declined to accompany me, so I walked up the ramp by myself. The truck, which smelled strongly of embalming fluid, was empty except for the open casket. In life Aunt Ruth had been silly and exasperating, but now she looked serene in the new pink suit she would have loved. My sister Marty and cousin Barbara leaned against each other. The casket was in plain view, and cars turning up my mother's street slowed as they drove past.

I walked down the ramp to where Jackie was standing alone. Our dads were brothers, and we had grown up living next door to each other. I told her how good her mom looked.

Afterward, we sat around the living room eating pie from the grocery-store bakery. My mother was delighted to have so much company. While Buddy was out in the truck tying down the casket, Jackie discussed getting Aunt Ruth over to the cemetery the next morning. "I thought we could stop by Uncle Ray's and Aunt Muriel's on the way," she said. "That way, they could see Mom before they leave for church."

Barbara raised her eyebrows. "You might want to call first," she suggested. "Some people are funny about that kind of thing." Jim got up to rescue a kitten that was dangling from a lampshade.

Later, back at our hotel, I apologized to him for my family. "I wouldn't have missed this for the world," he said. He was disappointed the next morning to hear that the truck had not been stolen during the night, as he had hoped. Apparently, there is a Chevy Chase movie with a similar plot twist.

—Fran Baxter-Guigli—

34

Battleship

*Siblings: children of the same parents, each of whom is
perfectly normal until they get together.*
~Sam Levenson

I t was a few days after Christmas, and I had gotten the electronic
version of *Battleship*. In the game, players enter in the coordinates of their ships to try and hit their opponents. Then they
are told whether it was a hit or a miss. I loved *Battleship* and
made my sister play it with me, promising in turn to play what she
wanted later.

She hit one of my ships, but I got distracted and didn't hear which
coordinate the game said. I asked her what coordinate she had hit me
on, and she said, "I won."

I shook my head, confused. "No, you didn't. You haven't sunk
my last ship yet. What coordinate did you just hit me on?"

"I won!" she said again.

Now, I was getting irritated. "No, you didn't! What coordinate?"

Again, "I won!"

Now, I was mad. "NO, YOU DIDN'T!"

My mom walked in. "What in the world is all this yelling about?
You were playing nicely not even two minutes ago!"

"Madelyn thinks she won, but she didn't! And she won't give
me the gosh-darn coordinate that she just hit me on!" I said angrily.

She sighed. "Madelyn, tell your sister the coordinate."

My sister glared at me. "I-1," she said slowly.
Oh.

—Mackenzie Conley—

35

Rusty Nails

Help one another is part of the religion of sisters.
~Louisa May Alcott

My mom picked up the phone and dialed my brother's number. "Leonard," she asked, "can you drive down here some Saturday and tear down an old shed for me? I'm tired of looking at it, and I'm scared for your little sisters to play near it."

Daddy had passed away the previous year, so my grown brother was quick to help anytime Mama called. That Saturday, after an early morning cup of coffee with Mama, he picked up his heavy black crowbar and headed out the front door.

"I'll help you," I said, following Leonard. I was twelve and dogged his every step. Angie, our six-year-old sister, insisted she wanted to help, too.

Mama told us we would be in the way, but Leonard said, "Oh, they'll be all right."

Mama blew out a sigh. "Well, alright, but you girls watch out for rusty nails." She didn't send us to our bedroom for shoes because everyone knows shoes and summertime in the South don't mix.

Each time Leonard pried a stubborn, gray board from the former henhouse, the wood creaked like it didn't want to let go. When Leonard paused and gave a nod, Angie and I carried the boards to a pile he would later burn.

Suddenly, Angie started shrieking and Mama came running. Sure enough, she had stepped on a rusty nail. Mama examined my sister's foot while Leonard looked at mine. On my way to see about Angie, I'd stepped on a nail, too. The grownups agreed we needed tetanus shots.

I hated shots. I would rather swallow a thousand pills for a thousand days than have one shot. Sitting between Leonard and Mama in his red pickup truck, holding onto my dirty bare foot, I leaned into Mama and whispered. "I don't want to get a shot."

Angie sat in Mama's lap, clutching her own hurt foot. Mama directed my sister's attention to cows grazing in a pasture and then cupped a hand around my ear. "Arlene, you and Angie have to get tetanus shots. I need you to be brave so she won't be too scared. If you take the shot without making a big fuss, maybe she won't pitch a fit when her turn comes. You know how strong she is and how she can put up a fight."

Mama had been through a lot of sadness since Daddy's death. My aunts often reminded me to be a good girl and not make things harder on her. I adored my mother and wanted to do what my aunts told me. I made up my mind to get that awful shot without crying a single tear.

At the hospital, Leonard lifted me onto a hard table. The tiny room had curtains instead of walls. Mama sat nearby in a metal folding chair with Angie in her lap. I tried not to squirm.

A nurse wearing a white dress and white hat walked in with a syringe. She cleaned my upper arm with a smelly cotton ball and told me I would feel "a little bite." Angie's big blue eyes studied the nurse's every move.

The needle hurt so much that I wanted to scream. Mama looked down at my sister and then back at me. I knew she was reminding me to be brave.

My arm felt like it was on fire, but I was brave. I didn't yell or shed a single tear. Mama smiled at me as I slid from the table onto my good foot and hopped over to Leonard. He held me against him and rubbed my back.

Mama lowered my sister onto the table. And that's when she made her big mistake. "See there, Angie. Your big sister wasn't afraid to get a shot. Arlene, tell Angie it didn't hurt at all."

Huge blue eyes stared into mine. I thought about how Angie trailed after me the way I trailed after Leonard. She trusted me the way I trusted him.

Mama waited for me to tell Angie that getting the shot wouldn't hurt. I wanted to do what she told me. *But if I tell Angie it won't hurt,* I thought, *she won't ever believe me again.*

I knew what I had to do. I cupped my hands around my mouth and yelled, "DON'T LET THEM DO IT TO YOU, ANGIE!"

Several things happened all at once. My sister screamed, bolted from the table, and took off down a long hall. Mama looked surprised, then angry, and then took off after little Angie. Leonard, Mama, and two nurses had to wrestle Angie back onto the table and hold her down while a doctor administered the shot.

On the way home, Angie buried her face in Mama's chest and sniffled. I tried to blink my own hot tears away. I didn't want to cry because of my hurting arm or my hurting foot. I wanted to cry because I'd made things harder on Mama.

And then a tiny finger touched my shoulder. I looked up and saw Angie's sweet face. A tear slid down her cheek as she reached out her hand. I took it in mine.

When Mama saw us holding hands, she smiled. Then she laughed. "Leonard, can you believe it took four of us to hold down this child?"

Leonard laughed, too. "I wish you could have seen the look on your face when she took off down the hall. The girl can move."

Mama and Leonard kept laughing and talking, but I don't remember what else they said. What I do remember is holding hands with Angie all the way home.

— Arlene Lassiter Ledbetter —

36

The Hot Dogger

Just because something is traditional
is no reason to do it, of course.
~Lemony Snicket, The Blank Book

The groom, Paul, had a confused look on his face, like he wanted to be gracious but was actually horrified by the gift he had just unwrapped. The raucous outburst of the crowd confused him even more. The box he held with trepidation said, "Presto Hot Dogger Electric Hot Dog Cooker — Cook 6 hot dogs in just 60 seconds." Paul and his bride, Vickie, had more refined taste. Although they might enjoy a hot dog occasionally, I imagine he could not think of an occasion for which they would need an electric appliance to cook six hot dogs at once, let alone six in sixty seconds.

The hooting, hollering and clapping that accompanied the unveiling of the Hot Dogger left a very perplexed look on Paul's face. He forced a little smile while clearly racking his brain to reconcile the tacky appliance with the overly enthusiastic response of the guests. Even more confusing was the tattered appearance of the Hot Dogger box, which was clearly of an earlier vintage. The Hot Dogger, a plastic gadget with six sets of prongs and an electric cord, manufactured in Eau Claire, Wisconsin, had first become popular about fifteen years earlier. Clearly, this one was not new. Why would a wedding guest give Paul and Vickie a Hot Dogger, let alone a used one? It did not make sense.

Unknown to Paul and Vickie, this Hot Dogger (a.k.a. HD) had quite a pedigree. Its story had begun innocently enough about fourteen years earlier on a bright, sunny Saturday afternoon in May 1982, when Sheila and Dick were endowed with the new Hot Dogger as a serious wedding gift. Realizing the great worth of the HD, Sheila wanted to share it with friends and quickly passed it along to Mary Beth and Peter when they wed a month later. Thus, the legendary Hot Dogger's amazing journey began.

In January 1983, Mary Beth and Peter bestowed the Hot Dogger on Patty and Neil on their wedding day. Then, just five months later, the HD was given to Lynn and Rick when they wed in June 1983. Later that same month (a record turnover rate that was hard to beat!), Marge and Clarence received the HD on their wedding day. Next, Beth and Jim received the HD in September 1983. Although they cherished this gift, they parted with it, giving it to Joyce and Dan in May 1985.

Until this time, the Hot Dogger was in Wisconsin, among friends who had all graduated from two high schools. But when given to Joyce and Dan, the HD crossed state lines for the first time, expanding its territory into Iowa. Joyce and Dan had the HD for almost three years, another record, but this time for longevity. When Debbie and Steve wed in April 1988, the Hot Dogger continued its cross-country trek, landing in Ohio.

In June 1988, Karen and Tim received the HD as a wedding gift back in Wisconsin. While in their care, the HD was almost opened once, which would have broken the tradition of keeping it pristine in its original package. But Karen and Tim passed the HD along to Ann and Vern when they wed two months later. After occupying an honored place in their home for almost a year, the Hot Dogger left Wisconsin once again and left the Midwest for the first time, landing in the mountains of Wyoming when BJ and Jay wed in August 1989. Their son, Cory, thought the Hot Dogger was a fantastic gift and really wanted to use it, but BJ and Jay decided to stick with tradition and keep the HD in its original package.

In December 1990, upon learning of my marriage to Jeff in Minnesota, BJ and Jay sent us the HD, returning it to the Midwest. The HD spent an uneventful six years with us in Minnesota, waiting for the late bloomers of the generation to finally get married.

And that is how, in June 1996, more than fourteen years and a dozen couples after the Hot Dogger first appeared as a serious wedding gift, it was unveiled as Paul and Vickie opened gifts in Madison, Wisconsin. The Hot Dogger's appearance was greeted with much pleasure by the gathering of friends and family, some of whom had been its previous recipients. But although Vickie had gone to high school with the group who had shared the HD, she had been away at college (where she met Paul) and living out of state during the Hot Dogger's wedding-gift tenure. Paul had never heard of the HD's legendary status, and nobody had warned him that it might appear as a wedding gift. Vickie's father, who loved hot dogs, eyed the HD with great anticipation. But her groom, Paul, eyed it with carefully veiled horror.

When finally told of the Hot Dogger's history and true sentimental value, Paul appeared relieved that it was not a serious gift and that he did not have to keep pretending to like it. For a moment, as we hooligans laughed uncontrollably while Paul unwrapped the white elephant, he must have wondered exactly what he had gotten himself into with this marriage! What kind of psychosis did these Wisconsin people share, anyway?

Once again, the HD left the Midwest, as Vickie and Paul took it home with them to Texas and then eventually to the West Coast when they moved to Oregon. They were the last of our generation to receive the Hot Dogger as a wedding gift and held onto it for many years until the first couple of the next generation was wed.

In August 2007, Vickie shipped the HD back to me so I could give it to my niece Joy and her groom James on their wedding day. The last time I saw the HD is when they unwrapped it and took it with them to New Mexico to start their new life.

Sometimes, the most memorable gifts are not the most elaborate or expensive but the gifts with the greatest stories, laughs, and traditions behind them. The very memorable Hot Dogger, which traveled thousands of miles to recipients in eight states, served that purpose among our group of friends.

I recently saw a similar Hot Dogger listed on eBay as "Vintage PRESTO HOT DOGGER Automatic Hot Dog Cooker." Could it be the very same one? Bitten by nostalgia, I'm thinking about snatching it up and starting another round of gift giving, just when my friends least expect it!

—Jenny Pavlovic—

Thanksgiving, Lost in Translation

It wouldn't be Thanksgiving without
a little emotional scarring.
~Timothy Burke, Friends

"You stuff *what* inside the bottom of a turkey?" my friend asked. She was quite serious.

"Stuffing," I said again. "That's right!"

She laughed.

It all began when the organization that supports our foreign missionary friends flew them to the U.S. for a conference the week of Thanksgiving. Picking them up at the airport, we couldn't have been more excited that they would be experiencing the U.S. and Thanksgiving for the very first time. I quickly discovered that Thanksgiving, a nostalgic holiday that makes perfect sense to Americans, seems like a bizarre ride on the crazy train to much of the rest of the world.

It had never occurred to me that, unlike Christmas or Easter, the rest of the world really has no ties to the holiday of Thanksgiving. Not only do they not celebrate it, but they don't really understand it either.

"The airport will be very packed," I warned them. "Thanksgiving week is the most heavily traveled time of the year in the States."

"Are people traveling to a place of worship to give thanks?" my friend asked.

"No, they're traveling to a place with turkey," I answered. "They travel once a year to eat a giant meal with their friends and family and give thanks that they don't live closer together."

"Why turkey?"

"Well, it's a traditional meal," I explained. "We take a turkey, cut its head off, pluck all its feathers, pull out its guts, and stuff its bottom full of bread."

"That sounds awful," she said, horrified. "Then what?"

"Well, we cook it. Traditionally, we bake it in our oven, but this year my husband is choosing to light a garbage can full of oil on fire in our driveway and dunk the bird in it instead."

Surprised, my friend commented, "That's how we cook sheep's heads in the township, but there are many accidents."

"We, too, have accidents," I said. "But Americans are often willing to risk life and limb in the pursuit of the perfectly cooked bird." Case in point: My Uncle Ted still has no eyebrows from last year's attempt at frying his turkey.

"That doesn't sound very appealing." She winced.

"Well, no worries. There are lots of other things to eat," I offered. "Americans take a variety of vegetables, especially gourds and pumpkins recycled from Halloween, and mash them up with enormous amounts of butter, sugar, and marshmallows that we deliberately burn before serving." I continued, "In fact, Americans consume on average some 5,000 calories on Thanksgiving day alone."

"Whoa!" she exclaimed, shaking her head in disbelief.

Not wanting to portray us all as irresponsible gluttons, I added, "Many of us go to the gym the next week to burn it off."

"What is this gym?" she asked.

"If Americans eat too much, they can go to the gym and pay money to run, jump, climb stairs, and lift heavy things in order to make sure all those calories do not stick to them."

"People are really motivated to do this?"

I could tell she couldn't fathom it. "Well, if they aren't motivated, they can pay the gym extra and have someone yell at them until they are."

The dumfounded look on my friend's face told me she viewed Thanksgiving as the strangest holiday she'd ever heard of, and the fact that it was celebrated nearly universally in the United States blew her mind.

I was tempted to go on discussing my love for Thanksgiving parades, where commentators give play-by-plays on the movement of enormous balloons, the tradition of tracing paper turkey hands, or watching football for hours until my family eventually becomes so inspired that we waddle onto the front lawn and recreate the game with Grandma as the quarterback.

But I realized I couldn't explain most of it and sound sane. I couldn't explain why my family loves space-age cranberry sauce that maintains its shape even after being poured from the can, or that at least three boxes of cereal mixed with Worcestershire sauce is a must.

I couldn't explain our obsession with shaping appetizers into balls — sausage balls, meatballs, and cheese balls.

Or why our dining room table would be beautifully set but then connected with a train of wobbly card tables extending to our coat closet.

Or why Thanksgiving is the first day it's acceptable to play Christmas music in our home even though Christmas is still a month away.

Or just try explaining why kids enjoy fighting over who gets the bigger side of a bone of the dead turkey carcass.

I thought about explaining all this to my foreign friend, but I decided not to — mostly because I didn't want her to think we were weirdos. And, at this point, I knew she would never understand.

To the rest of the world, I guess it really appears that Americans have lost their minds on Thanksgiving. But for those of us who grew up in the United States, we don't really care what the rest of the world thinks. We wait all year for that special day with family and friends where, once again, we repeat these unexplainable, bizarre, and nearly certifiable traditions.

Maybe it's not really about the traditions themselves. Maybe it's more about the way they make us all feel: grateful. Maybe, just for one day, it takes us all back to a time when the world was not nearly as uncertain and divisive as the one in which we live today. I know now that I can't explain American Thanksgiving to the rest of the world. I only know I love it — every crazy, wonderful, and certifiable part.

— Kimberly Avery —

38

Nerd Ensemble

Fashion is a form of ugliness so intolerable
that we have to alter it every six months.
~Oscar Wilde

My father was one of the most intelligent people I'd ever met, but his mind was so preoccupied with big issues and big problems that he often seemed oblivious about day-to-day stuff. He'd have to be reminded and cajoled into buying birthday and Christmas presents, but he would sometimes show up out of the blue with silver earrings for Mom or stained-glass keepsake boxes for my sister and me.

He was so thrifty that he never threw out anything, including clothes, and he was color-blind—a deadly combination, as far as his wardrobe was concerned. Despite our best efforts, my mom and I never managed to cure him of his fondness for pocket protectors. When he went to work each day, he always wore one in his shirt pocket, crammed full of pens and mechanical pencils. He also never noticed when his curly, mad-scientist-looking hair grew higher and higher, so my mom would have to wrestle him into a kitchen chair to cut it herself. "It looks fine," he'd protest.

One year on Halloween, my mother and I dressed him in a pair of too short plaid pants that he'd kept since high school, paired them with a shirt in clashing colors, added a bulging pocket protector, and wrapped tape around the middle of his heavy-framed glasses. His hair hadn't been cut in so long that it was reaching Einstein proportions.

Aside from the tape on his glasses, he thought he looked like he was dressed for a typical day at work.

Just imagine how insulted my dad was when his nerd ensemble won him the prize for best costume.

—Sheri Radford—

39

Photo Op

Some family trees bear an enormous crop of nuts.
~Wayne H.

The funeral of my husband's grandfather definitely takes the prize for the weirdest funeral I have ever attended. As a matter of fact, as we left the funeral my husband looked over at me and said, "If I hadn't known you so long I would be mortified."

Throughout the fifteen years we had been together I had never known my husband's grandmother to be affectionate, or even care what any of her five grandchildren were doing, but when Grandpa Hank was sick I witnessed her true colors. As Grandpa Hank lay dying, she often was caught saying, "If he doesn't die soon I may drive him off the pier." I was horrified by her comment but chalked it up to a tired woman who had taken care of a very sick man for a long time. Not to mention that she was never nice to anyone — so why should she start now?

Once Grandpa Hank finally passed away, the funeral arrangements were made. The services were to take place at the Mormon Church they attended, and after the service we were to make the thirty-minute drive to the burial site and then back to the church for a potluck lunch put on by the members of the church.

Walking into the church we were handed a pamphlet outlining Grandpa Hank's life, only Grandma didn't want to spend the extra money on printing so Grandpa's photo was completely black on the cheap Xeroxed copy. The flower arrangement that my mother-in-law had ordered on behalf of her kids from a local florist included a cheesy banner that incorrectly said "We Love You Gandpa" in glitter-covered letters. At this point my husband and I just started to laugh, as things were going from bad to worse. Once seated in the pew we saw the coffin sitting at the front of the room with an American flag draped over it. I had no idea Grandpa Hank had served in the military and it would have been a nice addition had Grandma spent the money they requested to iron the flag. The flag was completely wrinkled.

Again, we tried to stifle our laughter when the speaker began the eulogy. As he started speaking it was clear he had no idea who Grandpa Hank was. He went on and on about some random things that must have been listed on a sheet of paper until he came across the note that said Grandpa Hank was from Utah. He stopped mid-sentence and said, "Wow, who knew? I am from Utah too." He then picked up with the rest of his reading, often stopping to comment on the fact that he was surprised at how much they had in common. As he finished, he picked up his guitar and began singing a song. None of us knew the song and it soon became clear neither did he! As he got to certain verses he just stopped mid-verse and hummed until he was able to pick back up with familiar words. We could not contain ourselves any longer. I made eye contact with my "normal" sister-in-law and within seconds there was not a dry eye in our row — we were working so hard to hold in the laughter that we were crying.

Finally, the indoor ceremony ended and the family was to caravan to the burial where my husband, his father, and his two brothers would act as pallbearers. We were together on the freeway, but when we arrived at the cemetery my husband's older brother and his family were nowhere to be seen.

We waited and waited, worried that something had happened. We finally had to go on without them as Grandma had only budgeted a certain amount of time and money for this part of the ceremony. Because we were now missing one of the pallbearers, a random cemetery worker had to step in as the fourth pallbearer. A few words about Grandpa Hank were said and then to our horror… Grandma broke out her camera. She wanted us to sit on the coffin and take pictures! Each family member was instructed how to pose and she kept snapping. I felt like at any moment we would be on a *Candid Camera* episode where you find out it was all a really bad joke… but that was not to be. This was very real and although I tried to hide, the next thing I knew, I too was draped across Grandpa Hank's coffin. I am not sure what her reasoning was for the photo shoot, whether it was to confirm that Grandpa Hank for sure was dead and wouldn't be a bother to her anymore or to fill a page in her photo album of family memories.

Once the photo session ended, up pulled my husband's brother… he had gotten hungry on the way and pulled off the freeway for some mini corndogs!

As the day ended and we were driving home recapping the events of the day, my husband asked that I never discuss this with anyone! It has been almost ten years now and I have finally been given permission to share it. As we arrived home to pay the babysitter she commented on how sad the services must have been due to how red our eyes were from crying… if she only knew.

— May D. Sonnenfeld —

Marital Mishaps

The Night I Went a Little Too Far

I have an unhealthy addiction to space jokes,
but I believe that someday I will over-comet.
~Author Unknown

uch to the dismay of my wife and daughters, I'm a big fan of the "simple scare." That is, hiding and waiting for the hapless victim to enter a room, then shouting, blowing a trumpet, banging cymbals together—anything that will elicit the desired responses. A simultaneous jump and scream are great, but it's even better if they're carrying popcorn or something else that can be thrown into the air. It's like a piñata without the stick, and it never stops being funny (to me).

Over the years, however, my family has become almost completely immune to my sneak attacks. Too often, I jump out from behind a door or under a blanket, and they don't flinch or even look at me. All I receive for my efforts is, "Nice try, Daddy," usually accompanied by an eye roll.

Therefore, to avoid further disappointment, I found it necessary to improve my skills and up the ante by investing in props. One of these was a porcelain doll that I found in an antique store with a cracked face, disheveled hair, and a psychotic gaze. I occasionally put it on my wife's pillow and then wait for her to turn down the bedsheet at night. The only thing more exhilarating than that delicious moment when I know she's about to discover that nightmare of a doll is the blood-curdling scream when she does.

Other weapons in my arsenal are realistic-looking bugs pulled across the kitchen floor with fishing wire and a giant spider that descends upon her from a tree branch as she walks to or from her car. But the prize piece of my collection is a full-size, foam-rubber alien. I bought it for only five dollars at a garage sale, but if screams were a form of currency, it would be worth a fortune. The first time I employed my little pal, I laid the groundwork by casually mentioning to my wife earlier in the day that a UFO had been reported over town the night before. I have found this subtle, psychological preparation — planting the seed, so to speak — to be crucial for achieving maximum horrification later when the prank is actually carried out.

Knowing my wife would be giving our daughters a bath that evening, I propped the alien up against the bathroom window with a metal rake. When the bath was in progress, I went outside and tapped lightly on the window. However, I thought she couldn't hear it over all the talking and splashing, so I went back inside, opened the door and asked her if she had heard any "strange noises" in the yard. She said, "Yes, I thought I did a minute ago." To my great delight, she stood up and walked to the window (the delicious moment of anticipation I mentioned earlier). When she opened the window, she was greeted by the giant, black eyes of my extraterrestrial partner in crime staring at her.

Simply stating "she screamed" wouldn't begin to describe the other-worldly sound she produced. I think I tapped into her primal scream — the one even she had never heard before. I once watched a nature special where a walrus got into a scrap with a polar bear. The noise she made was very similar to one the walrus made when the polar bear latched onto one of its flippers. I was very impressed, though, because as she screamed, she delivered a straight right punch to the nose of the alien that would have made Wladimir Klitschko proud. The alien flew backward, but because the metal rake I propped it up with was in its lower back, it just bent backward and then popped right back into position, which elicited another, identical scream and a second punch to the nose. She was about to go for haymaker number three when she realized the alien wasn't reacting in any way.

Then came the aftermath that inevitably follows any high-level prank — the victim's wrath. This occurs when said victim realizes she has been duped and turns slowly toward the prankster with murder in her eyes. Having just witnessed my wife's surprising boxing ability, I decided to seek safety by running out of the house until she'd had ample time to calm down.

As I stood at a safe distance across the street, several neighbors who had heard her unearthly wails came out to investigate. I bragged about the prank, and they laughed unguardedly as my wife stood in the doorway yelling, "You've got to come home sometime!" Fortunately, she's a forgiving soul. When I came home after a two-hour walk around the neighborhood, she refrained from beating me about the head and neck for causing the horror that she swore shaved at least a year off her life. I also had a wonderful night's sleep and discovered that the couch is almost as comfortable as the bed. This was useful information because I spent the next few nights there. I also learned about a previously unknown ability of my own—sleeping with one eye open.

— Mark Rickerby —

I Am a Pickleball Putz

I did a push-up today. Well, actually I fell down, but I
had to use my arms to get back up, so close enough.
~Author Unknown

I am a proud pickleball dropout. After a brief attempt to learn the game from my husband Larry, I realized that being interested in something and having enough talent to play at the most basic level are two different things.

What? You haven't heard of pickleball? According to the 2022 Sports & Fitness Industry Association (SFIA), there are 4.8 million people who play the game in the United States alone. It is the fastest-growing sport in the country.

Until Larry and I retired, I had never heard about pickleball. Larry had been involved in sports his entire life — basketball, baseball, and track in his youth, and running and cycling as an adult. When he turned sixty-five, we both joined the local YMCA. While I took classes and swam laps in the Olympic-sized pool, Larry started playing the game with friends from Congregation Beth Shalom and other members of the Y.

Both competitive and athletic, Larry fell in love with the game immediately. When we moved to Florida, our criteria for where we would live included aerobic classes and a lap pool for me and pickleball courts for Larry. We both found what we were looking for in our 55+ active-adult community. Larry joined the Smashers and found players at his level. To make his life even better, Larry found the Summit

County Pickleball Club ("We play with altitude") near where we rent in Colorado every summer.

Pickleball not only provided Larry with a great form of exercise, but it also provided a social outlet. In Florida, the Smashers had dances and breakfasts; in Colorado, the players had picnics and cocktail parties.

As a matter of fact, it was the social aspect of "pb'ing" at 9,100 feet that got my interest. Larry was playing the game at least four mornings a week, and he was meeting lots of people. I, on the other hand, spent my mornings either hiking by myself or with my grand-dog or, occasionally, swimming lonely laps in a pool that accepted Silver Sneakers. Maybe learning the game would help me become part of a community.

So, one day, I asked Larry to take me onto the Colorado courts during a time set aside for beginners. After giving me some basic rules, Larry gently lobbed me a ball; I hit it. *Hey! This wasn't so bad! Slow lob, hit. Slow lob. I got this!* I thought.

When he started hitting the balls to me at the normal rate of speed, however, I could barely keep up. Only thirty minutes into my private lessons, a slim, athletic couple came onto the court.

"We'd love some lessons, too!" they said. Larry quickly repeated some of the basics, and the two of them took to it right away. At that point, they told us they had been playing tennis their whole lives, so this was an easy transition. Larry suggested the four of us play a game together.

Now, it was a completely different game. Fast lob, Marilyn miss. Fast lob, Marilyn miss. Soon, Larry was covering both sides of our court.

I wasn't even close to hitting the ball. My lifetime lack of hand-eye coordination, exacerbated by vision problems brought on by age, resulted in my swinging at lots of air. The ball was usually two feet above or two feet below my pathetic paddle.

So, I did what any normal mature adult would do in that situation: I told Larry I didn't want to play anymore, went back to our car, sat in the front seat, and cried.

"I can't do it," I told Larry after he finished his session with the two tennis pros. "I hate it! I can't see the ball. I can't hit the ball. I can't even move in time. I'm done."

I was. And I am. I am in the eighth decade of my life. Up until now, I had proven myself lousy at tennis, baseball, racquetball and squash. I have now proved myself to be lousy at pickleball. The benefits of being part of a large group — there are at least 1,000 members of Smashers — are totally outweighed by how much I hate trying to hit a stupid ball with a stupid paddle that may result in my breaking a stupid bone.

"You should try playing with us," some friends have told me. "None of us play that well, and we won't care if you're not great at it."

"No, thanks," I tell them. "I'd rather walk, swim, bike or do an exercise class."

And, after hearing about all my friends with pickleball-related injuries, I am happy to stick to what I am doing. None of them require hand-eye coordination. None of them are competitive, so I don't have to always lose. Better yet, I won't be the player who no one wants on their team. Yes, my short stint as a pickleball putz is over! From now on, my pickle of choice is a kosher one in a jar.

— Marilyn Cohen Shapiro —

42

Spy in the Sky

I love being married. It's so great to find one special
person you want to annoy for the rest of your life.
~Rita Rudner

I caught my husband five rungs up a ladder leaning against the carport, despite doctor's orders to stay off.

"What are you doing with all that white wire?" I asked.

He leaned more than an arm's length to his right to pound another nail overhead.

"Don't worry. I'm taking care of your safety," he claimed while disregarding his own. "I'm mounting motion cameras."

"Well, dismount! Get down."

Our grandson Kyle had forgotten his password, and the security-camera company could not save a digital copy of his videos, so he offered the cameras to Bill.

"Honey, this was all free. Kyle was going to throw them away. Trespassers won't even know they're being recorded."

Was he kidding? The four white, snowball-size cameras — not to mention the fifty-foot maze of white electrical wiring that snaked around the carport ceiling — were visible to any crook. Motion-activated flood lights already illuminated our front door every time our redbud tree rustled. The floodlight outside our bedroom window is triggered by moths playing tag. Critters visit the garden at night, lighting up the premises like it's midday instead of midnight. Our yard is so well-lit that the neighbor behind us bought room-darkening drapes.

"So, how will we catch an intruder?" I asked.

"I've rigged up a system in our bedroom. We can view everything in real time on a four-section split screen. The cameras don't save the data, but we can see the action."

I went indoors shaking my head and literally stumbled upon the recording device.

Proud as a producer, Bill came in and tried to demonstrate the results of "lights, camera, action."

"If a light comes on outdoors, all you have to do is flick off Netflix, tune into channel…" I walked away.

Kyle called a week later. "Gramps, last night my new security system captured a thief's every movement, sent a message to me, and stored the images. I viewed the tape remotely and called the cops, and they were at my business in a heartbeat."

I could hear the conversation on speakerphone. "How much did your new system cost? Yeah? I've been thinking about an upgrade. On sale? Today?"

Instant gratification was the incentive for my guy to buy. Bill climbed the ladder again and removed the old cameras and scads of wiring. He purchased battery-operated cameras that were dark as night and almost undetectable.

My honey assured me there would be no more TV interruptions in order to catch a thief. All I had to do was tap the app on my smartphone to view any activity. Movement would trigger a particular tone.

Every time he took out the trash, I heard the alarm. It was not a pleasant ping but a loud "bong." When I walked to the mailbox, my cellphone bing-bonged. All day, all evening, and all night, my phone sounded like the old *Gong Show*.

The sap-sucking hummingbirds flitted at sunset. Then a storm blew in, whipped up a frenzy, and triggered all four cameras simultaneously.

Bill decided to temporarily disarm the cameras. "How about I turn them off while we're at home, and then I'll turn them back on at night or if we leave the house? We can always view and access them remotely."

I could live with that. Later that evening, I headed to the basement laundry room to do hand-washables. While I was at it, I thought I might as well rinse the silky blouse I was wearing. I unbuttoned it and slipped it off. Then, I decided to launder my lingerie. When I unsnapped my bra, BONG! I frantically rubber-necked, searching for where the sound was coming from.

Bill shouted from upstairs, "You won't believe it. The cat's on my work bench."

My "girls" were hanging low when I realized Bill had mounted a fifth camera in the basement to monitor the cat's activity. He had not disarmed it. I covered my chest and made a beeline upstairs for my robe. As I entered the bedroom to close the blinds, the back yard lit up like high noon, spotlighting me. I ducked down and slinked out of the room, whining.

"I can't do this anymore! This is like living on the TV show *Big Brother*! Erase that tape. I mean it. Delete it. Now!"

"Aw, honey, don't worry. Nobody can see you. Our videos go to the cloud for seven days and then they're automatically deleted."

For an entire week, I looked to the sky, wondering which cloud was featuring my boobs.

—Linda O'Connell—

43

A Pregnant Pause

How do people make it through life without a sister?
~Sara Corpening Whiteford

We gathered at the outdoor venue for a wedding on an unusually warm and humid summer day in Minnesota.

Our niece Andrea, the bride, was stunning. Twenty-five years earlier, she had celebrated her fourth birthday by serving as a flower girl in my wedding along with her older sister. Today, she was the bride, and her sister, Cristina, her matron of honor. Her very pregnant matron of honor who was two weeks away from her due date!

To alleviate any concern, it was arranged that my husband Tom and I would be seated in the front row "just in case" Cristina should go into labor during the ceremony. We would be on standby, ready to leap into action to get her off the platform and to the hospital quickly. Cristina assured us she was feeling fine. No backache, no labor pains, no burst of "nesting" energy — nothing to be concerned about. This was her second child, and she was confident she was not going to have an issue. Nevertheless, we took our "baby emergency contingency plan" seriously.

The processional began, and the wedding party lined up on either side of the pastor. Andrea, the beautiful bride, made her entrance and met her groom at the altar. As the minister began his message, I noticed a look of sheer panic on Cristina's face. She turned and stepped off the stage and started to make her way over to us. Eyes in the audience moved from the bride and groom toward us. Fortunately, the couple reciting their vows was blissfully unaware of the unfolding drama.

I was now on full alert. *Oh, my goodness! The baby! It is really going to happen!* Tom and I quickly communicated with our eyes that we would exit to the left and try not to disrupt the ceremony.

Cristina was bent over with her hand on her bulging baby bump when she reached us.

"Are you okay?" I whispered as I grabbed my purse, ready to leap into action.

She nodded as Tom chimed in, "Do you want to sit, have a glass of water, go to the hospital? What do you need?"

Cristina leaned over and spoke softly. "Uncle Tom, I need your ring."

"What?" we replied in baffled unison.

"I forgot the ring!"

"You're bent over. We thought you were in labor!" I said, trying not to laugh.

Cristina's eyes widened. In her hurry to come up with a plan to fix the missing groom's ring situation, she forgot that we were poised to be her emergency escort to the hospital should the need arise. "I was trying to be discreet," she said as she shrugged.

Smothering our giggles, Tom struggled to remove his wedding ring from his finger, where it had resided for a quarter of a century. As he'd gained a little weight over time, the gold band, now misshapen and worn from years of wear and tear, was snug on his finger. The humidity in the air didn't help the swollen finger situation, either. He struggled to remove it, twisting, turning, and yanking it bit by bit over his knuckle. Somehow, he wrested it off and gave it to Cristina, who quietly returned to her place alongside the bride in the nick of time. She passed the ring to the minister at the appropriate moment.

The groom had selected a gorgeous platinum ring, and we got quite a chuckle out of the puzzled expression on his face when he saw the crooked gold ring that the minister held up to bless, and then handed the slightly less than circular symbol of eternal love to Andrea to place on his finger. The bewildered bride accepted the misshapen "token of her love," turned, and gave her sister a perplexed look before slipping the ring on her new husband's finger.

As the ceremony continued, I held Tom's now ringless hand and traced the red marks and white, untanned center that outlined where the gold band had been for the last two and a half decades.

The newlyweds and their matron of honor came to see us during the reception to thank us for saving the day. Cristina retrieved the forgotten band from the girls' dressing room, and the groom proudly wore it as he handed Tom his ring, saying, "I think this belongs to you." Then, looking at his own hand, he murmured, "I wonder if I'll ever get used to wearing this. It feels strange!"

Tom smiled as he placed his ring back on his finger and sighed, "Whew! I was feeling naked without it!"

— Donna Anderson —

44

See Cookie, Will Sneak

A balanced diet is a cookie in each hand.
~Barbara Johnson

For more years than I care to remember, I have been engaged in a diligent pursuit, and I won't stop until I reach my goal. My quest is to find a cookie I don't like. Throughout the years, I have eaten every cookie I could find and loved them all.

My biggest obstacle in this pursuit is The Gracious Mistress of the Parsonage. She has the crazy idea that I should limit my cookie consumption. I told her I will whenever I find a cookie that I don't like. So far, that hasn't happened.

My favorite time of the year is when the Girl Scouts are selling cookies. I love those little angels. I tell The Gracious Mistress of the Parsonage that I'm just supporting these lovely young girls, and that's all.

I don't think she believes me, but I will try anything I can get away with.

Recently, The Gracious Mistress of the Parsonage has been on a baking spree. She was baking cookies for various people — I have no idea who. My focus is not on the people she's baking for but on the cookies she's baking. As a faithful husband, I encourage her along these lines and congratulate her on a job well done.

One rule she has laid down is that I'm not allowed to have any cookie she does not give me personally. That is a very hard rule to keep with all the cookies in the kitchen. I try my hardest, but my hardest is not enough.

One of my favorite hymns has a line that says, "Yield not to temptation, for yielding is sin."

Last Tuesday, my wife planned to spend the day with one of our daughters. I was supportive of her activity and encouraged her to spend as much time as possible with our daughter. She looked at me suspiciously and said, "While I am away, I do not want you to eat any cookies in the kitchen." Then, she went to the kitchen, pulled out one cookie, handed it to me, and said, "This is the only cookie you are allowed for today."

Of course, I took the cookie, smiled as she left, and told her to have a great day.

Unfortunately, I did not know what kind of day I was facing and hummed the "Yield not to temptation" hymn all morning long.

For the first couple of hours, everything went well. I was working in my office, and things were just okay. Then, in the middle of the morning, I decided to take a break and get a cup of coffee. I can never have too much coffee on any day. I had forgotten about the cookies that were stacked up in the kitchen.

As I entered the kitchen, the aroma of all those freshly baked cookies slapped me in the face like I'd never been slapped before. Up to this point, I was able to "Yield not to temptation." But I am afraid that the "Yield not" had just expired.

As I was fixing my coffee, I thought it would not harm me to look at and admire those freshly baked cookies. After all, The Gracious Mistress of the Parsonage does a wonderful job in baking cookies. I just wanted to admire them and appreciate all the excellent work behind every one of those cookies.

I thought I could handle the situation, but I was wrong. I've been wrong on a lot of things; I was wrong on this thing.

With a cup of coffee in my hand, I began thinking that just one cookie wouldn't hurt me. I didn't think my wife would find out that I had one cookie because there were so many cookies in that kitchen.

I took one cookie very craftily and then walked back to my office, where I would drink my coffee and nibble on this delicious cookie. I thought I had solved the problem and gotten over any further thoughts

I had about another cookie.

After I finished that first cookie, I sat back in my chair and enjoyed swallowing the last crumb. How delicious it was. Of all the cookies in all the world, why did this cookie taste so delicious?

I thought it was over, but I could not get that cookie out of my head. Then, after lunch, I picked up another cookie, went to my office, and nibbled on it very slowly, enjoying every last crumb.

An hour went by, and I needed another cup of coffee. Walking through the kitchen, I smelled those delicious cookies. So, I decided I deserved two cookies this time because I was working so hard. After all, how would The Gracious Mistress of the Parsonage know I had two cookies?

Later that afternoon, I heard the front door open. My wife entered the kitchen, and I heard her say very loudly, "How many cookies did you eat?"

Then, I knew I was in trouble, but I didn't know how much trouble I was in.

I remembered the words of Jesus in Mark 14:38, "Watch ye and pray, lest ye enter into temptation. The spirit truly is ready, but the flesh is weak."

Everybody faces temptation in some form. The real issue has to do with yielding to that temptation. It's the weakness of my flesh.

—James L. Snyder—

45

Something Old, Something New

Weddings seem to be magnets for mishap and for
whatever craziness lurks in family closets.
~Robert Fulghum

Were it up to my sister, she would have eloped. But our parents would have none of that, and his parents said their relatives would never forgive them if they did. And, once that happened, they didn't have much to say about it.

They'd be married at the First Congregational Presbyterian Church. She'd have six bridesmaids, and little cousin Margaret would be the flower girl. Best Man would be her husband-to-be's best friend, Buddy. His little brother, Bart, would be the ring bearer. The reception would be at the Odd Fellows Hall downtown and catered by our dad's friend who has the Italian restaurant, and they would honeymoon in Niagara Falls, four days, three nights (compliments of our parents). My sister and her fiancé decided it was best to just let them do their thing. Keep the peace.

But then, on the day of the wedding, things took a turn for the weird.

While her future mother-in-law was helping her into her gown, she mentioned that one particular wedding tradition in her family dates back several generations: the "something old, something new, something borrowed, something blue" tradition. More than just an age-old tradition, a great deal of superstition had been attached through the years. At this time, the woman reached into a bag and took out a box tied with red ribbon. "Here's your something borrowed. Open it!" she said excitedly. So, my sister did.

Under a thick layer of tissue paper was a folded garment that she couldn't identify. "Those bloomers belonged to my great-great-great-grandmother! She wore them on her honeymoon night," the woman explained. My sister must have had a horrified look on her face because the woman quickly said, "Oh, don't worry. They've been thoroughly washed and disinfected!" It was one of the rare times in my sister's life when she was speechless. "Wear those on your honeymoon, and you're guaranteed to get pregnant! Every Murphy woman who's worn them has had huge litters!"

As my sister held the "something borrowed" up to the light, knowing the woman expected her to actually put them on, the thought of that yellowed, holey underwear touching her privates after all those women made her cringe. But even before she could process what was expected of her, her future mother-in-law reached into her bag and pulled out another box. "This is your 'something new'—for when Nicky goes away in the service!" Before my sister could explain that Nicky had no plans of joining the service, she pushed a long box into her hands and said, "That there's handmade. I, uh, guessed your size!"

Literally fearful to open it, my sister took a deep breath and slowly lifted off the lid. Inside was a beautiful, gold-inlaid wooden box, like an expensive comb or hairbrush might come in. Now feeling more relaxed about it, she removed the box and opened the lid. But it was no comb or hairbrush! "You know what that is, don't you, dear? To keep you from getting lonely—well, you know!" Now, my sister doesn't embarrass easily, but she wanted to run out of the room and hide! "My grandfather sent my grandmother one of those from Japan during World War II. Swears it saved her marriage! Since all the Murphy men go off to war, all the Murphy women get one of these on their wedding day. How you use it is entirely up to you!" she said, rolling her eyes.

While my sister searched her mind for the right words to say, "Gee, thanks for the beautiful dildo!" the woman again reached into her bag. "Now, this is your 'something old,'" she said, smiling for the first time. Figuring she'd better brace herself for what was coming next, my sister sat on the edge of the bed and forced a smile to match hers. To my sister's relief, the woman handed her a simple ring box. "Now, I know this doesn't look like much, but I promise you it has very special meaning!"

Expecting something jewelryish, what she found inside was a tiny glass vial on a gold chain containing something that looked like ink. "That, my dear girl, is some of granddaddy Murphy's blood!" the woman said, presenting the tiny vial she wore around her own neck for my sister to compare. My sister was sure her facial expression did nothing to hide the disgust she felt.

"His... blood?!"

"That's right, dear — oh, but nothing ghoulish happened!" the woman said, taking my sister's hand and patting it after seeing what my sister imagined was a look of pure horror on her face. "But now this makes you a blood relative — not just related by marriage. All us Murphy women have these!" she said as she continued to pat my sister's hand while gazing down into the bag one more time. "Now for 'something blue'!" Already in a state of shock, my sister kept herself from imagining what something blue might be. Her heart was pounding so hard in her chest that she knew she was visibly shaking. "So, are you familiar with the deadly Blue Viper from Australia?" she said, dipping her hand cautiously into the bag.

"No!" my sister screamed, getting up and dashing toward the door. "F**k, no! This is just too f**king weird! I love your son, but — this is just too f**king much!"

Just as she turned the knob and prepared to run out, she heard hysterical laughing behind her. This woman actually thought this was funny. She was clearly deranged!

"No, no, honey!" the woman said after her, still laughing — with more laughing coming from the other side of the door. "It's a joke! I was just putting you on, dear! Just the Murphy sense of humor!" she said, pulling a rubber snake from the bag. "It's our way of saying, 'Welcome to the family!'"

— James R. Coffey —

The Left-Handed Store

Keep your eyes wide open before marriage,
half shut afterwards.
~Benjamin Franklin

For our first anniversary, David and I planned a weekend trip to San Francisco. We booked a room in a quaint bed-and-breakfast in the heart of the city. On our first day, we decided to spend some time down at Fisherman's Wharf and PIER 39. The sun had burned off all the early morning fog. The smell of the sea air mixed with French bread and fresh seafood was intoxicating. The flowers displayed along the walk from wharf to pier were beautiful.

On PIER 39, we traveled from shop to shop, enjoying the wide variety of trinkets and treasures. Eventually, David spotted a shop he couldn't wait to explore. It was called The Left-Handed Store. David has always been very proud of being left-handed. He would tell me, "People who are left-handed are always in their right minds."

As we entered the shop, he was delighted to see many tools that were usually made only for those of us who are right-handed. He journeyed from display to display, thoroughly checking each item. Suddenly, he stopped at one case and patted me on the backside affectionately to point out something he thought was exceptional.

The only problem was, it wasn't me! I was still across the room and turned to him just as he realized he had just patted a lovely, older woman. The look of horror on his face combined with the smile on hers was more than I could take. I had to exit the store as tears rolled down my cheeks. As I stood there helplessly trying to control my laughter, I could hear David apologize to the woman profusely. She, of course, told him, "No harm done, Honey. You made my day!"

For the rest of our time on PIER 39, she was in every shop we entered, giving David a wicked wink and a little chuckle, to his red-faced chagrin.

—Janell Michael—

47

The Ideal Parking Spot

The misfortunes of mankind are of varied plumage.
~Aeschylus

My husband, Frank, loves cars. It is just that simple… and that difficult. He talks about cars, he reads car magazines, he belongs to car clubs and he tenderly washes and waxes his cars… by hand using only special soaps and cloths. And he has rules: no eating in the car, no drinking in the car (well water is okay but only on long trips), don't take the car through a car wash, and try your very best not to park in parking lots. This last rule is a little bit flexible because sometimes the only available parking is in a lot. But, if you must park in a lot, park as far away from other cars as possible so that no one opens his car door and dings the side of our car.

It was a nice summer day. We had a date to meet some friends for lunch. Frank got the car ready — tires, windows, mirrors and all — and then we drove off. We checked the streets in the neighborhood surrounding the restaurant for parking, but with nothing available, and following his rules, we pulled into a parking lot and parked as far away from everyone and everything as possible. No cars were on either side of us and no cars were in front or in back of us. We were safe. That also meant that we were three long blocks away from the restaurant, but we walked fast and got there on time.

We had a nice relaxing lunch with our friends, said goodbye and started walking back to our car. Way off in the distance we could see it… his beautiful car. It was still by itself with no one nearby. What luck. Frank was so pleased; his precious car had enjoyed another dingless outing. Never mind that his precious wife was now limping in her dressy shoes because of the long distance between the restaurant and the car.

But, wait. Something was not right. Our car was a medium silver-blue color. The car we were heading towards seemed to be a different color — kind of a creamy color. And wait. What was wrong with the windows? They seemed kind of opaque rather than the sparkling clear windows Frank had washed carefully before we left. Frank started to walk a little faster and then started to run towards his car. I did my best to keep up but soon I was half a block behind. I couldn't see his face when he reached the car but I sure could hear him yelling. #&%$#!*%&*@*! or something to that effect.

I arrived at the car, huffing and puffing. And what did I see? Was it our car? Oh yes, it was our car and it was parked right where we left it — inconveniently far away. But… oh my… it was covered in pigeon poop! COVERED!! Can you picture it? Thick, gloppy, runny pigeon poop. What Frank hadn't realized when he found his ideal spot was that he had parked beneath a whole host of electrical wires. And you know that birds love to congregate on wires. I think that while we were in the restaurant, a whole flock of pigeons, probably seventeen generations of them, had a family reunion on the wires above our car and then they let go with everything that they had. Do you think that was why we had this perfect dingless portion of the parking lot to ourselves?

It was a sight to behold. Frank couldn't speak and was beyond being rational at that point. He was sputtering, spewing, yelling and was practically in tears. And I, his loving, devoted, understanding, caring wife was… in hysterics. This was the funniest thing I had ever seen.

Now I had been married to Frank long enough to know that the one thing you don't do when he is upset is laugh. It's best to just be quiet and let him process what is happening. I tried but… I couldn't help myself. I was screaming with laughter. You know, the kind that comes from your toes and explodes. I was doubled over with laughter and gasping for breath.

We still had to get home. How? The front window was totally covered; there was no way to see so Frank could drive. Another question: how were we even going to get into the car? The doors were covered too. Frank checked and found that one of the back doors was not as bad as the others and so, using a tissue I found in my purse, he opened that door very carefully. We both got in and then we had to climb over the seat to get into the front. I was trying to control myself and was doing a pretty good job.

Then Frank turned on the windshield wipers and pigeon poop flew everywhere! It's a good thing that no one was parked near us. Frank turned on the engine and slowly backed up, since he couldn't see out the rear window either. Then we slowly made our way forward, out of the parking lot, onto the street and headed for home. Frank had to sit at a funny angle the whole way home in order to see out the front window through a tiny poop-free opening.

The ride home was slow, long and not very pleasant. Frank was mumbling to himself and I just kept my head bowed and stared at my knees. But every once in a while I would look up, try to look out the window, see all of that poop and just burst out laughing. Frank would mumble louder and say in his angry voice, "Barbara, it's not funny." Of course that made it even funnier and I'd laugh louder.

We did make it home. Frank immediately washed the car. The car survived the attack of the pigeon poop and so did our marriage. Every once in a while I'll tell the story about the pigeon poop. It still makes me laugh. (I'm laughing right now.) Frank, on the other hand, still doesn't find it amusing at all and still mumbles, "Barbara, it's not funny."

— Barbara LoMonaco —

48

The Pendulum of the Mind

I think the next best thing to solving a problem
is finding some humor in it.
~Frank A. Clark

Tick, tock, tick, tock. The sound in my dream grew louder and louder until, in a foggy daze, I realized it wasn't a dream but a clock beating so noisily that it woke me from a sound sleep.

I lay with my head on the pillow, trying to figure out where the sound was coming from. Neither Tom nor the dogs seemed to be bothered. I listened… *Tick, tock, tick, tock.* Was it the clock in the hall? Tom had changed the batteries recently. Could the fresh cells be giving the clock extra tick-tock power?

Tick, tock, tick, tock… I realized with a start that the sound was not in the hall but in the room. *TICK, TOCK, TICK, TOCK.* It seemed even louder now. I looked over at my sleeping husband. Above his side table is an art piece he created from the innards of an old grandfather clock we'd found in a dusty corner of a flea market years earlier. He'd wound it once with an antique key he found, and it worked for about fifteen minutes before coming to a halt. Now, out of the blue, the clock parts were ticking.

Was this thing haunted? Why would it suddenly start working? Why now? My mom had recently passed away. I thought maybe it was a friendly, heavenly hello. After all, in recent years, Mom had a habit of calling her kids in the middle of the night. More than once, my phone had rung with Mom calling between 1:00 and 4:00 in the morning just to say hello. Oh, and she and Dad would tell us to behave in school because they could see us through the face of the clock. Maybe they were in this late-night visitation thing together! In the darkest wee hours, all these strange thoughts and more seemed plausible.

I got out of bed and walked around in the dark to be certain. Yes, it was the "artwork." *Tick, tock, tick, tock*, super-creepy art clock. It was like a metronome, and my racing pulse was pulled into its rhythm.

I couldn't sleep, so I left the room, taking comfort in the fact that the dogs and Tom were sleeping soundly and apparently unbothered by the noise. I was then struck by the thought that I should film the phenomenon in case it stopped before Tom woke up, and he didn't believe me.

I went back with my cellphone and recorded the booming sound. Of course, in a dark room, you can't see anything, so I also filmed the electric clock with the illuminated time and date display. I was amazed that, despite my moving around, Tom was still out cold.

An hour or so later, I had the bright idea to film again, but this time armed with a flashlight. I knew the clock was still ticking because I could hear it from where I was camped out in the family room. Seriously, this was getting unnerving. With my lantern in one hand and cellphone poised to record in the other, I tiptoed back in and captured the beating clock.

Back in my recliner, sleep refused to come. *Tick, tock, tick, tock...* "Woo, woooo, woof!" I jumped at the sound. Ohbe, our Golden Retriever, was having one of his nightmares. "It's okay, Ohbe, you're okay," I called out to him in the dark. Usually that calms him down. It took me several tries until he stopped whimpering. I'm embarrassed to say that I was too chicken to go see if he was crying in his sleep or was awake and "seeing" something that scared him.

Tick, tock, tick, tock... The time passed slowly as I waited for dawn to break. I amused myself by posting the videos to Facebook, where the consensus was that I should get rid of the clock, incinerate it, or move out of the house. I still wanted to believe it was a sign from heaven rather than a nefarious spirit on the loose. At least that thought was more comforting in the darkness.

Tick, tock, tick, tock... How was Tom sleeping through all this? I sent him a few text messages, hoping the dinging on his phone would wake him. He'd been up late packing for a last-minute trip he was making to California, so I knew he was probably sleeping in a little later than usual before going to the airport. *Oh, man,* I thought, *he's going to leave me here alone with a haunted clock.* I decided I would have him move it out to the garage before he left town.

Getting impatient, I wanted to see if he was still sleeping. I tiptoed into the room and could not believe my eyes. There he was in the bed, calmly reading e-mails on his phone.

"How on earth are you just lying there? Haven't you noticed that your crazy clock guts are ticking? How do you sleep through this noise? I haven't slept all night!" I couldn't understand how he wasn't even reacting to his artwork suddenly moving and ticking.

"Oh, that. I'm surprised it's still going."

"Excuse me?"

"Well, right before I went to bed, I tapped it," he said.

"You tapped it?"

"Yeah, I tapped the pendulum. It usually stops after about twenty minutes."

"You've done this before?"

"A couple of times, but I haven't done it in a while."

"It's been going for hours. HOURS." I was indignant.

"I know! That's incredible!" He sounded pleased. Obviously, he missed the annoyance in my voice.

"I haven't slept at all. You had me thinking the clock was haunted!"

"Oops. Sorry. You know you could have stopped it at any time."

"No, I didn't know that," I snorted. "I thought it was possessed! What if I reached out to touch the pendulum, and it grabbed my hand and pulled me in?" I might have veered a little toward melodramatic at that point, but he made it sound like my sleep deprivation was all my fault for not stopping the clock.

"I really am surprised how long it has been going." He looked at the clock with pride and then gave a shrug and said, "At least it didn't chime at the top of each hour."

I returned his shrug with a raised eyebrow. "Have you noticed the time is an hour ahead? It's actually the correct time for the East Coast." I didn't voice my continued thought out loud, but that was my parents' time zone — another reason to let my mind believe this could have been a sign from heaven. Not haunted, just husband. Not a sign. I sighed.

Tom left for the airport, and I listened to that clock *tick, tock* all day. I finally stopped the pendulum at about 10:30 P.M. when I was trying to go to sleep. A part of me almost let it go on ticking, just to see how long it would run. But the side of me that was going to be alone all night in a dark house… Well, that side won the argument for silence.

While my husband was out of town, I created a sign for the clock: *Do not touch or your wife might tick, tock, BOOM!* It features an image of a ticking time bomb with an angry expression. We can now safely go back to the usual nocturnal noises that wake me: Tom's snoring and Ohbe's dreams.

— Donna Anderson —

Adventures in Living

Summer Love Revisited

Learn to laugh at yourself. Life will be a lot funnier.
~Author Unknown

I'm fourteen, sitting at my kitchen table and staring out the window. I'm gritting my teeth and praying that I can make it through the next few hours without throwing up or, even worse, killing my father. Without asking my permission, he invited a business friend and his son to dinner. Dad and his buddy discovered that both of them have teenage kids who are going to the same summer camp. They are hoping we'll become friends and travel together.

Camp is six hours away. We have to take a train, a bus, and a boat to get there. My best friend and I have been plotting every night about how to use the long trip to make new connections and check out crush-worthy boys. Now, my dad is forcing me to babysit the ugly, creepy, nerdy son of his friend. How can he do this to me?

Finally, their car pulls into the driveway. I consider developing a migraine or a sudden case of the stomach flu. Finally, the passenger door opens and out comes a perfect, drop-dead gorgeous hunk named Jimmy. I can see his biceps bulging under his T-shirt.

I quickly update my mental scenarios. This trip to camp will not be torture. It will be awesome. Jimmy and I will surely sit together on the train, the bus and the boat. By the time we reach camp, I figure, we will be madly in love.

Incredibly, this comes true. We become a couple. We swim, canoe, sail, and hike together.

At night, after the evening program, he walks me home, or as far as guys are allowed to go into the girls' camp. The end zone is "The Kissing Bridge." I'm not completely new at this. I've played Spin the Bottle several times. But those slobbery smooches were never like this. Every night, Jimmy and I experiment with new ways to touch tongues. We are in the throes of summer love.

I've never been so happy in my life.

Then they hold tryouts for the camp musical. This year, we are doing *The Sound of Music*. I take a chance and audition, but apparently I am tone deaf and can't carry a tune. I'm given a small part in the chorus with no lines — and directions to only mouth the words during "Do-Re-Mi."

But Jimmy can sing like Johnny Mathis. He is cast as Rolf, the Nazi who falls in love with Liesl, Captain von Trapp's eldest daughter. Sue Ellen, one of the most beautiful girls in camp, gets the Liesl part. They harmonize during the famous duet, "I Am Sixteen, Going on Seventeen," where he sings, "You need someone older and wiser, telling you what to do. I am seventeen going on eighteen, I'll take care of you." And soon he is doing just that.

Well before opening night, Jimmy and Sue Ellen are an item. I have to walk myself over The Kissing Bridge. My heart is broken. I cry myself to sleep when no one can hear me.

The good news is that since this tragedy occurs when I am fourteen going on fifteen, I get over Jimmy. I grow up, finish college, and move to Washington, D.C. for an exciting job as press secretary to a politician. Now and then, I hear from old camp friends about what everyone is doing. I learn that Jimmy is married, although not to Sue Ellen. He lives in the Bay Area.

Coincidentally, I am scheduled to go on a business trip to San Francisco. I decide it will be fun to see Jimmy since it's been around twenty years. I take a chance and call him. He is super friendly, says it's great to hear from me, and wonders if I have time to meet him for dinner. We make a date.

I put on my best suit with my sexiest blouse under the jacket.

I do my hair and apply my make-up perfectly. And then I set out to make Jimmy totally forget Sue Ellen. And possibly his wife.

When I get to the restaurant, I see him at a corner table. He already has a bottle of Cabernet and two glasses. He stands and gives me a hug and kiss. We catch up on the last two decades, and soon it is as if no time has passed at all. He is still gorgeous, charming, funny and, well, perfect.

We drink, laugh and trade stories about what our old friends are up to. My brain fast-forwards to many possibilities. I confess that some are X-rated.

Then he says he wants to ask me a question. *Oh, boy*, I think.

"What kind of insurance do you have?" he says.

"Huh?" I answer.

"Well," he explains, "you're a single woman, making a good salary. What if something happens to you, and you lose your job? Did you ever wonder how you could pay your rent or your mortgage if you couldn't work?"

"Huh?" I repeat.

He goes on. "It's really important for you to have protection from unanticipated events that might happen in the future."

Then, it dawns on me. Through the cloud induced by a half-bottle of wine, my woozy brain begins to realize this dinner is not a prelude to a torrid night at the Ritz. There will be no confession that Jimmy has never forgotten me. He will not tell me that he regrets dumping me for Sue Ellen. He is not stuck in an unhappy marriage and hopes this dinner can be the start of a romance that picks up where we left off.

Nope, he took me out to dinner in order to sell me insurance.

He did not make a sale, but I still acquired a new policy: I will never again call an ex-boyfriend.

— Maureen Rubin —

Locked In

*I believe that the ability to laugh at oneself is fundamental
to the resiliency of the human spirit.*
~Jill Conner Browne

t 8:00 in the morning, I was in my two-year-old granddaughter's room getting her ready to come to my house to be taken care of for the day. My daughter Megi had an early morning meeting and a very long day of teaching ahead, and would not be back for ten hours or so. So, granddaughter Maci and I were in for a fun but very long day together. A cat named Cheeto and a Chihuahua named Snickers were also in the room with us that fateful day. I am not particularly fond of cats, but Cheeto is okay as far as cats go. And I can't resist a three-legged Chihuahua. (Can anyone?)

It was a freezing day with temperatures around zero degrees. My plans were to bring Maci to my home, give her a nice breakfast, work on the potty training, read books, color some pages, and maybe paint a little picture or two. I also hoped a long nap would be part of the day. But this was not to happen anytime soon, much to my dismay.

We were in Maci's room getting her dressed, her hair combed, and her big-girl panties on. She had recently graduated out of diapers but was at the stage when she needed to go to the bathroom every hour or so. No worries because Grandma Ginny could take her to the potty several times a day.

Then, all of a sudden, I heard, *Slam!* Playing around, Maci had closed the door to her room. My daughter had warned me not to let the door close tightly because the door was not working properly.

Because Maci's bedroom had been rented out to a tenant before Maci came along, there was a bolt lock on the door. That bolt lock was locked, and the key to open it was inserted in the keyhole on the other side of the door. As I scrutinized the door, I realized that I was locked in the bedroom with no way to get out. There was no lever to turn, no lock to unbolt, nothing!

I was not alone, however. I was accompanied by my granddaughter saying she had to go potty right now, a scared three-legged Chihuahua, and a cat wanting to get out of there, too.

Since I am a take-control type of person, I did not panic right away. I thought I would just call my daughter to come get us out. Then I realized my cellphone was down on the first floor. It was nowhere near this second-floor bedroom.

Another thought came to me. Perhaps I could somehow put a credit card in the space between the door and lock. But that won't work with a deadbolt, and I didn't have a credit card with me. It was also on the first floor. However, I did find a few pages of a coloring book I had ripped out. I put them together and tried to stick them in the door by the lock. Needless to say, that did not work.

My next plan was to try to pick up the door from the floor, undo the screws in the hinges holding it in place, and remove the whole door. Of course, I had no tools, only toys in that room. The closest thing I could find to a screwdriver was a Barbie doll leg. Obviously, I did not have much luck with that method of escape, even if I could have lifted the entire door.

In the meantime, three creatures were really getting on my nerves. Maci still had to go potty, Snickers was barking, and Cheeto was trying to escape by clawing on the curtains. And it was only 9:00 A.M.!

Perhaps I could holler at somebody walking by in the greenbelt behind the house or get a neighbor to rescue us. Well, I found that when it is zero degrees outside, there are no joggers or signs of human life anywhere nearby.

I thought maybe I could climb out the window and go get help like they do in the movies. But I could see I didn't have enough sheets to tie together for my great escape from the second floor. Plus, the Hello Kitty toddler bed that I planned to tie the sheets to did not look heavy enough to hold me. The thought of me falling down twenty feet, breaking my leg or back, and lying in the snow to freeze to death made me abandon that plan.

All of a sudden, I got a terrible case of claustrophobia. The thought of staying in that room for ten hours with Maci, Snickers, and Cheeto was more than I could bear.

Then I saw it… my escape! A little, pink-polka-dot broomstick horse. *That should do it.* It was the best thing I had ever seen. I knew it was a drastic plan, but we were getting out of there soon.

I grabbed the broomstick horse's little head with its wiggly eyes and used the broomstick as a battering ram. After a little work, I made a hole through the drywall near the door handle. I was shocked to find an inner wall and an outer wall. After I hit a hole in the second outer wall, I found that I still could not reach the door handle. *Oh, well, no stopping me now.*

I smashed two more large holes in the drywall with my beloved horse. They were each about a foot wide and a foot high. All three of my companions were crying, barking, and hissing by now because of the loud noise.

The holes were finally big enough for me to stick my whole arm through to the outside of the door. I played with that lock forever. Somehow, miraculously, I was able to unlock the bolt lock so that the door would open. We could finally escape from our prison.

Believe it or not, we made it to the bathroom for the potty training. I do have to admit that the dog and cat steer clear of me nowadays. They think I am crazy. I prefer to think of myself as a very creative problem-solver.

I did feel a little embarrassed about having a drywall worker come out and repair the walls, patch the holes, texturize, and repaint.

— Ginny Huff Conahan —

Five-Star Hotel

If happiness is the goal — and it should be — then
adventures should be top priority.
~Richard Branson

We watched in disbelief as our cabdriver turned off the main road and headed through a creepy part of town. Old, decaying buildings. Not many streetlights. Definitely not the type of area we'd pictured ourselves traveling through in the dark on our way to our hotel.

Our sons had invited us to fly to Okinawa with them to attend a concert by HY, our family's favorite J-pop band. Toby and Paul had frequently flown to Japan, but this was a first for David and me. I offered to book the hotel since our sons had their hands full finding four concert tickets and making airline reservations. "Don't worry," I said. "I'll find the perfect place to stay."

Full of excitement, I had a blast as I searched online. I waded through hundreds of reviews, looked at pictures, and found a hotel in our price range that rated better than most of the fancier, more expensive hotels in Okinawa. It boasted nothing but five-star reviews, looked nice, and was close to the sights we planned on seeing, plus they allowed us to reserve four beds in one room. I felt pretty proud of myself for finding such a gem. But I hadn't imagined us driving through such a shady-looking area to get there.

Our cab made its way down a narrow road lined with outdoor booths of some kind. Blankets hung on each side to divide them, and makeshift curtains covered the fronts so we couldn't see inside. At first, I assumed homeless people must live in these makeshift rooms. But, as we continued, several young men in white dress shirts and black pants appeared and hovered near our cab. I held my breath and thought we might get robbed.

The men in the white shirts seemed shocked to find our family inside. The cabdriver waved, and we continued our trip. By now, we had a pretty good idea that the huts weren't sheltering homeless people.

Earlier, back at the airport, the taxi dispatcher had given us a strange look when we told him our hotel's address in order to find us a cab. We ended up pulling out the receipt so he could see we had it right. Now, his reaction made sense.

I held my breath, expecting to drive out of this area, but minutes later our cab parked in front of our hotel. All we could do was laugh at my grand hotel plan. I'd made reservations smack dab in the middle of Okinawa's red-light district.

None of us knew what to expect, but our stay in the red-light district was actually rather fun. Each night, as we got a cab after sightseeing, we got a kick from watching the driver's expression when we said the address of our hotel.

And, each night, the white shirts appeared, only to find the same American family driving through, instead of a paying customer.

Although we had bars on our windows, the room was clean, and not once did we feel unsafe. Throughout the night, we heard people coming and going, but we were so tired from sightseeing that we still drifted off to sleep.

The people who ran the hotel were warm and friendly. Although our friendly cleaning lady didn't speak English, we loved greeting her each day on our way out. We had complimentary tea in our refrigerator and a vending machine in the hallway so my husband could buy Japanese beer after a long day in the heat.

My husband and I fell in love with Okinawa. HY put on a spectacular concert. The sights were breathtaking. We finally had the pleasure of meeting the many friends our sons had made in Japan over the years. And our little, red-light hotel added an unforgettable splash of spice and a lot of laughter to the perfect trip. In the end, I had no choice but to give our hotel the five-star rating it deserved!

—Jill Burns—

Wisecracks on the Whiteboard

Being a good neighbor is an art
which makes life richer.
~Gladys Taber

During the lockdown, my wife and I tried to pull our daughter away from screens and take her for a walk every day. Staying inside all the time isn't good for a ten-year-old. She needed air, sun, and blue skies. We all did.

We had regular spots we visited around the neighborhood, which we may not have noticed before the lockdown made our worlds smaller and forced us to pay closer attention to the people and places around us.

We might have stopped by the town's common and seen what was happening: adults sprawled on blankets, kids learning to ride bikes, teenagers hanging at the gazebo. We might have stopped by the house with the pet ducks, Waddles and Gideon, which was a special sight as pet ducks are not something you see every day. The ducks have their own hatch and pen, though they sometimes roam free on the lawn, or their owner may pick them up and put them on her lap.

The previous occupant of the hutch was a rabbit, but it vanished one day. We didn't know what became of it, and we didn't ask.

Some days, our daughter brought her scooter along, and as she hurled ahead, gliding along, we scurried to catch up. Along the way, we passed the neighbors sitting on sidewalks in lawn chairs, talking to other neighbors doing the same. Along the way, we passed the woman living on the corner, who has a dog that looks like a mop with legs.

One particular place we always made sure to stop was a cozy, beige house near the baseball and soccer fields, where women did yoga six feet apart, close to a pond full of frogs making a glorious cacophony of croaking.

At this beige house, along the railing on the front porch, a whiteboard was fastened. And that whiteboard provided an essential public service, one just as important as the post office or fire department, particularly in a time when the world felt so out of sorts.

The service the beige house provided? Jokes. Every day, the people in the house wrote a new joke on the board. Walk by that house, and you were promised a chance to laugh every day.

"Why did the stadium get hot after the game?" said the words on the board written in marker. "All the fans left."

"What did one eye say to the other?" the board announced another day. "Something smells between us."

"Why don't scientists trust atoms?" it said, delivering the setup before hitting us with a punch line so silly that it might bomb in a kindergarten. "They make up everything."

The jokes were groaners that would barely provoke a knee slap. They were dad jokes that elicited eye rolls. And yet, we couldn't help but laugh, or at least smile. It felt good to smirk and snort and chuckle with everything seemingly turned upside down.

So, we stopped by the board and read, "What did the pepperoni say to the mozzarella? You want a piece of me."

And, another day, we read, "Why are police officers so good at volleyball? They can serve and protect."

Another day, we read one that seemed a little too apropos for those days of masks and hand sanitizer: "Did you hear the joke about the germ? Never mind, we don't want to spread it around."

And on and on it goes. In a never-ending quest for comedic gold, I imagined the occupants of the house scouring the Internet or reaching out to grandchildren, neighbors, or anyone who might have heard a good joke lately. I was grateful for their efforts. The yuks, quips, and jests offered us a small respite, a diversion from our days. We read the wisecracks on the whiteboard and then turned around and headed home to be inside once again.

—John Crawford—

The Wedding Crasher

Strangers are just friends waiting to happen.
~Rod McKuen

I brought a close girlfriend as my date to a friend's wedding reception. I wasn't getting married yet, but I was certainly going to enjoy dressing up, meeting people and partying away the evening.

My "plus one" and I found my name on the board of table assignments but did not recognize any of the other names at our table. We made our way over to our seats where two men were already sitting. They were a bit older than the rest of the couple's friends, but they were ready to have a fun night, which was all that mattered.

We began getting to know each other with the usual questions. One of the men revealed he was a doctor. My friend and her new husband were nurses, so I figured they were friends through work. However, I never requested more specifics.

The conversation evolved, and our night of fun was off to a great start. Neither of the men seemed like the type of person my friend would invite to her wedding, but I couldn't say for sure about the groom. We shared a lot of laughs, enjoyed delicious food, and took a lot of photos of us having a carefree and wonderful time. I remember thinking that my friend must have put all of us together at the same table because she knew we would all hit it off.

Finally, after the speeches were over and we all got up to mingle, one of the bridesmaids approached me.

"Who are those guys at your table? I don't recognize them," she said.

"The one said he was a doctor, but that's all I know," I replied.

The bridal party had been staring at them throughout the speeches wondering who they were. It finally clicked.

"WEDDING CRASHERS!" the bridesmaid said, outraged. Then, she ran them straight out the door.

We thought it was hilarious and plastered all the photos of our night with the wedding crashers on Facebook. They aren't a mythical thing, we joked. People are actually doing this. And, for most of the night, they actually got away with it.

Nearly seven years after this wedding, I found myself needing to take my one-year-old daughter to an appointment at a children's hospital to see a dermatologist. We waited in the exam room for the doctor to come in. But, first, a man came in introducing himself as a resident. He explained he would see us first and then come back with the attending physician.

We went through the typical appointment questions, but something about him just felt off. He eventually left and said he would return shortly with the dermatologist.

"That guy seemed so familiar," I told my husband. "Where could I know him from?"

As we waited for them to come back, my mind raced through where I could have possibly met this man.

And then it hit me.

"He was one of the wedding crashers!" I declared. And I knew I could prove it!

I pulled open Facebook on my phone. Thankfully, the album of photos from that night was still there. We looked closely at the man from the wedding.

"That is definitely him," I proclaimed. "See this mole on his face? If that mole is there, then this confirms the resident is the wedding crasher."

The resident returned with the dermatologist and, sure enough, there it was: the mole. Exactly where it was in the photo.

He wasn't a doctor at the wedding seven years earlier, maybe just a med student, but one thing was for sure: he was definitely a wedding crasher.

—Katie Bergen—

54

Perfect Timing

It's as if the Universe has a sense of humor.
~Deepak Chopra

In the summer of 1967, my sisters Karen and Nancy and I went with my grandparents, Nanny and Poppa, to the Lake of the Ozarks. With no real plan except that they wanted to fish, Poppa waited until we got to the Ozarks to look for a place to stay. Pulling into a little, one-pump gas station with a sign that read "Vacation Rentals," Poppa went inside and, sight unseen, paid for a cabin described as "two bedrooms on the lake." Following a map, we drove through a heavily wooded area and got lost twice, but we finally found it. Located only a few yards from the lake's shore, it was small but had a fishing dock and a swimming area. It was perfect.

I have wonderful memories of the time we spent there, fishing with Nanny and Poppa under pink-rimmed skies at dawn and hearing the occasional splash of a fish as it jumped from the water and fell back in. I remember how grownup I felt about making my own decisions. Cold cereal, or bacon, eggs and pancakes for breakfast? Wear my swimsuit all day or change into shorts and a T-shirt? I remember the excitement I felt at the idea of swimming in a lake and my scream of surprise at its arctic chill. The evenings were wonderful, too. Having packed his grill, Poppa cooked hamburgers and hot dogs for dinner, which we ate while sitting together at the picnic table in the cabin's front yard.

Our evenings were spent chasing lightning bugs and then going inside to play go fish, old maid and dominoes with Nanny while Poppa relaxed in the recliner, drinking a beer and watching us through the hazy fog of cigarette smoke. From its very beginning, it was a wonderful vacation. But what made it legendary was its ending.

On our last full vacation day, Poppa shifted from relaxed grandpa to drill sergeant. That night, there were no games with Nanny because Poppa had us busy packing up so we could get an early start the following morning. By bedtime, the grill, bag of charcoal, lawn chairs, fishing poles, and ice chests were all cleaned up and nicely organized by the front door. Our blue suitcase, lying on the floor of our bedroom, was packed and ready to go except for the things we still needed or would need the next day (i.e., our pajamas, toothbrushes, travel clothes and Nancy's doll, Drowsy).

I thought the next morning would be less busy, but it wasn't. While Nanny was washing the breakfast dishes, the rest of us were carrying everything to the car so Poppa could fit it into the trunk. When he came to our suitcase, he said, "Are you sure you packed everything?" I told him I was sure. "Well," he said, "go back in. Look under the couch, chairs and beds, and then open all the drawers and make sure they're empty." I wanted to say that I was sure there was nothing left in the cabin, but one did not argue with Poppa. So, my inner rebel and I went back and looked under the couch, chair and beds. But I didn't open the drawers.

Poppa finished packing and yelled that it was time to go. Nanny came out of the cabin, firmly closing its door. Karen, Nancy and I followed her down to the car and opened the back doors to climb in.

"I have to go to the bathroom," Nancy said. Poppa muttered something. But Nanny smiled and said, "Well, the door's not locked. Go on in. But hurry." Poppa looked at Karen and me. "You two might as well go in and use the bathroom, too." We told him we didn't need to do that. "Well, do it anyway. I don't want to get twenty minutes down the road and have one of you telling me you need to use the bathroom."

Finally, we were all in the car — Karen and I with books to read and Nancy with her "baby."

"Everybody ready?" Poppa asked. "Once I start driving, I don't want to hear one person say 'I'm thirsty,' or 'I have to go to the bathroom,' or cry because something got left behind." We said we were fine. Poppa started the car and put it in Drive.

"I want another drink of water," a tiny voice in the back seat said.

Poppa hit the brakes. And faster than I've ever seen anybody move before, he flung open his door. Jumped out. Flung the back door open. Leaned in and roared, "Dangit! ('Dang' was not the word he used.) Who the heck (he didn't use the word 'heck' either) said that?" We were too scared to answer. "Well," he bellowed, "which one of you was it?"

Turning from the front seat, Nanny looked at him and said, "Poppa, it was Nancy's Drowsy doll."

Poppa didn't say a word. He just got back in the car and drove down the road.

I don't know what the odds are of that doll saying that phrase at that exact moment, but I do know that Drowsy's string did not get pulled again for a very long time.

— Crystal Hodge —

55

A Diamond in the Rough

*The trick to being smart is knowing
when to play dumb.*
~V. Alexander

My son has always been a great student. He was always in advanced placement classes in high school. My husband and I have always said he is "book smart" and we are very proud of him but, on the other hand, he doesn't have much in the way of "street smarts." And we all know that you need "street smarts" to get along in the world.

When you have a responsible son, you can trust him with things like credit cards, even in high school. So we gave him a Chevron gas card. But our son couldn't get it to work, no matter how hard he tried. Finally, my husband went to see what the problem was — was our book smart son putting the card in the gas pump upside down or backwards?

My son had a sheepish grin on his face when he came back home. My husband just smirked. Of course the Chevron gas card hadn't worked… my son tried to use it at a Shell station.

I tried to do everything I could to prepare our son for life away at college. I taught him about banking, cooking, which gas card went with which gas station, and even sent him off with a first-aid kit.

I must have done a good job. The first quarter of college went off without a hitch. He did very well in his classes and seemed to settle into college life without too many questions or problems. My husband and I felt great about how mature our son had become and were so proud of his ability to live independently.

Thanksgiving came along, and our son was coming home, flying alone for the first time. Still not ready to completely give up my "mother" responsibilities, I checked him in for his flight from my computer, texted his boarding pass to him, and arranged for the shuttle service to pick him up at his dorm and take him to the airport. All went well. I met him at the airport when his flight landed and he proceeded to share his flight experience with me on our drive home.

"I really lucked out, Mom," he said. "I was seated between two hot girls."

This surprised me because he is on the shy side, so my question was, "Did you talk with them?"

"Yes, I did."

He then told me the three of them talked about a bunch of different things until one of them started feeling sick. The plane was almost empty, and with so many rows of vacant seats, she decided to lie down in her own row. He and the other girl kept talking.

We got home and as our conversation continued, we heard lots of stories about school and college life. Then we all went to bed. While lying in bed, I reflected on the many stories he had shared, including the one about the "hot girls" on his flight... and then it hit me. Why did he sit between the two girls with all the empty seats that were available on the plane? That would be very out of character for my shy son.

In the morning I met him in the kitchen and asked, "Why did you sit between those girls if there were so many empty seats?"

His response was: "I had to sit there. That was my seat number."

Seat number? Your seat number? I began to laugh so hard.

You see Southwest Airlines does not have assigned seats. Between giggles, I explained that Southwest has what they call "festival" seating. Another foreign word to him. He didn't have a clue. I explained that is what it's called when you go to a concert but do not have an assigned seat. You sit anywhere.

He looked at me with a confused look on his face. "But Mom, I checked and the boarding pass you gave me had my seat assignment... B12."

"Oh no! That was not your seat number; that was your boarding group number."

The reality of the situation hit him. We laughed until tears were running down our faces. Those girls must have thought this 6'2" cute guy was so self-assured and bold… or crazy… that he wedged himself between them in a middle seat on an almost empty plane. When we finished laughing my son said that he had actually never felt so confident and he had even asked one of the girls for her phone number. I guess in this case it was good that he wasn't so street smart.

And I guess no matter how hard we try to prepare our kids for life's adventures there are always things a mother forgets to teach her kids. Again, in this case… maybe that's not such a bad thing!

— Michelle Campbell —

56

R You Listening?

For years, I'd go to the movies and see guys doing
Boston accents and think, "Oh please, God,
I hope I never have to do that."
~Michael Keaton

I am the product of a mixed marriage — my mother was a Red Sox fan from Boston and my father was born and bred in New York City. I live in Greenwich, Connecticut, in staunch Yankees territory, but only twenty miles south of the Red Sox Nation border. The American League East is at war in my blood. My cousin on my mother's side has worked at Fenway Park his whole life and he gave me a Red Sox hoodie that I love wearing when I am safely outside my local area.

But where I live? Forget it. I dared to wear my Red Sox hat *once* while walking in our neighborhood. And sure enough, I took it off for one second when I got hot, and a bird pooped right on my head — a big pile right where the emblem with the two red socks had been. Even the local birds had noted my treachery.

Boston is on my mind a lot because my son and daughter-in-law live there now, surrounded by people who sound just like my mother. Why do I bring this up? Because I remember fondly the day more than twenty years ago when I was talking to the kids about "foreign countries" and they insisted they had already been to one. They explained that every time we visited my parents we went to a foreign country.

In reality, my parents lived twenty minutes away. Where had they gotten the idea that Grandma and Grandpa lived in a foreign country? Well, they explained, Grandma had a foreign accent and she lived in a place with a foreign name — Chappaqua — in New York State. So "New York" must be a foreign country. I had no idea that for years I was getting credit for taking my children on exciting weekend trips out of the country!

My mother's "foreign" accent was always a source of amusement in our family. When she drove me to my freshman year of college, she actually said the very clichéd "oh look, they opened the gates so we can pahk the cah in Hahvahd Yahd" as we pulled up to the front of my dorm. I always teased my mother and dared her to pronounce words with an "r." She would struggle and slowly enunciate the words, with only the faintest trace of an "r" no matter how hard she tried. But give her a word like "idea" and up popped an "r" right where it didn't belong. What's an "idear" anyway?

One of my favorite stories about my mother's accent was when she tried to buy some dark chocolate bark a few years ago in a candy store in touristy Annapolis, Maryland. Mom told the salesclerk that she wanted some of the "dahk bahk" in the glass case. Considering all the foreign tourists who visit Annapolis, the home of the Naval Academy, the clerk assumed that English was not my mother's first language. She explained that she couldn't understand my mother's accent, so would she please spell what she wanted? My mother proceeded: "D-A-AH-K B-A-AH-K." No luck. She left the store empty-handed, foiled by her Boston accent.

After my mother had a stroke, which resulted in her losing some language skills, I had to pull the speech therapists aside and explain to them that her Boston accent was not the result of aphasia. I didn't want them to try to reinstate an "r" sound that had never been there anyway. They had actually been trying to teach her how to say words with R's in them, so they appreciated the heads-up.

At my mother's memorial service I told some stories about her various unique characteristics, including her Boston accent and how she was often misunderstood. My cousin who works at Fenway "Pahk" came up to me after and said it was the best funeral speech he ever heard but he didn't really understand my comments about my mother's accent because he "had never noticed that she had one."

And that's why I love going to Boston, where the pahking is difficult and the snowy, cold winters are hahd. In the meantime, I still get to talk to the other side of the family, the New York side, which can't pronounce R's either. It wasn't until my Park Avenue aunt died that I learned that her best friend's last name wasn't "Shera," but was "Sherer." And we love to tease my Brooklyn-born husband about his R's. And his L's too. He can't for the life of him pronounce one of his favorite beverages, the "Arnold Palmer," so he always has to order a half-iced-tea-half-lemonade.

— Amy Newmark —

Mistaken Identity

57

Lost My Car and My Mind

Sometimes crying or laughing are the only options left,
and laughing feels better right now.
~Veronica Roth, Divergent

Our part of the world is famous for its heat and humidity. On this particular day, I surmised that the heat and humidity called for a dip in the pool. As I floated in the cool water, I daydreamed about the plans for our son's birthday party later that evening. It would be hot as it always was this time of year, but hopefully the food, balloons, and ice cream would distract from the boiling heat.

After backstroking to the side of the pool, I checked my phone. It was much later than I had imagined, and I still had a lot to prepare. I was going to have to hurry. I threw on a cover-up, slipped on flip-flops, and tied my hair in a wet knot, mimicking the "Messy Bun" hair tutorial I had watched the night before on Instagram.

Pulling into the grocery store parking lot, I realized I was not the only one who had begun my weekend with a supply run. The parking lot was packed. I finally located an open space by not-so-stealthily stalking an exiting shopper. Pulling in and exiting the car with fifty-year-old-cheetah-like speed, I ran in and around the store collecting what I needed.

After checking out, I grabbed my receipt and nodded to the young man who had bagged my groceries and offered to push the cart to my car. *Perfect! That might save some time,* I thought as I jogged past him, leading the way with my messy bun unraveling and now living up to its name. Before heading out the door, I checked my receipt to ensure I wasn't missing anything: ice cream, cake, wine, and balloons.

I was proud of myself for making good time. The sweltering heat hit us both as the supermarket doors sprang open. Fumbling in my purse for my keys, I saw a sea of hundreds of shiny cars like a mirage baking in the sun. Keys in hand, I picked up speed. The only things slowing me down now were my flip-flops, which were beginning to stick to the melting tar of the parking lot.

At that moment, it dawned on me that I had no idea which car was mine. My husband worked for a car manufacturer, and the vehicles we drove as a family would often change when he brought home different ones. I racked my brain. I had not paid attention to the car I had hopped into back in my driveway. This was worse than trying to find a needle in a haystack — at least I know what a needle looks like! Deciding not to worry just yet, I pushed the key fob. Silence. I tested it repeatedly. *How is this possible? Perhaps the battery is dead.* Glancing back at the bag boy I had left in the dust, I cut to the next aisle, squeezing between a camper and a 4x4 parked closely together.

"This way," I yelled, knowing the cart would not fit through, and he would be forced to go all the way around, hopefully giving me time to locate my stupid car. No such luck.

Do all car manufacturers conspire to ensure all cars look just similar enough to appear camouflaged when parked together? After twenty minutes of chasing me through nine aisles of the parking lot, the bag boy finally caught me with the cart. "Ma'am, did you lose your car? If you describe it to me, I'll help you find it." How could I possibly explain to this young man that I drove here in a car and parked it in the parking lot, but I had no idea of the make, model, or color of the car? I think I mumbled something like "black wheels" and "rectangle." We were both melting in the sun. Looking down at my cart, I noticed that my cake and ice cream were suffering, too, as they began to pool in the bottom of the cart. Shaking his head, he looked at me as if he now believed I had a lower I.Q. than the radishes he had bagged for me earlier.

Of course! I thought. *My husband! He knows which car I'm currently driving. As I see it, this is all his fault!* I grabbed my phone and quickly called him. No answer.

It had been forty-five minutes of inspecting cars, and I was sweating, exhausted, and limping with a broken flip-flop. No explanation at this point would make me appear sane. The bag boy agreed. "Ma'am, have you been drinking?" he quietly asked. I was looking down at the bottles of Chardonnay in my cart.

"No, not yet," I said, desperately trying my husband's number again. "I'll be fine," I told him. I collapsed onto the curb to adjust my toasted, melted flip-flops and bun that now resembled a bird's nest.

It seemed the bag boy, too, had had enough. "I'm going back inside. I need to refuel with a drink," he announced as if he was part of a rotating parking-lot pit crew for lost shoppers.

The parking-lot temperature kept rising, and so did my temper. Why wouldn't my husband answer? Connecting to his voicemail for the tenth time, I left a message he couldn't ignore. "There has been an incident. I'm sitting on the curb in the grocery-store parking lot, slurping melted ice cream from a straw while drinking wine directly out of the bottle. A woman just handed me a ten-dollar bill and said, 'God bless.' If you don't call me back soon, I'll throw off this cover-up, hitchhike to a corner in the red-light district, and embrace my new life. CALL ME BACK!"

After eating half the cake and drinking half the wine, I was losing both hope and my mind. I took out my receipt and scratched a few final words on it.

"If you are reading this, you've probably found my body in the grocery-store parking lot. I tried to be a good mother and put on a great birthday party for my son, but instead I died of heat, humidity, and humiliation because I could not identify my car, and my husband didn't call me back."

I untied the balloons from the grocery cart, attached the receipt, let them go, and watched them float away. I glanced down in time to see an older gentleman in overalls crossing the parking lot toward me. He had a friendly smile and kind eyes.

"Young lady, I noticed you can't find your car." I nodded in absolute defeat. "I can help you," he said with calm assurance.

For a moment, I felt new hope. He seemed so confident. Alas, staring at my shopping cart, I realized it now contained only part of a cake, no ice cream, no wine, and no balloons. If he could help me find my car, I could at least drag myself home.

"No problem," he said. "Now, what does your car look like?"

— Kimberly Avery —

58

Oh, Henry!

If cats could talk, they wouldn't.
~Nan Porter

Shortly after settling into our new Florida home, my husband Dave and I unexpectedly became foster parents to a couple of feral cats living in our subdivision. We didn't set out to become their primary caregivers. It transpired as they repeatedly showed up at our front door for a bite to eat. We didn't know if the previous owners had fed them or if someone else living in the community had moved and the cats were searching for another place to get some food. Anyway, we fed them, and, in time we named them Tiger and Midnight.

As they became comfortable around us, Dave and I trapped them and brought them to get spayed and neutered. To keep down the feral-cat population, the Humane Society provides these services for free. Although they remained outdoor cats, Tiger and Midnight became part of our family. We didn't mind tending to their needs: providing food, water, and shelter outside. After all, it wasn't their fault they were homeless with no one to care for them.

A few years later, another cat showed up at our door. We didn't know where he came from. We never saw him roaming the neighborhood. I felt sad for him. He looked tired and hungry with his big, puffy-looking face and scrawny body. We fed him with the other two. And soon they became a pack of three. We named him Henry.

Unlike Tiger and Midnight, whom we could catch and bring

in to get fixed, Henry apparently knew better. I suppose his age and familiarity kept him from biting the bait. Another thing that was different about Henry was that he roamed the neighborhood, and he would stay away for days on end. Tiger and Midnight stayed within the boundaries of our property.

One morning, upon opening my front door, I spotted Henry. Immediately, I blurted out, "Oh, Henry! What happened to you?" I thought, *Boys will be boys, and feral cats will be feral cats.* By the looks of him, he must have gotten into a ruckus with another cat. He had an open wound on his neck. The best I could do was to give him some food while feeding the other two. As I placed his dish in front of him, I said, "Henry, if you stop prowling around at night and stay around here, you won't get hurt."

Two days later, Henry showed up for a bite to eat. I was shocked when I saw him. The open wound had miraculously healed. I couldn't believe my eyes! I shouted to Dave, who was inside the house, "Honey, you've got to get out here and see Henry. You won't believe this! He's all better."

After inspecting Henry, Dave said, "Wow! He heals quickly." Being naïve, I assumed the same. We fed him, along with the other two, and left it at that. For several days, Henry stayed around our house and remained injury-free.

However, after being AWOL for a while again, I spotted Henry limping toward my front door. Immediately, I said, "Oh, Henry! What happened to you now?" I thought, *Maybe he fell from a tree or sprained his leg trying to get away from another cat.* I felt bad for him because he could not put any weight on the injured leg. Since we couldn't catch him to bring him to the Humane Society to get checked out, we did the best we could by feeding him some good, high-quality food.

A few days later, Henry showed up at our house, but he was not limping. I thought, *Wow! This cat heals quickly.* I asked Dave, "How can he be better that quickly?"

Dave responded, "I don't know. Maybe the chicken we fed him two nights ago helped him."

"I don't know about that," I replied. "But, anyway, I'm glad he's better."

For months, this happened over and over — injuries followed by miraculously quick healing. Dave and I were dumfounded by what was taking place. We knew there was no way that Henry could heal from his injuries that quickly. Yet, he did!

It wasn't until one morning, after Dave came in the back door and I came in the front, that we figured out how Henry was healing so quickly. Dave commented, "Henry's in the back yard waiting for food."

Surprised, I responded, "No, he's not. I just left him at the front of the house."

Pointing out the back window, Dave said, "Look, he's sitting right there." As I peered outside, realizing Henry was there, I thought to myself, *Then, who's in the front?* Quickly, we headed to the front to see if the Henry I saw was still there. To our surprise, he was. Turning to Dave, I exclaimed, "There are two Henrys!"

Those two cats were identical. It was odd because few cats look like them, with their big puffy faces and scrawny bodies.

As both cats began coming around at the same time to eat, I could distinguish one from the other. Henry #1 has eyes that are open wider than Henry #2, who looks like he's squinting. To this day, Dave still struggles with figuring out which is Henry #1 and which is Henry #2.

And, yes, when one of our Henrys shows up with a bruise, I still say, "Oh, Henry! What happened to you?"

— Barbara Alpert —

59

The Birthday Dress

What are sisters for if not to point out the things
the rest of the world is too polite to mention.
~Claire Cook

When I moved from a big city to a small town located hours away from my family, I knew I wouldn't see my siblings as often as I had in the past. I still visited the city every so often because many of my relatives lived there, but I no longer spent every holiday with them the way I had before.

A few weeks before my birthday, I did manage to visit my sister in the city. As I left her place, she handed me a gift bag with a bunch of presents inside. They were all wrapped in bright pink tissue paper and looked very chic. My sister has an eye for design, and everything she puts together always looks impressive. That's part of the reason I didn't want to open my gift right away. I asked her if it was okay if I waited until my birthday to open my present, and she agreed.

I opened it while my partner and I ate breakfast on the morning of my birthday.

My sister had managed to fit quite a number of presents inside that gift bag. I pulled them out one by one, unwrapped the hot-pink tissue paper, and enjoyed the thoughtful items she'd chosen for me. There was a box of salted-caramel chocolates, which I opened immediately, even though it was 8:00 in the morning. Why not have dessert after breakfast?

She'd given me a number of other gifts, including a warm and comfy scarf, lip balm, and a long purple dress. The dress surprised me. In all our decades as sisters, I couldn't remember another time she'd bought me an item of clothing. Accessories? Sure. Scarves, hats, mitts — she'd bought me those gifts before. Never a dress, though.

I tried it on immediately. The dress was a dark shade of purple with a floral pattern that was even darker. It had long sleeves and came down past my knees. According to the tag, it was a size that ought to fit me. Even so, the fit was a little large. That didn't matter, though. The dress felt quite cozy. As soon as I put it on, I didn't want to take it off — and I didn't!

When I asked my partner what he thought of the birthday dress, he agreed that it was a tad billowy but looked quite elegant. It was a great choice of attire for a birthday. So, I pulled on a pair of tights and decided to wear the dress for the rest of the day.

Before heading out, I wrote my sister a quick e-mail to thank her for the birthday gifts. In particular, I told her that I'd already started in on the chocolates and loved the dress. "I'm wearing it right now." Those were my exact words.

She replied to say that it's never too early for chocolate, but she made no mention of the dress. I thought that was a little strange, but I went on with my birthday, feeling pleased that my sister had picked out so many lovely things for me.

Later that day, my partner cooked dinner, and we cut into the delicious chocolate-mousse cake he'd picked up at the bakery in town. We'd just sat down to work on our after-dinner crossword puzzle when the phone rang. It was my mother calling to wish me a happy birthday.

"I talked to your sister," my mother said. "I heard you opened your presents from her this morning. I heard you liked the chocolates she gave you."

I agreed that I did, and I put her on speakerphone so my partner could be in on the conversation.

My mother then said, "And I heard you liked the nightgown, too."

"The nightgown?" I asked, looking to my partner in confusion.

My partner and I gazed down at the dress I'd been wearing all day. We both burst out laughing.

"What?" my mother asked. "What's so funny?"

My partner could not stop laughing as I said, "This dress is a nightgown? I've been wearing it all day!"

That's when my mother erupted in laughter, too. It's a good thing I don't take myself too seriously, or I would still be hiding under a rock after going about my entire day — and my birthday, of all days — wearing what turned out to be sleepwear.

"But how would I know it's a nightgown?" I asked, rushing to the garbage to pull out the tag I'd thrown away. "It doesn't say anywhere that it's a nightgown."

My mother asked what it looked like, and I described it: purple, long sleeves, a little billowy, stretchy cotton-blend material. What made it a nightgown and not a dress? My mother simply said that my sister told her it was a nightgown, and she had bought it, so she would know.

Even after I said goodnight to my mother, my partner kept laughing. He thought it was hilarious that I'd been wearing a nightie all day. Luckily, I thought it was pretty funny, too. I just couldn't understand why, when I e-mailed my sister to say thank you, she didn't warn me that I was wearing a nightie and not a dress.

Later, when my sister came to visit my new home, I made sure to show her around town wearing my billowy yet elegant birthday dress.

— Tanya Janke —

60

Upon Reflection

Look in the mirror, and laugh at yourself.
~Bernie Glassman

I t was a cold winter evening in the kitchen of my raised ranch. I had just clomped up the snowy deck stairs to the back door of the kitchen with grocery bags. It was getting dark outside but light enough for me to find the keyhole in our recently replaced glass-pane back door.

I put down the bags inside, turned around and saw to my horror that someone was standing motionless on the deck on the other side of the glass door where I had stood moments ago. I couldn't distinguish the features of the person. It all happened in a flash, but it appeared to be someone about my height in a jacket looking in, staring back at me. I screamed and galloped down the three steps toward the front door, swung it open and scrambled across my lawn — snow crunching under my boots — to the neighbors across the street.

"Oh, my God," I muttered under my frosty breath. "He's probably broken into the house by now." I couldn't stop shaking.

Thank goodness the Gilberts were home. With my heart thumping, I breathlessly gestured and explained what had happened. Mr. Gilbert reacted to the panic in my eyes. He put his arms around me and told me not to worry, reassuring me that he and his two sons would check it out. His sons, two burly guys in their late twenties, would scare off anyone!

Mr. Gilbert grabbed a heavy shovel and flashlight and led his sons back across the street. Too nervous to remain stationary, I followed a distance behind them, quaking but feeling a bit relieved.

The Gilberts boldly opened my front door and climbed the three steps to the hallway across from the kitchen. Not a sound was heard. No one was in sight. We walked into the kitchen where I stopped suddenly, startled, gasped and pointed to the door. The figure was still out there pointing at me! And then panic turned to relief, to laughter and, finally, to embarrassment when we all realized what I had seen: my own reflection in my new glass door!

—Judy Stengel—

61

Yankee Doctor Down South

Laughter is the shortest distance between two people.
~Victor Borge

He was one of the first patients I saw during my first week on the job at the Veterans Medical Center in a small North Carolina town in August 2003. We'd just moved there from New York City, and my Brooklyn accent was still pretty strong. My patient had his own thick Southern accent, making it hard for me to understand him.

The fifty-eight-year-old veteran had been through some tough times. Clearly, his lower back pain was only part of his problems. He now lived alone in a trailer with no television and told me he could use some inexpensive home entertainment.

"Have you thought about visiting a pawn shop?" I suggested. The man's dull demeanor turned sharp, and his face flushed.

"Well, I'd be too embarrassed," he said, but I could tell he liked the idea.

Encouraging him, I noted, "I've been to many pawn shops in my life. I was a bit embarrassed to be seen going into one the first time, but then I got over it. There's nothing to be ashamed about."

A bit of gleam shot into the melancholic eyes. "You're a real respectable-looking lady. If you can do it, I guess I could, too. But I imagine where you went in New York City, no one knew you."

"That's true," I replied. "However, I wouldn't be embarrassed to enter a pawn shop here in Salisbury."

"Maybe," he said, "that's because you don't know anybody here yet, so there's no one to catch you doing it."

I contemplated that thought. "Well, I do know some people here now, and I wouldn't mind any of them seeing me enter a pawn shop."

"It sure would perk me up," the fellow said, warming to the idea. "Do you think the VA would pay for it?" I doubted that, and he said he doubted it, too, but he just had to ask.

"I can afford to buy new things, but I still like going to secondhand stores," I told him. "There's no reason to be embarrassed about being careful with your money."

"Oh, lawd," said the patient. "I couldn't see buying one of them things used!"

"Why wouldn't you want to buy a used T.V.?" I asked.

"T.V.? You mean to play adult videos?" he answered uncertainly.

Then it dawned on me: This patient heard my Brooklyn-accented "pawn" as "porn." I explained the misunderstanding.

Three seconds later, the front-desk person came bursting into the exam room to see what the loud screaming was about. She was shocked to see us both doubled over in laughter, with tears streaming down our faces. Standing up and wiping his eyes, the patient said, "This is the best damn visit to the VA I ever had."

— Susan Jensen —

Cloaked in Mystery

Absence of proof is not proof of absence.
~Michael Crichton, The Lost World

The alarm rang out at a deafening volume, shocking everyone in the gallery. We all covered our ears and looked inquiringly at each other, wondering what in the world was happening.

I was a university art student in Canada, contentedly working part-time at the nearby National Art Gallery for the art experience and some spending money. Serving as student gallery interns, those of us who worked there did a little bit of everything. We would greet people coming into the various galleries, give them information about the different articles and artistic items on display, and serve refreshments at opening shows. We helped dismantle the past shows and assemble the upcoming ones. We guided tours and acted as security guards. We also cleaned up as needed.

There were several main galleries in the building, as well as a couple of smaller side areas that were used for art shows and displays. So, there was always quite a bit going on there and plenty of people visiting. When a new, popular show opened, wine, cheese and a variety of other goodies were usually served as refreshments, making for much bigger crowds.

On this particular weekend, a new show had opened, so we were busy attending to our list of duties. One unusual aspect of this show was a floor piece that looked just like a black cloth cloak lying bunched up on the pavement. It was cordoned off with burgundy rope, like the other sculptures, but being a dark, crumpled fabric on the floor, it looked very different from any other art piece.

The alarm went off without warning, completely stunning all of us because it was incredibly loud. We couldn't escape it because the whole building went into complete lockdown, securing all the doors to prevent theft. Finally, an administrator punched in the code to turn off the blasted thing. We breathed a collective sigh of relief.

Then, we quickly looked around to see if anything was missing or someone had accidentally tripped the alarm by trying to sneak out the back emergency exit for a cigarette. Everything seemed to be in order until we noticed that the black cloth piece that had been displayed on the floor was missing.

The police arrived, and everyone was questioned while the whole place was searched. We came up empty-handed, so eventually everyone was allowed to get their coats and go home, although we were disheartened at not finding the missing piece.

Since we were employed there, we were the last to go, still excitedly chatting about the missing art cloak as we got our coats from the cloakroom.

Putting on our jackets, we noticed that someone had forgotten their coat. Looking at it more closely, we realized that it was the missing art piece that we had been searching for all evening. It had been hidden in plain sight among the other coats on the rack.

Some good Samaritan had picked up the art piece that looked like a cloak and hung it up in the cloakroom! They were probably thinking that it was someone's coat that had been taken off and forgotten, and then had slipped to the floor. That set off the alarm and the whole series of events that followed.

Mystery solved. All's well that ends well.

— Sergio Del Bianco —

63

The Creature That Moaned in the Night

There is no such thing as fun for the whole family.
~Jerry Seinfeld

It started with a growl, a deep, guttural cry that shook the air with its sound of pain.

"What is that?" my husband AJ asked.

The kids were finally in bed, and the puppy was sleeping with our middle daughter. It was just AJ and me sharing a couch in the sunroom with our second dog asleep on the other sofa.

Chloe, our old dinosaur of a dog, paid the sound no attention. She had been obnoxious as a younger dog but now, with limited hearing, was a gentle giant.

"What is that?" he repeated.

I heard the pained cries: one short wail, a larger cry, and a fading moan to the wind.

"I'm not sure," I said. "It's not a fox." I had seen one earlier that day at his parents' house, asleep on the cover of their pool, nestled up as if in a dog bed.

The air was silent.

"An owl?" I guessed.

"No."

The night outside was dark. A crescent moon competed with the stars and Jupiter.

Chloe lifted her head and looked at us, disinterested.

The animal wailed again as she settled back to sleep.

"Why don't you see if you can see it?" I said.

"Maybe you should text Hector," he suggested, referring to the neighbor I have never, not once in my life, texted or called.

"Um, he's your friend."

"Then Kim?" I was not about to text my new friend about an animal outside. We texted about whether my first-grade son had escaped our house to play in their yard, not about a dying animal at ten o'clock at night.

"Just go outside," I suggested. I imagined him approaching a dying fawn, attacked by an owl or hit by a car.

Chloe looked up as AJ reluctantly got up from the couch and moved to the door. The animal howled again in pain.

AJ opened the slider to silence and let Chloe out.

"I can't even tell where it's coming from," I said.

"Check out Nextdoor," he said, referring to the community chat board.

"Already am," I retorted. "Nothing there. I just can't figure it out."

"Why don't you ask them what it is?"

"And look like an idiot?"

Chloe scratched at the door to be let back in.

"Are we sure it's an animal?" AJ asked. "Maybe it's some kind of machine." We listened again, careful to be silent against Chloe's snoring that had resumed.

"Like, what kind of machine? A lawnmower? And who would do that at this time?" I got up from the couch to check the window on the other side of the room. But the animal was silent again.

"North American animal sounds," I typed into a search engine.

A seal barked back at me.

AJ and I sat there for ten minutes (there are a lot of animals in North America) determining whether the creature we heard was a raccoon or a coyote. Definitely not a mouse or a bat.

"Wow," he said. "Bobcats sound really scary. Wouldn't want to be alone with one of those at night."

"I really think it's a deer. I bet a baby is injured or lost its mom or something." In my head, I formed a story. The baby had gotten stuck in a sewer hole. Maybe it broke its leg. Or maybe two bucks were fighting to the death. Perhaps all my deer stories shouldn't come from movies.

"Deer crying sound," I typed into the search engine. A coughing sound spit back at me. "We're getting close," I said. "This might be it. I really think this has to be it." I heard our youngest cough from the other room. I needed to check on her so she wouldn't wake one of her siblings. "Anyway, I need to go to bed. Are you sure you don't want to go outside and see if you can find it?" AJ shook his head.

"I'm going to take Chloe out and come to bed," he said.

"Okay, good night." I started to leave the room. Chloe reluctantly jumped off the couch with a butt push from AJ. We heard the roar again.

"What is this?" he said, pointing to a palm-sized toy nestled between the cushions of the couch.

"Lucas's toy," I responded. "The dinosaur toy he got in Montana." I paused a second. "Are you kidding me? The sound is a T-Rex." I pressed the button on the remote-shaped toy. A T-Rex moaned. He cried out in his deer cough. He barked like a seal. And he tricked us both into thinking we had heard a dying T-Rex in our back yard.

Chloe looked at us in disgust at moving her and ambled toward her bed.

— Kaitlyn Jain —

64

There's Something Wrong with This Joint

A subtle thought that is in error may yet give rise to fruitful inquiry that can establish truths of great value.

~Isaac Asimov

With her hands on her hips, my mother waylaid me. "Show me." Usually, my mother paid no attention to my reading materials, so I guessed she was "showing an interest." But she couldn't have picked a more inconvenient time. I was heading for my bedroom with my latest purchase firmly tucked under my arm.

I sighed, crossed my fingers, and hoped this interruption wouldn't take long.

My mother read the back, opened to a random page, and scanned it. Then, she shook her head. "I think this book is too old for you."

What?

My book disappeared into my mother's room, leaving my reading plans in ruins.

Fortunately, I knew where my mother's secret hidey stash lived. All I needed to read was time and a chair. I couldn't take the risk that my mother would discover the book missing from her hidey hole or, worse, find it in my room. So I'd have to sneak my reading in when she left the house.

Each afternoon, as my mother headed to the stables, I'd streak into the kitchen, grab a chair, and head into her bedroom. I'd climb up, stand on tippy toes, and then stretch my hand over the top of the cupboard to grab my book. I didn't have time to be greedy, so I'd read five pages at a time. Then, I'd stash the book back in its place, climb down, and pop the chair away.

One day, close to the end of the book, the characters headed off to a beach party, and I couldn't for the life of me understand why they'd taken a joint with them.

Joint? Like a lamb joint? That's what we'd roast for a Sunday dinner, a lamb joint.

It made no sense. Why would you take a lamb joint to a fun-filled beach party? Sure, they probably cooked it first, so it was a juicy, tender roast, but even so, that's not picnic food, is it? It wasn't like they'd cut it up for sandwiches. Instead, they shared their lamb joint around like they were playing Pass the Parcel.

Images of teenagers flooded my mind for the next few days. They sat on the beach, grinning as they took a mouthful of juicy meat before passing on the lamb joint. The salty smell of the sea and the sound of waves crashing against the shore filled the air. The wind whipped up a frenzy and blew sand around as the sun beat down on them.

Each image would raise more and more questions.

Was that even hygienic?

Did sand get in the way of their feast?

And weren't their hands getting grotty and slimy?

Who wants to nibble on the same lamb bone as everyone else?

The rest of the book shed no light on the mysteries of why a group of teenagers would share a roast lamb joint on the beach. It bothered me, but I couldn't ask. I'd read a banned book whose contents were taboo. So, my lips stayed zipped.

Over the next few years, the lamb joint conundrum popped into my head whenever I helped prepare a Sunday roast. I still couldn't grasp the point of sharing a roast lamb joint at the beach.

At nineteen, I found myself at an unforgettable beach party. The music was pumping, the beers were flowing, and the sun was beating down. It was just like the beach party I'd imagined all those years ago.

A shaggy-haired guy asked me if I wanted any of his weed. He crumpled an empty beer can, popped some tufts of weed on the top, lit it, and took a hit.

I was eager to try, but the beer can… *Eeeewww!*

My face must have displayed my mixed emotions. The shaggy-haired guy said, "I'll roll you a joint."

My eyes popped open as I watched him roll the weed into the tobacco paper. I couldn't help but laugh at the sight.

As I sat on the beach and lifted the joint to my lips, I noted there wasn't a single roast lamb in sight. Perhaps my mother was right: That book had been way too old for me.

— Sandi Parsons —

Club Connie

Laughter has no foreign accent.
~Paul Lowney

Ring, ring. In a thick Japanese accent, my father began the phone call in his usual abrupt, get-to-the-point-fast manner. "Karyn. Okay-uh, Michael there?"

Sighing, I replied, "Hi, Dad, nice to hear from you, too. Actually, Michael is in the shower, but I can have him call you back in a little while."

"Okay-uh, my friend, Waki, coming. He like a club. You know good club?"

Remembering that his Japanese friend, Waki, was coming to visit, and that we had planned to take him out to dinner in Long Beach one night, I tried to wrap my head around this unexpected change in plans. "Well, I will have to give that some thought. What kind of music does Waki like?"

"No, no. Club, club," he repeated.

"Yes, I heard that you want to find a good club, but there are lots of different kinds of clubs. Does your friend like jazz or blues or rock music?"

"No, no. Club, club. Club, Connie," my dad stated emphatically.

Happily, I breathed a sigh of relief. "Oh! You already know the name of the club you want to take him to? I've never heard of Club Connie. Where is it? Is it in Long Beach?"

Exasperated, my dad whined, "NOOOOOOO! Connie, Connie. Club, Connie."

Trying to keep my composure, I said slowly, "I heard the name: Club Connie. But I'm not familiar with Club Connie. Perhaps Michael will have heard of it. I will ask him when he gets out of the shower, okay?"

"NOOOOOOO!" he insisted desperately. "Connie, Connie! Club, Connie!"

Feeling at a loss as to what to say next, I paused. After a few uncomfortable seconds, I heard my mother enunciate clearly in the background, "Crab."

Suddenly, the light bulb went on as it dawned on me: Kani, which sounds like Connie to an American ear, is the Japanese word for crab. And, in his struggle to pronounce the word "crab" in English, anyone would have mistaken it for "club."

"Oh, now I get it. You want to take Waki to a good restaurant that serves crab. Okay, I will let Michael know. Oh, I see he's out of the shower, so I'll put him on the phone."

Covering the receiver, I looked my husband in the eye and clearly introduced the situation, telling him, "My dad is on the phone, and he wants you to recommend a good restaurant that serves CRAB."

Taking the phone from me, Michael jovially greeted my dad. After hearing a few words on the other end, he replied, "What kind of music does he like?... I've never heard of Club Connie. Where is that?"

— Karyn Hirsch —

Chapter 8

I Kid You Not

66

Do as I Say...

Children have never been very good at listening to their elders,
but they have never failed to imitate them.
~James Baldwin

"Okay, you kids! I just finished cleaning the bathroom, and it already looks like a pigpen. I am getting sick and tired of this. This bathroom is off-limits."

Four sets of large blue eyes roamed the floor, the ceiling, each other... anywhere but my stern face.

I glanced at the clock and panicked. In thirty minutes, my husband and I would be hosting the annual potluck for the local dentists, and I would barely have time to shower and put on a clean shirt.

The party was a success, the food tasty, and the weather balmy. As I was cleaning up, a friend tapped my shoulder. "Your little girl is so polite," she said as she doubled over with laughter.

"Thank you?" I said with a question in my voice.

Still laughing, my friend said, "She was quite the hostess when people asked her where the bathroom was. She took them back to the master bath and added this warning...." I felt my breath catch. My friend continued, "She told your guests, 'My mama is sick and tired of cleaning the bathroom and then having it look like a pigpen. So, DO NOT use that one. Use this bathroom.'"

I took a good look at the mess before me: damp towels in the sink, toothpaste oozing out on the counter, curling-iron cords tangled together, a stray shoe hiding under the bed, clothes that didn't make the cut for my outfit tossed on the floor. But the pièce de résistance was my husband's boxers hanging on the doorknob.

Even though I was embarrassed beyond belief, I had no grounds to be angry with my four-year-old daughter. After all, I did say that the bathroom was off-limits.

— Sharon Landeen —

67

Define "Emergency"

*You know you're potty training when you have a potty
in the kitchen and candy in the bathroom.*
~Huggies

I don't remember whose brilliant idea it was to adopt a dog and potty train a child at the same time (oh, yeah, it was me), but I may have been in over my head.

My daughter and I had really been focusing on potty training the past couple of weeks, and I was sure we were on the cusp of a breakthrough.

"Tell Mommy when you have to go potty, and I can help you, okay?" I'd often remind her.

This particular morning was no different.

"I have to take the dog outside. I'll be right back."

I left her in her Baby Shark PJs eating cereal from the box, watching *Monsters Inc.* My eighteen-year-old son was also in the living room on his computer.

Marah, our dog, was taking her time finding "the spot." Circle after circle, she padded, wearing a path through the frozen snow.

I was shivering in the February air, wondering how her butt could be so sensitive to any certain spot in the wintry tundra of the front lawn.

Then I saw them, though not clearly, across the blacktop. They were walking toward me.

I live in a confusing configuration of townhomes and assumed they were lost and looking for directions. They headed straight for me.

Now, I could see the badges. The uniforms. The serious cop expressions.

"Do you live here?" one officer asked, pointing to my front door.

"Yes…"

"Do you have children at home?"

"That depends on why you're here." I laughed nervously.

One of them cracked a smile.

I ran down a mental list of why they could possibly be here.

Tom's music is too loud? No, he wears headphones. Vandalism? No, that would require he leave his bedroom. Oh, and he's not that kind of kid.

"Dispatch received a call from a young child saying they needed their mommy because they had to go pee."

Shock and embarrassment engulfed me like the flames of a fire. It was only ten degrees outside, but I started to sweat.

"Do you want to go check on her?" he asked, motioning to the door where my dog danced around, finally ready to be let in.

"Uh, yeah…" I opened the door and saw my daughter standing there naked.

"Mommy, I have to go potty REALLY BAD!"

"Did you call the police?" I asked.

"Yep, it's a 'mergency!" she said with her hands between her legs.

I slowly shook my head and turned reluctantly toward the door.

"Everything okay?" the officers asked.

"Yeah, thanks for asking. I'm sorry you had to come out here for nothing."

"Oh, don't worry about it. This is one of the better kinds of calls we get!"

The other officer chimed in, "Just be careful when you're in the line of doody." He chuckled.

I forced a half-hearted laugh/groan and went back inside.

As I was leading Olivia to the bathroom, she asked me if, since the police were already here, they could help her find her pacifier.

"Sure. I bet they'll put a detective on the case right away. In the meantime, let's talk about what an emergency is."

— Melanie Brening —

68

Fourth of July Chaos

Kids are the tiniest and deadliest army in a house.
~Author Unknown

"It's just for the afternoon. A little lunch and a swim. What's the worst that can happen?" says my ever-optimistic husband, Sean.

"What's the worst that can happen? Have you met our boys? Your mother's house is not set up for toddlers!" I reply.

"My sisters and their kids will be there. My family wants to spend the Fourth of July with us. We can make it through the afternoon. It will be fine."

"Famous last words," I reply dejectedly.

After years of infertility, my husband and I had been blessed with two wonderful boys. Our one-year-old, Carter, and our three-year-old, Jackson, were non-stop, rough-and-tumble toddlers. Our house had every cabinet and drawer locked, every outlet plugged, and everything breakable locked away. My mother-in-law's beautiful new home had expensive oriental rugs, beautiful china, and amazing knickknacks displayed from her travels.

My mother-in-law dearly loves our family. I am terrified of the chaos that my running, touching, climbing sons can wreak in one afternoon. I reluctantly agree to the afternoon festivities and carefully put together bags of toys, food and clothes to ensure we have a successful afternoon.

When we arrive, my mother-in-law is ecstatic to see us. She warmly welcomes us in and tells me not to fret. She is so excited to spend the afternoon with us. We hug and chat with my sisters-in-law and their husbands and children. It is nice to see everyone and spend time with family.

My mother-in-law has created the perfect Fourth of July feast. Sean and I carefully prepare the boys' plates to avoid anything too messy and try to keep the sugar to a minimum. We manage to keep all the rugs safe and not break any dishes. A successful lunch!

Now, onto swimming. Sean and I lather up the boys with sunscreen. We strap them into their life vests, and Sean and the boys begin swimming. I quickly help my mother-in-law and sisters-in-law clean up lunch. We then sit on the edge of the pool and watch Sean and all the kids swim. We laugh and chat and have a great time.

As dinner approaches, I let Sean know that it is time to get the boys home for the evening. We wrap the kids in towels and carry them upstairs to the bathroom to change them. Sean and I do a quick high-five. We made it through the afternoon. There were no breaks or messes or chaos. As we are dressing the boys, I realize the bag with changes of clothing has been left in the car. I quickly run downstairs and out to the car.

As I re-enter my mother-in-law's home, I notice that everyone is looking shocked at the second-floor landing where my one-year-old son is standing... naked. My brother-in-law is laughing hysterically. I look from my brother-in-law to my son to my mother-in-law. I am not sure what has happened. I feel pretty sure it cannot be good, though.

I quietly whisper in my sister-in-law's ear, "What happened?"

Eyes wide, she says, "Well... umm." She hesitates.

I look over at my brother-in-law for some clarification.

"He just peed off the landing," my brother-in-law says between laughing fits. "He just walked right up to the edge and peed between the slats."

"Oh, no!" I yell and quickly begin running up the stairs toward my son.

"He did! He just peed off the landing," he repeats, still cackling.

I grab one-year-old Carter's hand and pull him into the bathroom.

Sean and I dress the boys as I, red from embarrassment, tell Sean about the peeing incident.

As we leave, I apologize again to my mother-in-law.

"Oh, sweetheart, it's not a problem. What's a Fourth of July without a bit of excitement?" she says, smiling.

I hug her and walk my sweet little chaos creators to the car.

"We almost made it without incident," says Sean.

"Almost. Never a dull moment with our crew," I reply, shaking my head.

—Marie Loper-Maxwell—

I Pinched That Kid

There's nothing like a grandchild
to put a smile on your face.
~Author Unknown

My husband and I have fourteen wonderful grandchildren. We enjoy taking them one at a time to spend a week alone with us. When Gino was three years old, it was his turn for a visit. He happened to be with us on July Fourth, so we took him to the Independence Day festival at the park. Booths were set up for games, arts and crafts, and food. Later in the day, a country band was going to set up on the outdoor stage and perform for us, followed by fireworks across the lake.

Gino was having a grand time but became bored and cranky after a while. We decided to go over to the playground and let him play with other children. At first, he was the only child on the curvy slide. I carefully watched him climb the steep stairs and stood below him in case he slipped. Then, as he slid down the slide, I ran to the end to catch him.

We continued doing this for a few minutes before another boy close to Gino's age joined us. The child's parents watched us from their blanket on the ground a few feet away.

This child was very aggressive. He didn't want to take his turn at all. He'd run from the end of the slide, hurriedly climb the steps behind Gino, and try pushing him aside so that he could go ahead of him. Gino comes from a family of six boys and knows very well how to stand his ground and defend himself. So, I was surprised when I watched him let the boy pass him a few times.

I was standing below the steps watching when I saw this boy almost push Gino off the top platform as he cut the line once again.

"Oh, no," I mumbled under my breath. "This kid is asking for it." I was expecting the inevitable at any moment. Maybe I could prevent an altercation. "Gino, let's go play on the swings for a while," I suggested. I half-hoped the little boy would run to the swings… but he didn't.

Suddenly, we heard the most ear-piercing scream from the boy. His parents came running. Gino ignored him and went down the slide. I had not taken my eyes from the two of them at any time and had not seen any misfortune befall the child.

The father climbed the steps, enveloped his son in his arms and descended. The high-pitched screams continued even louder, accompanied by flailing arms and legs.

I was dumfounded. "I was watching, and I don't think Gino touched him," I said to the father. "Perhaps he bumped his head?"

"No, no. My wife and I were watching also, and we didn't see any foul play. Like you say, he probably bumped his head. We'd just commented on your boy's patience. He must have siblings," said the father.

"Yes, he's one of six boys," I replied. "I'm surprised, too. Patience has never been one of Gino's virtues."

Taking Gino by the hand, I said, "Since it looks like your boy is uninjured, we'll head on over to the music stands."

Gino was noticeably quiet and attentive as we stood in front of the bandstand watching the musicians set up their equipment. Then, looking straight ahead, completely out of the blue, came this confession: "I pinched that kid." It wasn't actually a confession when I consider it now. It was more like a proud announcement, even though it was quietly spoken.

I was so surprised that I wasn't sure if I'd heard him correctly. "What did you just say, Gino?" I asked.

He looked up at me with a sly grin and repeated just as quietly as before but very proudly, "I pinched that kid."

It had been several minutes since the episode. The child and his parents had disappeared into the crowd. It was too late to make any apologies. Why was he telling me now? He had gotten away with it. No one was the wiser. I pondered my choices. As an adult, I knew that I really should reprimand my grandson for his pinching... and especially for not confessing sooner. Yet, neither the child's parents nor I had, at any time, asked Gino if he had touched the boy. So, he hadn't lied.

I glanced down at him. He was watching the musicians, his confession forgotten, and pleased with himself... more or less. I remembered the tolerance that Gino had shown for the boy for so long without retaliation. Perhaps it was best to leave well enough alone, I decided.

I took Gino's hand, and we walked to the stands to look for Grandpa and find seats for the performance. And, shamefully, I admit, I couldn't erase the slight grin from my own face as I replayed Gino's little voice announcing to no one in particular, "I pinched that kid."

— Christine M. Smith —

70

From the Mouths of Babes

You can learn many things from children.
How much patience you have, for instance.
~Franklin P. Adams

When my son Leo was two and a half years old, his favorite word was "balloon." Sometimes, he would randomly shout it as an expression of joy. This was a wonderful word, and I felt confident about him repeating it anywhere, in public or at home.

Then, at age three, his favorite word became "buttocks," which isn't exactly a vulgar word but is not the most appropriate thing to shout at random, especially at church.

Leo would usually say it whenever he undressed to take a bath, but there were other occasions, especially ones that involved dancing and hip-shaking, that would also cause him to loudly proclaim, "Buttocks!" This was awkward since we attend a church that features lively worship, and a young child happily shouting "Buttocks!" definitely stands out against the reverent shouts of praise.

I thought I had had my share of Leo's awkward, funny proclamations, but I was wrong.

One night as we were eating dinner, someone knocked over a glass of water. Leo jumped up and, to all of our surprise, screamed, "Holy s***!"

First, we all had to stifle our laughs, knowing it would only encourage him to say this phrase even more. After we all managed straight faces, we tried to clean up the water, and my older kids began to encourage Leo to say something more appropriate.

I observed my two teenagers as they attempted to get Leo to say another phrase instead.

"Say, 'Holy guacamole!'"

"Say, 'Holly, jolly Christmas!' instead."

"Leo! Leo! Say, 'Holy pizza pops!'"

Their enthusiasm made me suspect that one or two of their teen movies might have introduced this new word to Leo's vocabulary. I made myself a mental note to discuss it with them—after Leo was asleep, of course.

Over the next few days, we all took opportunities to give Leo appropriate expressions of surprise. He seemed to particularly like "Holy cow!" over all the rest, so whenever something was spilled or Leo had a funny mishap, I would exclaim, "Holy cow!" with enthusiasm.

I thought it was starting to catch on, but the real test would be if Leo would spontaneously use it without prompting.

A week or so later, we had a little family get-together with aunts and cousins. The table was packed with nearly fifteen people, including a toddler the same age as Leo.

Inevitably, during the meal, someone knocked over a cup. Once again, Leo sprang to his feet, and, in front of his aunts, uncle and cousins, he happily shouted, "Holy cow s***!"

I guess it's something we've still got to work on.

—Ree Pashley—

71

Conned

*Back of every mistaken venture and defeat
is the laughter of wisdom, if you listen.*
~Carl Sandburg

A few months into our relationship, my girlfriend called to ask if I would mind watching her seven-year-old son while she worked a late shift at the hospital. "You'll have to sleep over," she said. "I'll be working until two or three in the morning."

"No problem," I replied, seeing this as a great opportunity to impress her. "It will be fun. We'll have a guys' night. Get a pizza and pick up a movie or two at the video store."

Yes, I said "video store." It was that long ago.

"Oh, by the way, he's supposed to have a friend sleep over tonight," she added. "You don't mind, do you?"

I would end up marrying my girlfriend and adopting her son, but at the time, I admittedly hesitated. Just for a moment, though.

"No, I don't mind at all."

I wasn't an expert on children, but how difficult could it be to take care of a couple of seven-year-olds for a few hours?

The evening started off great. We watched the first movie while stuffing ourselves with pizza and soda. Then, I opened the sleeper couch and got it all set up for them with sheets, blankets and loads of pillows. The boys changed into their pajamas and got into the sofa bed while I set up the second movie for them.

Once they were settled, I turned off the living room light, said goodnight, and went upstairs to do some reading. It was all going according to plan. This parenting thing didn't seem as difficult as everyone made it out to be.

About an hour later, the sounds of excited chatter carried up the stairway. They called my name and said to hurry. I took the stairs two at a time. When I asked what was wrong, my son's friend proudly held up a small, bloody tooth. With his gap-toothed grin, he looked like a miniature hockey player raising the Stanley Cup.

This was an unexpected event, for sure. They talked excitedly while I just stood there, wondering what to do. The last time I had seen a tooth fall out was thirty years earlier, and that tooth was my own. I considered calling my girlfriend at work, but I didn't want to appear helpless. No, I would deal with this on my own.

I rinsed the tooth and placed it in a tissue, as I remembered my mother doing all those years ago. Then we put it under the boy's pillow for the Tooth Fairy.

As I headed back upstairs, hoping I had a dollar bill in my wallet, I heard the friend say, "Wow, this is great! I'm going to get another five bucks from the Tooth Fairy!"

I stopped and turned back around, hoping I had not heard him correctly. Five dollars? Per tooth? I got a quarter a tooth when I was a kid. I assumed, accounting for inflation, that the going rate would be a dollar. He flashed that innocent, gap-toothed smile and assured me that, yes, the Tooth Fairy gave him five dollars per tooth. I smiled back and told them to try to get to sleep.

Then, I ran upstairs and frantically dug through my pockets.

I found four one-dollar bills in my pocket and another one on the dresser. Phew! After the boys fell asleep, I quietly went downstairs and slipped the five bills under his pillow. I was halfway upstairs when I remembered to go back and take the tooth. For that price, I figured I'd earned it.

I was asleep when my girlfriend returned from work. In the morning, I told her about the tooth incident, emphasizing my competence in managing the situation. When I asked if five dollars per tooth was normal, she said that most children she knew received a dollar per tooth. She seemed surprised that the boy's mother, who was a friend and co-worker, would give five dollars per tooth. She and her husband had five young children. That's a lot of teeth.

The boy's mother came to pick him up later that morning. I handed her the tooth and asked why the Tooth Fairy placed such value on her children's teeth. She stared at me for a moment and then burst out laughing.

"My kids only get a dollar a tooth," she said, turning to give her son the "mom look." He grinned and ran off.

It was official. I'd been conned by a seven-year-old.

— Gary Sprague —

The Empty Nest Quest

Your child's life will be filled with fresh experiences.
It's good if yours is as well.
~Dr. Margaret Rutherford

fter dropping off our last child at college, we sat in silence on the long drive home. "What now?" I wondered. Glancing at my husband John I noticed an ear hair was beginning to curl out of his ear and down into his collar. Sure, he would need me to pull the hair he couldn't reach, help keep his eyebrows separated, and signal him when he had spinach between his teeth, but sadly he wouldn't need me the same way the kids had.

The next day, I was catching up with an old friend when she caught me off-guard. "Now that you're an empty nester, what are you planning to do with yourself?"

Do with myself? She spoke with urgency as if my warranty was about to expire, and I risked quickly becoming as obsolete as Blockbuster.

"I have no idea," I told her. "Perhaps I'll skip this phase of life entirely and move into assisted living early."

After being a full-time mom for nearly thirty years, the thought of sitting and rocking peacefully alone with my thoughts — assuming I still had any — was somewhat alluring. I could attend field trips I didn't plan, dine on food I didn't cook, and lounge in bed all day binge-watching Netflix in my comfy pajamas without anyone worrying that hell has frozen over or pigs now fly. "You must admit that it has an underappreciated appeal," I told her.

"Seriously, what employable skills do you have?" she asked.

"As a mom, I have got skills," I told her confidently. "I'm just not sure how employable they are."

"Any particular field?" she asked.

"I have a lot of experience in health care."

Let's see, I have administered 1,728 doses of Tylenol. I have kissed and applied bandages to 1,200 boo-boos. I can tell a child's temperature with just my elbow and sense when they are about to throw up in traffic. I once performed surgery with only Super Glue when my son's knuckle was shaved off during an apple-peeling debacle. I have extracted seventy-two splinters and eighteen fishhooks. I saved one hamster that was headed toward the light with mouth-to-mouth resuscitation, and I have removed thirty-seven ticks, not counting the one I tried to remove from the dog that turned out to be a nipple.

"Bill's half-brother Steve is starting a late-life career as an Uber driver," my friend informed me.

"I have a lot of experience in transportation, too."

I can drive a school carpool with my eyes closed, often backward and uphill in the snow. I can also dislocate my own shoulder in order to retrieve a screaming child's sippy cup from the floor of the back seat while never taking my eyes off the road. I can probably drive Uber at night and still get a full eight hours of sleep. I am trained to nap sitting straight up with my eyes open in order to give my offspring the impression I am watching them from the car as they spend hours practicing sports they will never be good enough in to translate into a profession.

"What about working with food? You make a fairly edible meat-loaf," she said.

"I have experience in the culinary arts, too."

I can slap together a school lunch in under fifteen seconds — thirty seconds if we are out of Lunchables. I have a talent for locating items in our refrigerator that are invisible to everyone else in the family. I can make leftovers last for a week by dressing them up and disguising them as new meals. When the kids announce there is nothing in the house to eat, I'm able to discover vegetables no one recognized as food.

Is there a job that requires knowing which culprit has mud on their shoes or predicting when the dog is about to poop on the living room carpet?

I'm bilingual. I also speak fluent two-year-old.

What about something in accounting? "Accounting? You're terrible at math," my friend pointed out. That actually works in my favor, I told her, as the IRS is now hiring eighty-seven thousand new agents. Plus, I'm great at estimating what people owe. I can tell you my kids each owe us eight million dollars. "Eight million?" she asked. Obviously, that accounts for inflation and pain and suffering.

I was actually thinking the military might be interested in employing me. "Seriously? You're joking." My friend laughed.

"Go ahead and laugh," I said, "but I have developed a few rare abilities the Navy seals might be very interested in."

I have overdeveloped olfactory senses that can sniff out potentially lethal substances. I once identified dirty gym socks and a bag of Doritos under a bed three rooms away.

I am an avid multitasker. I can talk on the phone, fold laundry with my toes, swill wine, and help two kids with their homework all at the same time.

I'm skilled at employing bribery and negotiating with tiny hostage-takers. I know when a teen isn't telling the truth without a lie-detector machine and have held interrogations that resulted in the suspect confessing and begging for their father in less than five minutes flat. "Impressive," she said.

If they still underestimate the extent of my unique skills acquired in thirty years of parenting, I may need to arrange an in-person interview in order to demonstrate my superhero speed that kicks in when chasing a missed school bus or garbage truck. And they could observe the most extraordinary trait I have developed as a mom: eyes in the back of my head.

— Kimberly Avery —

73

There's a Cow in My Room

The innocence of children is what makes them stand
out as a shining example to the rest of mankind.
~Kurt Chambers

When my mom was little, she and her parents lived in a trailer on her grandparents' farm. One day, when she was a toddler, her exhausted mother put her down for a nap. Shortly after, my mom came wandering out of her room.

"Go back to bed, Lynne! It's naptime!"

My mom replied, "I can't sleep. There's a cow in my room."

Now, little kids have been known to say crazy things, but my grandma thought this was just the most ridiculous excuse she had ever heard. A plea for a glass of water or one more story might have worked, but not this.

"There is not a cow in your room. There is no way a cow could possibly have gotten into your room. It wouldn't fit through the door! Go back to bed."

Reluctantly, my mom returned to her room.

A couple of minutes later, she emerged.

"It's naptime. Get back to your room."

"I can't," she whined. "There's still a cow in my room."

By this point, my grandma was more fed up than amused. This kid was not going to get out of naptime that easily. She was not about to deal with an overtired, grumpy kid because of some made-up story about a cow. She scooped up my mom and marched her to her room.

But then, as she opened the door, she heard a strange sound: "Mooooooo!"

Startled, she glanced over to my mom's window. Sure enough, standing outside, with its head poking all the way into the room, was a gigantic cow.

She stared at the cow.

The cow stared at her.

Smugly, my mom proclaimed, "I told you!"

Sometimes, it pays to listen to preschoolers.

—Jillian Bell—

74

The Grandma Name Game

It ain't what they call you, it's what you answer to.
~W.C. Fields

"I'm going to be a grandmother," I proudly announced to my friends over lunch. I could hardly contain my excitement. No longer would I have to resort to showing screenshots of my grand-dogs when my friends bragged about their grandchildren. After the cheers and congratulations, a friend who was already a veteran grandmother asked, "Well, what's your name going to be?"

"Name?"

"What are your grandkids going to call you?" she asked.

No one had ever prepared me for that question. I shook my shoulders and answered, "I guess Grandma."

"Oh, that's no good." My friend frowned. "It makes you seem old."

"I think the fact that I am now old enough to have a child that is old enough to have a child makes me seem old," I quipped.

A few days later, I mentioned it to my sister-in-law, who agreed with my friend that picking a name was a must. "In fact," she told me, "you need to pick it soon. You don't want to be stuck with a name that is the only one left after all the family's other grandmas and aunts choose theirs." Then, as if suddenly remembering, she warned, "In fact, I know a friend who ended up being NeeNaa because everything good was already taken."

"NeeNaa the grandma" for the rest of my days? That prospect

seemed absolutely terrifying.

Driving my younger son to practice, I decided to enlist a more youthful perspective. "What do you think might be a good name for my grandchildren to call me?" I asked.

"Let's ask Google," he suggested. "Not to worry, Mom. They have a list. Mi Mi, Gi Gi, De De, Minie, Honey, Queenie, Marmie, Kitty, Lolly…"

"So, it must end with E and sound like the name of candy or a stripper?" This was no help.

"This site suggests you add 'mama' in front of the first letter of your first name. So, you would be Mama K," he laughed.

"That sounds like a rapper, not a grandmother," I told him. "I can hear it now: 'Mama K is in the house.'"

"So, give it up for Mama K and the grands!" He laughed.

"Hard pass!" I told him disapprovingly.

"Kim Kardashian's kids call their grandma Lovey," he read.

"I doubt I should take my grandma's name from the suggestion of a woman who broke the Internet with her bottom," I snapped.

"Hey, I didn't write it. I'm just reading it."

"Besides, Lovey reminds me of *Gilligan's Island*," I told him.

"Gilligan's what?" he asked. "Is that a grandma thing?"

A friend of mine had picked Ki Ki as her grandma's name. I wouldn't suggest it, she said. "The other day, my three-year-old granddaughter asked, 'Ki Ki, are you my grandma?'"

Wow, so much pressure to pick a name.

"Just remember that everyone will be calling you that for the rest of your life," she warned.

Remembering that I wasn't exactly alone in this, I asked my husband, "Have you come up with your grandparent name yet?"

"Sure," he responded immediately. "Barry is taking Paw Paw, and I'm going with Grandpa." I was stunned. This was the same man who took one month to settle on a good name for his truck and one week to pick a clever enough name for his fantasy football league. But this he had already picked?

Weighing the gravity of this decision, I spent the next seven months contemplating the suitability of grandma names. I conducted polls and asked the experts at my mother's water-aerobics class. It should be a name that describes me but doesn't define me. Something simple yet dignified. Original but not overused. I imagined a word I could live with being called until my dying day and possibly etched on my tombstone.

Finally, by the time my first grandchild, little Gerald, who goes by G, arrived, I had settled on the very simple, understated, and unoriginal name of "Grandma." I felt I had made the right decision. Grandma couldn't be rhymed with, made fun of, or misunderstood. Also, I had waited so long to decide that everything else was taken.

"I'm going to be called Grandma," I announced confidently to everyone I believed could help reinforce the name. Unfortunately, a year later, it became apparent I had made a grave miscalculation. Try as he may, little Gerald can't pronounce Grandma, so instead I am now "Bumpah" for the rest of my days.

— Kimberly Avery —

75

Big Boy in the Hot Seat

Remember, as far as anyone knows,
we're a nice, normal family.
~Homer Simpson

S ummers in North Carolina can be miserable. It's hot, humid and sticky, with temperatures often in the low 100's. But our family will not be stopped by the heat and most weekends you can find us gathered for some type of fun. Whether it's by the pool, at the beach, or just gathered around the firepit. We love laughter and there is always something going on to keep us giggling. I often say we'd make the perfect reality show.

Several years ago, after a day of fun, my daughter, my son and I were headed back to Wilmington after one of our family days. My son Will is a big boy. I'm talking 6'5", 300 pounds. He's a jokester and always has something going on. My daughter loves playing pranks on him any chance she can get.

We are all piled into her Black Jetta, not a big car so we were literally jammed in. I was riding in the back with Tiffany at the wheel. Will was in the front passenger seat, as there was no way he'd ever fit in back. Tiffany had the air blasting; it was an extremely hot day, and that black car had sat in the heat for most of the afternoon.

About ten minutes into the ride, Will asked if she even had the air on because it was so hot. (I was sitting in the back feeling comfortable so I didn't know why he was complaining). She turned it up higher and told him that was as high as it would go. I noticed that Will was squirming in his seat. Big Will, as we call him, was miserable. I also notice that Tiffany has a smirk on her face!

A few more miles down the road Will began twisting in the seat, complaining about how hot it was, and next thing I knew he was rolling the window down. The poor guy was sweating up a storm. Not to mention some of the language he was beginning to use! Tiffany had a smirk on her face, and I could tell she was about to burst out laughing. She turned around and looked in my direction, and instantly I knew. She had the heated seat on!

I was trying so hard not to laugh. Imagine that 300-pound guy twisting and turning in his seat, sweat pouring off him, and for the life of him he couldn't figure out why he was so hot. Tiffany had literally been adjusting the heated seat temperature back and forth so he wasn't able to pinpoint the problem. After a few minutes, we both broke out in hysterical laughter and Tiffany confessed the truth. The names Will called her I will not repeat, but after his rage he found it as funny as we did. We laughed all the way home.

— Teresa B. Hovatter —

That Was Embarrassing

76

Down the Dark, Dark Stairs...

I love practical jokes, but I don't like being scared.
~Mitt Romney

Moving slowly toward the old, wooden door, I whispered to my husband, "Mike, do you think this is a good idea—to take Adam and Lizzie down into that dungeon?"

As we entered the dimly lit staircase, he replied, "Yeah, I'm sure they'll be okay. Everyone else is going down there. We have already paid for this part of the tour. They have been through haunted houses before. This tour can't be as bad as those."

Placing my hand on his arm and looking him in the eye, I said, "Well, if you think it's okay..." I glanced nervously toward Adam and Lizzie, praying they would want to go back, but as typical teens, they rushed past me eagerly, nodding their heads.

We slowly followed the rest of our tour down the dark, dark staircase to see the jail cells where young women accused of being witches in 1692 awaited their sentencing. We had just heard the gruesome history of the Salem Witch Trials in the courtroom where it all happened.

Bringing up the rear, we silently wound around and down the stairs into the dungeon. The closer we were to the bottom, the mustier the air became. We ducked our heads under rotten, wooden beams as we walked down the narrow, dirt passageway. Turning a sharp corner, we came to jail cells on each side.

Each cell had a full-sized, wax figure dressed in period clothes. Several were sitting on their cots reading the Bible. Some were working on their stitchery, and others were staring off into space, contemplating their fate. They gave the air a chill in the dim light of the candles.

I moved closer to the metal bars separating us to get a better look. The creepiest part was the faces of the figures. They weren't the smooth faces of a typical wax museum but were a shriveled-up, yellow color with crevices and ridges. Looking closely, they were wrinkly, as if their heads were basketball-sized apples, peeled and dried.

Standing at the last cell, I stopped and stared at the figures. The ones in this jail cell didn't look like the others we had seen. Gone were the crevices and ridges in their dried, apple-like heads. Their faces seemed almost natural.

I stepped as close as possible to the metal bars, pushing my face toward them, and stared. Why were they different? No one else had noticed the difference.

Suddenly, one of the figure's hands moved up toward me, beckoning for me to come closer. Shocked, I jumped back toward the other side of the corridor and let out a bloodcurdling scream. Mike stopped in his tracks, looked back at me, and began to holler, "Move, move, move. Let's get out of here." Adam began to yell, and Lizzie shrieked as loud as she could. We rushed out of the chamber as we heard screams moving from us to the head of the tour group. Everyone began waving their arms, urging the people in front of them to get up and out of the dungeon.

As I finally stumbled through the door into a brightly lit room at the top of the dungeon stairs, everyone in the tour group turned to face me. "Why did you scream? What happened down there? Did you see a ghost?"

I bent over, gasping, and held up my hand, motioning for them to wait a second. I needed to catch my breath. Everyone stopped, waiting to hear the horror I had experienced.

Just then, two ladies dressed in period clothes came up from the cellar, bent over with laughter. "That was the best one yet. She was so scared when you raised your hand to her!" Still giggling, they headed out of the building and off to lunch.

They had been looking for the perfect unsuspecting person in our tour group, and I was it.

—Valli Cowan—

Stuck

Laugh at yourself first, before anyone else can.
~Elsa Maxwell

It was getting close to rush hour, and I was in a hurry to beat the traffic. I'd promised to stop at the post office to mail two packages and drop off a few letters for my parents. I considered driving up to the outside mailbox and taking care of the packages the next day. But, ever the dutiful daughter, I pulled the car into a parking spot. Tucking the packages under my left arm, I grabbed the letters from the passenger's seat and dashed inside. Before going to the counter to have the packages weighed and paying for them, I figured I'd get rid of the letters first. With a quick flourish of the wrist, I pushed the letters into a narrow mail slot and swiftly turned toward the main lobby's automatic doors.

"Ouch!" My right hand didn't come back out. "What the heck?" I stopped and stared at my hand, assessing the situation. Gingerly, I attempted to pull my hand back, but my finger caught. *This is ridiculous. I can't actually be stuck.* I tried again. After a few moments of denial, I realized my middle finger—yes, the curse-word finger—was caught. It had slid into the slot but would not slide out.

I'd been recently diagnosed with rheumatoid arthritis and the knuckle of my right middle finger was one of the joints affected. At this moment it was quite swollen. I am five feet tall and had to reach up to mail the letters, leaving my arm stuck in a raised position. I attempted to slide and jiggle my hand from side to side. There was no escape.

"Ahem," said an impatient voice behind me. I glanced over my shoulder. There stood a woman, holding up her letters.

I looked at the identical mail slot beside me and then back at her. "Um, I'm sorry, ma'am, but if you're in a hurry, I think you may have to use the other slot." I nodded my head in the direction of the twin mail slot. "I'm pretty sure I'm stuck." Perspiration broke out all over my body.

"You're really stuck?"

I pulled my hand a little more desperately. "Ow! Yes, I'm pretty sure I'm stuck." I let out a nervous chuckle. "I'm so embarrassed."

The woman moved over to the other mail slot and deposited her letters. I stretched and straightened my fingers, convinced they would come out. They didn't. "Crap!"

The woman stared at me for a few minutes, watching me struggle. "Do you think I should go inside and get someone to help?"

I hated to admit it, but things weren't going well for me. "I guess so. I'd really appreciate it."

The interior sliding doors opened as she hustled inside.

"Excuse me!" I heard. "There's a lady out here with her hand stuck in the mail slot!"

"Did you say a woman's hand is stuck in the mail slot? What the heck was she trying to do?"

Geez. Like a mail robber would really choose to rob the post office through this skinny mail slot and in broad daylight! Perspiration ran down my back and chest.

A regular door with a glass window was located a few feet away from me. It opened just enough for a postal clerk to gawk. Realizing I could see her, she rolled her eyes and said, "Are you REALLY stuck?"

"Yes, I'm stuck. Do you have some soap back there? Maybe in the bathroom?" The clerk didn't answer. Instead, she simply closed the door. I lost my grip on the two packages I'd been holding under my left arm. I sighed. Suddenly, the automatic doors opened, and out came the postmaster. I prayed he wouldn't recognize me from a complaint I'd made a few months ago. Instead, the postmaster raced to my side. He grabbed my arm and yanked.

"Ouch! You're hurting me!" I yelled.

"I'm sorry," he said. Then he reached up and held onto my hand. He tried, a little more gently, to pull out my hand.

"It's really stuck," I repeated. "Does anyone have lotion? Soap? Hand sanitizer?"

"We don't have anything."

Seriously, don't all restrooms have soap?

The postmaster had me move to the left a bit. He stood to my right and placed the fingers of both his hands into the slot. He yanked, pulling down on the metal as hard as he could. "Pull! Pull!" he shouted, grunting with the effort. Unfortunately, the heavy metal did not bend.

"It's not moving," I said. Again, the postmaster pulled down on the slot with all his might. He pulled so hard that his feet left the floor, and he was literally hanging from the mail slot.

"Pull... out... your... hand!"

"I can't. The metal is NOT bending!" As sore as my knuckle had become, I was doing my best not to laugh. Seeing the postmaster, with knees bent, dangling from the mail slot was truly a sight. Meanwhile, a young postal worker had gotten in on the action. He was behind the wall on the other side of the mail slot. He'd taken hold of my finger and gently tried to urge my hand through.

"Ouch! No, no, no. You're cutting my finger on the metal."

The young postal worker's eyes peeked through the slot. Then, he said, "Stop trying. Your finger is really swelling up. We'll never get it out."

"I think I'm going to have to call 911," said the postmaster.

Oh, no! I had visions of a fire truck showing up since the firehouse is about five minutes from the post office. My ladylike perspiration turned into full-out sweating, and my hair was soaked. In my little town, this incident would surely make the newspaper!

"Doesn't anyone have any hand lotion, soap, hand sanitizer... anything?"

"Oil!" shouted the postmaster, and he ran back through the automatic doors. In a flash, he raced toward me, screaming, "WD-40! Stand back and close your eyes!" Oil sprayed from the long, red straw attached to the can. The postal worker on the other side of the wall grabbed the large canvas bins filled with mail and jumped back. WD-40 flowed all over the slot, inside and out, down the wall, and around my fingers. For a moment, nothing happened. And then, miraculously, the oil spilled under and over my swollen finger, and it slipped out. Cheering with relief, we had a good laugh.

I thanked the postmaster profusely. My finger throbbed and was turning red and purple. I started to leave and then remembered my packages lying on the floor. I approached the main lobby. As the doors slid open, behind the counter, I heard a postal clerk telling her customer about the crazy lady who'd gotten her hand stuck.

"She's right here," another clerk said, alerting the first clerk that I was standing in line. Smiling sweetly, she asked if I was alright. I sweetly smiled back and then lifted my middle finger to show her the bruising.

I laughed all the way home.

— Mary J. Staller —

The Bird and the Biscuits

The rate at which a person can mature is directly
proportional to the embarrassment he can tolerate.
~Douglas Engelbart

I grew up outside of Boston and I was a big basketball fan. Larry Bird was an iconic name in my home. So, it was an amazing moment for me when I got to meet Larry through a friend associated with the Celtics team. It was so amazing that I never thought to tell him hello from my mother, whom he had never met. The next time I saw him, I explained that my mother was upset with me because I didn't say "hi" to him for her. From then on, Larry would always tell me, "Make sure you say 'hi' to Mom this time."

My mother finally got the chance to come to a game with me, and I had the opportunity to make one of her dreams come true when I introduced her to her favorite player in all of sports. She was so excited. He looked at her and said, "You get the hello right from me this time." With a big smile on her face, she put out her arms and gave Larry a hug. There was a problem, though. She didn't adjust for the proportions of a man standing six feet, nine inches tall. As she wrapped her arms around him, his bum was right at arm level, and my mother accidentally grabbed onto both biscuits.

When she realized what she did, her smile was replaced by a look of absolute shock. Her jaw dropped, and her eyes opened as wide as they possibly could. Instead of letting go, she panicked. She clenched her hands tighter and squeezed her arms even harder until she started to laugh uncontrollably at what was happening, all without ever letting go. Thankfully, Larry patted her on the back and laughed along with her as he nonchalantly backed away, removing her hands from his backside.

It was a year or so before I saw him again. When I did, he immediately cracked a smile and asked if Mom was here. She was not, so he said, "Tell her I said 'hi' and give her a big hug for me, but be careful where you put your hands."

— Elton A. Dean —

Forgive and Forget?

The day the child realizes that all adults are imperfect,
he becomes an adolescent; the day he forgives them, he
becomes an adult; the day he forgives himself,
he becomes wise.
~Alden Nowlan

My sweet little grandson, Henry, came to visit me, so I decided to make his favorite dish of baked macaroni and cheese for dinner. I pulled out a pan and an assortment of ingredients while he sat at the dining room table to color pictures. When I turned on the oven to preheat it, a small voice interrupted me.

"Mee-maw, can I have that candy?" He pointed toward a crystal dish sitting in the middle of the table that contained a single piece from my favorite brand of assorted chocolates.

"No, honey. We don't eat candy before dinner. I'll turn a video on for you, and by the time it's over, our macaroni will be ready."

He looked longingly at the chocolate but nodded his agreement and settled himself in front of the television set. As he watched, I worked on grating cheese, boiling noodles, and making a roux. When everything had been put together, I slid the pan into the oven and got to work on my kitchen mess. Then, I cleared Henry's crayons and papers from the table. Wetting a cloth to wipe down the tabletop, I picked up the candy dish and put it on the counter.

A mouth-watering fragrance from the oven wafted through the house, and my stomach rumbled. The lone piece of chocolate called to me. If I ate it, I could put the bowl in the dishwasher, and no one would be the wiser. With that rationale, I grabbed the piece of candy and popped it into my mouth just as Henry's video ended. He scurried in my direction.

That's when I discovered the piece of candy in my mouth had a caramel center—a rather old caramel center. Henry's gaze immediately went to the empty dish in my hand, and he said, "Where's the candy?"

There were a hundred excuses I might have used, but I couldn't answer. My jaws were stuck together tighter than if they'd been super-glued. I felt like we were playing out a scene from an old sitcom.

"Mmmph, mmmph," I finally managed to say.

His eyes narrowed accusingly as he studied my face. "Did you eat it?"

I had no choice but to nod.

"We don't eat candy before dinner, Mee-maw," he pronounced sternly.

With my cheeks hotter than fire, I nodded again and choked down the sticky lump of candy—the one I now realized that Henry had hoped to receive after dinner. When I could speak, I said, "You're right. I shouldn't have taken it. Tell you what. After we eat, let's go out and get ice cream. Deal?"

For a moment, he gave me the Evil Eye, but then, to my relief, Henry graciously agreed to the suggested course of action.

As soon as our plates were clean, this repentant Mee-maw bought her grandson the ice cream of his choice, paying extra to add choco-late chips on top. I pointed out the addition, and he laughed, so I've apparently been forgiven—although I'm not sure he's ever going to let me forget.

— Pat Wahler —

The Day I Dropped the Ball

It's a great thing about being pregnant — you don't need excuses to pee or to eat.
~Angelina Jolie

The week before my baby was due, I took my nine-year-old son Brian and his friend bowling. I knew that after the baby was born I wouldn't be able to get out for a while, so I wanted to take them somewhere fun while I could.

Of course, I didn't plan to bowl myself. In my condition, throwing a heavy ball could set me off balance. That's why bowling was on my obstetrician's list of things to avoid. The truth was, I couldn't have bowled if I'd wanted to. My feet were too swollen to fit into the shoes. So, I just sat on the bench with my mother-in-law, who was visiting at the time. We cheered for the boys.

My son was new to bowling. Every time Brian threw the ball, it swung to the far left and missed the pins completely. "Please don't curve!" he'd yell, gesturing with his hand for the ball to go the other way. But it invariably rolled into the gutter. This alley didn't have bumpers.

"Line up your thumb with the center pin," I said. "And keep your arm straight."

No matter how many pointers I gave him, Brian's bowling balls ended up in the gutters. He'd see where the ball was heading again and cover his eyes with both hands. Walking back to the bench, his upper lip quivered. Yet when his friend managed to knock down some pins, my son gave him a high-five and said, "Good job!"

By the seventh frame, Brian still had a zero. I couldn't bear it anymore. Weren't we here to have fun? When it was his turn, I stood up. "Let me show you how to hold the ball," I said.

I stuck my two fingers and thumb into the holes and lifted the ball in front of me. Little did I realize that I could lose my balance simply by picking it up. I wobbled like a bowling pin. Then, my legs collapsed, and I dropped onto my bottom. The ball slammed onto the wooden floor with a thud.

"Are you all right?" my mother-in-law asked.

"I think so." I wasn't hurt, just surprised that I'd ended up on the floor. I felt something odd underneath me. The back of my maternity pants was sopping wet. Why was I sitting in a puddle?

"Oh, no!" I said. "My water broke!"

My son looked confused. "What do you mean, Mom?"

"Remember that I told you the baby grows in a sac of water? When I fell, the sac must have torn, so I need to go see Doctor Wilson. Hurry! Take off the bowling shoes and put on your sneakers."

Sure that my baby was ready to be born, I called my obstetrician's office and told the receptionist what had happened. "Come in as soon as possible," she said.

My mother-in-law drove me there and waited in the car with the kids. Dr. Wilson put his other patients on hold and saw me right away. The doctor looked serious while he examined me, but I noticed him smiling as he washed his hands. "It wasn't amniotic fluid," he said.

"What was it?"

"Urine."

It took me a few seconds to comprehend what he'd said. "Oh!" My face felt hot. I'd made such a fuss, and all I'd done was pee!

When I came out, my mother-in-law was ready to rush me to the hospital. I explained why we didn't need to go, trying to word it in a way that my son and his friend wouldn't understand. "False alarm. When I fell, the baby hit against my bladder."

My mother-in-law stifled a chuckle. "I guess we can go home."

"The sac didn't break?" Brian asked.

"No," I said. "It actually cushioned the baby."

He frowned. "Then where did all the water come from?"

There was no escaping the truth. "Honey, I wet my pants."

Brian's eyes lit up, and a grin spread across his face. It was the first time all day that I'd seen my son happy. His laughter shook the back seat. I didn't think he'd ever stop. Bowling with his pregnant Mom proved to be quite entertaining!

— Mary Elizabeth Laufer —

81

An Elegant Horror Story

The best way to handle awkward moments
is to gracefully move on, and, if possible,
try to find humor in the situation.
~Diane Domeyer Kock

It had been a grueling afternoon. The dentist had had to extract a tooth, and as I made my way back to the car, I was grateful that the Novocain was still in effect.

The dentist's location in a complex next to the elegant, upscale Brookwood Mall set me to thinking: It would be a long trip home back across Birmingham, and I wasn't looking forward to fighting the traffic.

I almost never got the chance to shop at Brookwood. Surely, after what I'd been through, I deserved a treat.

My husband didn't enjoy window shopping, but I loved it, so I gave myself an hour to roam the halls and ride the escalator of the beautifully appointed mall.

Everything I saw there was way beyond the budget of a young mom with two small children, but it occurred to me that, as an avid letter writer, I could at least afford a new box of stationery.

The store I entered was tiny, but the walls were filled with beautiful paper creations of all sorts. Quickly, I selected a box decorated with roses and stepped up to the register.

"What a beautiful store you have here," I commented as I handed the clerk a twenty. The elegant young woman's response was a curt nod. As she worked the cash register, she kept giving me sidelong glances and frowning.

"Thank you," I said, collecting my change and trying to elicit a friendly reply. None was forthcoming, just a sober stare.

How snobbish was that? I thought to myself in disgust as I left the store. The coat I was wearing was pretty old, but my money was as green as anyone else's!

I sighed. It was time to head home, but first I needed to pay a visit to the ladies' restroom.

Still smarting from the snub I'd experienced, I ducked into a stall and was quickly out again. As I stepped to the sink to wash my hands, I glanced up at the tall mirror and froze.

There, trickling from a corner of my mouth and extending down and around my chin was a bright red path of blood, only just now beginning to congeal!

I leaned forward and looked in my mouth. Yes, there it was. I'd been bleeding the whole time but didn't realize it because of the numbing effect of the Novocain.

What I took for snobbishness was more than likely horror!

Quickly, I scrubbed the blood from my face and replaced the roll of gauze given to me by the dentist. Then, I scurried out of Dodge before anybody called security to warn of a roaming vampire!

—Ellen Edwards Kennedy—

82

Lunchtime Lockout

*Embarrassment is the worst! It's the feeling of having
your entire body go numb and not knowing what to do
with yourself for that one moment.*
~Miley Cyrus

lancing at the clock on my computer screen, I was thrilled
to see it was finally lunchtime. Getting stuck in traffic during my commute into work had just been the beginning of a
stressful morning, so I was more than ready for a break. A big
salad topped with grilled chicken was waiting for me just outside the
Navy base's main entrance, plus I would pick up some food for my
co-workers.

I parked in one of the few open spots at the restaurant, exited my
SUV, and locked the doors. My keys were left in the center console
since there was a keypad on the door for keyless entry. As usual, it
was crowded inside. The tables were all full, and many people were
standing around, waiting for their orders to be ready or in line to place
orders. After waiting for what seemed like half an hour (it was less
than ten minutes, I'm sure), I placed the orders, paid, and was handed
cups for my drinks. I decided to fix the drinks and carry them out to
the car since it would be a while for the food to be ready.

When I got to my car, I placed the tray of drinks on the hood so
they wouldn't topple over when I entered my code into the keypad.
They were all large drinks and a bit wobbly in the tray. I punched
in the numbers on the door and pulled the handle. It did not open.

Thinking I had incorrectly entered the code, I tried again. Nothing.

Oh, no! I wondered if my car battery was dead or something. I tried again. It still did not unlock. Would it lock me out if I entered the wrong code too many times? I did not know because this had never happened before.

My phone and keys were in there. I was going to have to go back inside and borrow a phone to call work. Then, I noticed the phone in the car had the cord attached to charge. I was not charging my phone when I went inside. Then, I saw a briefcase on the passenger seat. Not mine. Wait a minute. I slowly turned around to discover my SUV right behind me. Oh, no! I had been trying to break into someone else's car!

I walked around my vehicle to get to the driver's side, punched in my code, and opened my door. Hallelujah! I placed the drinks inside and walked back to the restaurant to get the food, which was surely ready by now. As I entered through the door, I heard a man's voice say, "They look alike, don't they?" Even though the establishment was full of talking people, I knew that was directed at me.

Turning my head to my left, I saw a booth filled with four men staring back at me with eyes twinkling and huge grins on their faces. Their booth had a big window providing a nice view of the parking lot. It was obvious they had had a good laugh while watching me struggle. I'm sure they were taking bets on how long it would take me to realize I was trying to get into their car. My face surely turned as red as a ripe tomato.

I picked up my food from the counter, left the building, and paid close attention to which car I approached. I could hardly see through my tears of laughter as I drove back to work. It would be a story to share when I got back to the office. *They might as well get a good laugh at my expense, too,* I told myself. I have no doubt those guys at the restaurant enjoyed telling their co-workers about my faux pas when they got back to their own office.

— Debbi Mavity —

83

A Secluded Meadow

*Thinking, not for the first time, that life should come
with a trapdoor. Just a little exit hatch you could
disappear through when you'd utterly
and completely mortified yourself.*
~Michele Jaffe, Prom Nights from Hell

My heart thumped as we searched through the woods for my older sister. Concern sounded in my parents' voices as they yelled my sister's name. When she didn't answer, their faces filled with worry.

Of course, my imagination ran wild as I thought of the stories I'd heard over the years about hikers getting lost or even attacked by a bear or mountain lion. My sister and I were in our early teens but had learned to respect the wilderness, and the idea of an animal attack or losing our way still terrified us.

"Let's stick together," Dad said. "We don't need anyone else getting lost."

Earlier, I'd watched with envy as my sister left camp, lugging our new portable potty with her. Normally, on a trip, we would find a secluded spot close to camp and squat to do our business, but Mom claimed she was getting too old for that and had purchased the new camping toilet to try out on this trip. With first dibs on the toilet, my sister would miss out on the grueling work of unloading the car and setting up camp—a task that always took forever.

Before my sister left, Dad had reminded her to make sure she placed the toilet out of view in case other campers or hikers were around. With plenty of privacy in the woods, she should have stayed close enough to hear our calls. And the farther we walked, the more we worried.

Out of breath, I kept thinking this was crazy. I could not imagine my sister lugging that potty this far. We reached the end of the wooded area where we had to wade through an almost impenetrable wall of tall, thick brush and scrubby bushes before we broke through the mess.

"Now, there's something you don't see every day," Dad said, relieved but now laughing at the sight before us.

When my sister spotted the family gawking at her, she freaked. "What are you doing?" she shouted as she waved her hands to shoo us away. "Get out of here! Go on! Gee, can't I go in private?"

All worries evaporated as the chuckles started. She looked hilarious sitting on a throne in the middle of a meadow, and as we took a closer look, we laughed so hard that we had tears in our eyes and couldn't speak. All we could do was point, which embarrassed my sister more because she thought we were pointing at her.

Other than walking way too far, my sister had taken my father's earlier words to heart and found a secluded meadow hidden on all sides by the tall, dense, scrubby bushes with a vertical rock wall located well behind her. Later, she explained that she had put the toilet in the middle of the meadow so she wouldn't have to worry about snakes or animals creeping up on her.

But had my sister looked up at the ridge top behind her, she would have seen the busy road we had driven on earlier packed with weekend travelers who had an incredible view of the vista and the lush green meadow below where my sister sat for all to see.

Before we turned to head back to camp, my dad, still in hysterics, pointed once more and managed to shout to my sister, "Look up behind you!"

Her expression was priceless!

— Jill Burns —

84

Impressing the In-Laws

If embarrassment were a muscle, I'd be huge.
~Brent Weeks

My future husband, Mike, and I had flown out to Oregon so I could meet some of Mike's family members for the first time. We were staying with Mike's brother and his wife, and Mike's parents had flown in from their home in Alaska.

Naturally, I worried about making a good first impression. After all, I was serious about this guy, and we'd flown all the way from Florida to Oregon for my "debut" as Mike's girlfriend.

I also wanted to impress my boyfriend, if you know what I mean.... This was our first solo trip together, which I thought was so romantic. Therefore, to surprise him, I had purchased all-new panties and bras for the trip. I could hear my mother's words in my head, "You don't want to have ugly granny panties on if you're taken to the hospital." So, I splurged on some pretty, delicate underwear at Victoria's Secret — for his eyes only, of course.

The week passed quickly, and everyone got along well. We saw the sights in southern Oregon. We went to a play and saw some fall colors. We played card games and ate plenty of delicious food. Mike's family was even forgiving when they taught me how to play poker and I beat them all — taking the whole pot of $27! I got a lot of ribbing about "beginner's luck," but it was all in good fun.

At the end of the first week, we were getting low on clean clothes, and my sister-in-law offered her washer and dryer for our use. I laundered our clothes and carried them back to the bedroom where we were staying. Mike and I were folding the clothes when we heard a knock on the door.

"Come in!" we called, thinking we were being summoned for dinner. Much to our surprise, Mike's sister-in-law and his mother were standing in the doorway with giant grins on their faces. There was something dangling from my future mother-in-law's finger.

"Did somebody lose something?" she teased. She and her daughter-in-law broke out in giggles.

I took a closer look at what was hanging from her hand. In shock, I realized that it was a pair of my new, extremely skimpy thong panties! My face must have turned ten shades of red because everyone — including Mike — pointed at me and started laughing.

Needless to say, that wasn't the kind of first impression I had hoped to make! Twenty years later, I no longer wear thong underwear, but I still make sure to account for every piece of laundry when I'm with my in-laws!

— Susan M. Heim —

Pawsitive Thinking

85

What's in a Name

Names have power.
~Rick Riordan, The Lightning Thief

My wife Louise was always thinking of others as evidenced by her insistence that we needed to get a dog so I wouldn't be alone if I ever lost her. This wasn't just some obscure thought. We'd been living with the knowledge for some time that her cancer was spreading. What was heartbreaking for me to contemplate was just a simple matter of kindness for Louise. She was genuinely concerned for my wellbeing. So, one spring day in 2017, we set out to find a small, easily trainable dog.

Louise's insistence on a small dog derived from the fact that she was having difficulty walking and felt she could only help care for a smaller dog. But small dogs were in high demand, so we got to the shelter early to browse without feeling rushed by the competition.

We soon joined a group of ridiculous-looking humans poking their fingers into the pen of one desirable small dog, talking baby talk in the hope that the dog would pick them.

While participating in this undignified ritual, I saw a large hound watching us from another pen. Nobody was looking at her. She was a new arrival who still showed the signs of being abandoned. Her coat was filthy, and we could see her ribs. Her face looked blank like her mind was elsewhere. But there was nothing wrong with her nose. She focused that nose at every invisible scent that passed by. With each one, her tail would wag with excitement.

Louise saw me looking at the dog and warned me to stay away because it might be sick. But I liked underdogs; I walked over to the pen anyway.

The dog acknowledged me long enough to "see" my scent and then turned her nose to more interesting smells. I read the information on the clipboard. It seemed unremarkable: "Plott Hound/Coonhound Mix, Arrival Date March 22, Stray." But unlike most of the other dogs, this one already had a name: Louise.

That was it: This was my dog.

Two years passed. I attempted to teach Louise (the dog, not the wife) several commands that she dutifully learned to ignore. I made her a luxury dog run from a long zipline that ran the entire length of our property. She became a happy, healthy albeit large dog with complete run of the house and an ample choice of furniture to sleep on.

But sadly, as she had warned, my wife passed away, leaving me with this silly hound dog for comfort. Nothing can prepare you for a loss like that, not even a thoughtful spouse.

Mourning is a personal thing; there's no prescription or set of directions. Everyone mourns in their own way and at their own pace. For me, finding out why someone would name a dog "Louise" became an obsession. It shouldn't have mattered; I wasn't going to get my wife back. Yet, somehow, I felt that knowing why this dog was named Louise would ease my pain. So, I began a months-long quest to find the answer.

The shelter where we got her was very helpful. Their records showed that Louise had arrived already named. They provided the name of the agency where she came from half a country away, and after several lengthy phone calls and e-mails, they reminded me, "We rely heavily on donations...." So, I had the first lead in my search and my first tax deduction for the year!

The agency down south told me that Louise came through yet another rescue organization, and she had already been named when they got her. They were happy to provide the name of the previous rescue organization for me to contact but freely added, "We rely heavily on donations...."

This continued for several more organizations and several more donations that I was happy to trade for information. But time was passing, and with each new contact, I could feel my voice breaking. I didn't know if I was getting closer to an answer. I might never find out the reason my dog had the same name as my late wife. I was in mourning and getting desperate.

Finally, about six months after I started my search, I was put in touch with a self-described elderly woman in South Carolina who fostered dogs while they were awaiting transport north. She seemed to understand my pain. I was very emotional, but she talked with a soft, calming voice. "Yes," she began our conversation, "I remember Louise. She was a nice dog."

The woman never asked for donations. Instead, she was genuinely interested in helping me. Her voice was kind and reminded me of the lost generations of grandmothers and aunties in my own family who always kept a warm house full of teddy bears and fed ice cream to little boys who probably didn't deserve it.

"Why did you name my dog Louise?" I asked, my voice breaking.

"That was my mother's name," she said.

Almost sobbing, I said, "But why this dog? Why did you name this particular dog Louise?"

A heavy silence came over the phone. She knew this was important to me. This was the answer I had been searching for. This was what would give some meaning to my loss.

After several seconds of uncomfortable silence, the woman spoke in her soft, gentle voice, choosing her words slowly.

"Oh, honey," she said in a low whisper, "I name them *all* Louise."

— Tom Armstrong —

86

Ninja Cat

Nothing inspires forgiveness quite like revenge.
~Scott Adams

Sammie was a stinker. Our middle-aged orange tabby loved to play his own brand of feline practical jokes on us whenever the opportunity arose. And the opportunity seemed to be arising more and more every day.

Whether Sammie was leaping from atop the stairs onto my head, grabbing my foot from underneath the sofa, or jumping on my back when I bent down, he never failed to shock me. The most terrifying move of all, though, was what my husband Bill called "The Ninja." In this maneuver, Sammie would wait patiently around a corner or behind a piece of furniture until one of us passed by. Then, he would literally fly through the air and land on a thigh, securing all four sets of claws into it. It was unnerving.

One day, I heard strange growling emanating from our basement. Never imagining that it could be coming from our usually silent tabby, I crept down the stairs to find him sitting on a window ledge, eye-to-eye with a neighborhood cat on the other side of the glass. The growling increased as the other cat taunted Sammie with his presence, moving this way and that. Yet, when Sammie hissed and smacked the window with his paw, the other cat ran for his life.

Ninja Cat, proud of his brave efforts, refused to leave his stronghold. He pressed against the window, craning his neck to the left and the right, searching for any sign of the other cat's return. Even an hour later, Sammie still held guard at the basement window. Promise of dinner and the shaking of the treats bag could not entice him back to the first floor. I climbed halfway down the stairs and beckoned him to come back up. He never flinched. Then, I got an idea.

In my bedroom, I have one of the famous FAO Schwarz toy lions that sat regally in their display near the entrance of the Manhattan store. Sammie may have had the courage to face off with a neighborhood cat, but a lion several times his size? I didn't think so. From there, I formulated a plan for Sammie to receive his comeuppance for all the ninja attacks we had endured through the years.

I interrupted Bill as he watched the evening news and held up the stuffed lion. "I'm going to play a trick on Sammie with this, and I need you to help me."

With the memory of Sammie's most recent hijinks still fresh in his mind, Bill responded eagerly, "Count me in. What do you need me to do?"

"I'm going to sneak outside and move the lion around in front to the basement window. I need you to grab your cellphone and go downstairs and record Sammie's reaction on video. That," I said, "I've got to see."

With that, Bill proceeded to his spot in the basement as I crawled outside, next to the window, with the lion in my arms. Then, with all the stealth of a Nighthawk attack, I shook the lion in front of Sammie's face. Ha ha! I'd done it! I'd finally given Sammie a dose of his own medicine. I ran into the house and straight into Bill.

"Show me the video! Show me the video!" I exclaimed.

"You're going to be disappointed," Bill replied. "I couldn't get very much."

"I want to see it! I want to see it!" I cried with all the enthusiasm of a five-year-old being handed a gift-wrapped box at Christmas.

So, Bill played the video.

He was right. There wasn't much to see.

"Play it again," I instructed. I looked closer. All I could see was a two-second video of a giant, puffed-up tabby tail trailing behind a rocket-ship blast of orange cat running for cover. The video may have been short, but it was enough. I had beaten Sammie at his own game, and I even had proof. Ahhh, sweet victory was mine! Finally.

—Monica A. Andermann—

87

Does That Come with Sides?

A cat will do what it wants when it wants,
and there's not a thing you can do about it.
~Frank Perkins

I grew up in a family of five children, all perfectly spaced three years apart. On top of that, my father was a veterinarian, so we always had at least a dog and a cat, if not also a gerbil, hamster or rabbit.

My mom did her very best to keep the house and us kids under control, which was especially difficult around the holidays. But she was an expert hostess, and she always planned and executed holiday meals perfectly.

One particular Thanksgiving, Mom had set the table a week in advance, putting a king-sized sheet over it so that dust and pet hair wouldn't settle onto the beautiful china and crystal. She made a list of all the dishes she would be preparing, changing it until she was satisfied with the spread. She was also an excellent time manager and had baked the pumpkin and apple pies several weeks in advance and frozen them.

Her Thanksgiving routine had been meticulously crafted over the years, and she stuck with the same agenda every year. It began, of course, with the turkey. It was usually at least twenty pounds, and she would dress it and truss it the night before, and then get up early in the morning to put it into the oven for slow roasting. Then, she would take a break to have a cup of tea, eat breakfast, and scan the newspaper.

Afterward, she would finish prepping the side dishes and rolls.

As she whizzed around the kitchen, my siblings and I were prohibited from staying there longer than the time it took to eat a bowl of cereal and take on our chores for the day. My dad made the floral arrangements fresh from his garden, taking up most of the kitchen table. He had prize-winning mums for a burst of autumn color on the table and hutch.

By mid-afternoon, everything was prepared, and the aroma of roasting turkey with butter, rosemary and garlic filled the air. Only then could my mother retreat to her bedroom to get ready for our company. Just before our guests were due to arrive, she pulled the turkey out of the oven to baste one last time, tented it with aluminum foil, and placed it on the kitchen counter to cool. She said this would make it juicier before my dad began carving. This also gave her time to increase the heat of the oven for the side dishes and gave her a break from the kitchen to return to her guests.

My final job before dinner was filling up the crystal goblets with ice water. When it was time, I left the living room and headed back down to the kitchen. And, oh, what a sight awaited me. Our cat, Funny Girl, had managed to climb up on the counter where the turkey had once been resting, and I saw nothing but her tail sticking out from the tented aluminum foil! On the floor below her, our German Shepherd, Samantha, was licking up the bits of turkey that had dropped on the floor. I ran and lifted the foil to discover that more than half of the turkey had been eaten. Funny Girl stared directly at me, cool and aloof, before jumping down off the counter and sauntering away.

"MOOOMMM!" I yelled again and again.

"Adrienne, why are you yelling?" she asked, rounding the corner.

However, before I could even say, "Funny Girl ate your turkey," I could tell by the horrified look on her face that she already knew. Then, she did something I had rarely seen her do. She broke down and cried. "My dinner is ruined," she said as tears streaked down her cheeks. "I can't believe that darn cat." I tried my best to console her by wrapping her in a hug. We clung together for a moment as I tried to blot her tears with a napkin. I asked if we could still serve the remaining half of the turkey, but when we saw the cat hair where she had sat atop the carcass, we knew that it was inedible.

"Mom, at least we have the side dishes," I offered. They were all still browning in the oven. That's when she burst out laughing. The tears were gone. She knew that there was nothing left to do except move on and deal with the problem. She removed the sides from the oven and the salad from the refrigerator.

"Adrienne, go get your father — quietly!"

My dad came into the kitchen and surveyed the damage. "Well," he said, "at least we have the sides." Gratefully, my mother broke out into another big laugh as she plated what was left of our meal. Dad threw the turkey into the trash outside and went to offer more drinks and wine to our guests. "It won't hurt to get everyone a bit more relaxed before we tell them that there's no turkey this Thanksgiving!"

Finally, I felt like I could laugh, too, as I helped my mother finish getting dinner on the table.

That was truly the most memorable Thanksgiving, especially for Funny Girl, who spent the rest of the evening locked in my parents' bedroom, vomiting up her feast... all over my mother's side of the bed!

— Adrienne Matthews —

88

Terror on a Country Road

A smile starts on the lips, a grin spreads to the eyes, a chuckle comes from the belly; but a good laugh bursts forth from the soul, overflows, and bubbles all around.
~Carolyn Birmingham

I jerked my head up from the flower bed I was weeding when I heard the screams of terror. I saw a car parked on the side of the road with its driver's door open. I sprinted toward the sound, fearful of what had caused such panic. My feet froze about twenty feet from the car, horrified by what was in the front seat. The screams intensified.

We lived on a gravel road in the country. While speeding down the rough terrain, the car lost a hubcap. When the driver pulled over to retrieve it, he left his door open.

The scene inside the car sounded terrifying. Screams from the hysterical mother in the front seat harmonized with the kids' shrieks from the back seat, increasing in volume and intensity with every second that went by. Snuggled up to the mother was our Samoyed/Malamute, Mindy, with her nose affectionately nuzzled into the poor lady's neck. Pressed against Mindy was Jake, our German Shepherd pup, who weighed about seventy pounds at the time, proudly sitting behind the steering wheel with his tongue hanging out and a very jolly look on his face.

I was shocked. My dogs love to go for rides, but they had never done anything like this before. Apparently, they had interpreted the open door as an invitation. Apprehensively, I glanced toward the father. Surely, he would run to his family's defense. I braced myself for whatever harsh words he would fling at me for this offense and hoped it would not get physical.

There he was — on the side of the road, still holding the hubcap in his hand. Would he hit me with it? Should I run for the protection of our house? Were my dogs in danger of his wrath? Now, I was the one engulfed in panic.

Instead of malice or any ill intent, he was doubled over in laughter as if his knees might buckle under him. The retrieved hubcap was firmly sandwiched between his body and his arms as if to shield the pain in his stomach from laughing. While his terrorized wife and kids were "trapped" in the car, he was laughing so hard that he couldn't even walk.

I commanded my dogs to exit the car, apologizing profusely. Reluctantly, they slid out, disappointment clearly visible on their faces. Once relieved of the two dogs pressed up against her, the mother calmed down. Still hyperventilating, she glared at me.

Stifling his laughter, the father said to me, "No need to apologize. Honestly. I haven't laughed that hard in a long, long time. So, thanks, I needed that." He was still laughing as he closed the car door and drove away.

With the disaster averted, I returned to my flower bed. Throughout the afternoon, uncontrollable laughter continued to bubble up as the scene replayed in my mind. He was right. I needed that, too — although I'm not sure his wife would agree.

— Marie T. Palecek —

89

The Dog Days of Summer

Everything is funny as long as it is
happening to someone else.
~Will Rogers

When my friends David and Sally told me they were going on a fabulous, two-week summer vacation to Europe, I was jealous. But when they asked me to house-sit their very respectable, Spanish-style beach house, my jealousy quickly turned to excitement. I couldn't wait.

It was the mid-1990s, and they'd just acquired two adorable Dachshunds: Betsy, a jolly, roly-poly ball of energy who looked like a misshapen sack of new potatoes, and salt-and-pepper Billy (age unknown), small, thin and very nervous, who was purported to have been a show dog back in the day but was probably not cut out for pageant life.

I say they were "acquired" because, after Sally's aunt died, she drove to Denver, packed up the two dogs, and brought them back to Los Angeles. Sally loves animals; she had five cats already. When visiting her home, it wasn't unusual to see a bluebird eating peanuts off the dining room table, a couple of possums having dinner on the patio or meet a newly rescued feral cat.

The dogs came with no papers, vet records, or record of their existence except a single Polaroid picture of a rigid Billy posing as he received a blue ribbon at a local dog show back before he had gray hairs.

In the past couple of months, I'd gotten to know and love the two dogs. They were lovable — Betsy for her positive attitude and Billy for his world-weariness. And the five cats — well, they were cats.

I was also happy to have a break from my small studio apartment and be able to lounge in this beautiful house with its refreshing sea breeze just steps away from the ocean. It was sure to be a much-needed vacation for me, as well.

The day David and Sally left, I dropped them at the airport and went back to walk the dogs. The cats were easy. They kept to themselves and only became finicky when they weren't fed on time.

All went well for the first three days. Betsy, Billy and I would sit on the couch and watch our favorite shows at night. During the day, we'd wander around the boardwalk at the beach, stopping to have some lunch.

But on the fourth day I noticed some unruly behavior from Betsy. She kept jumping on Billy, but not just a playful jumping on and off. This was a jumping and humping. And humping and more humping. Poor old Billy looked so put upon and didn't know what to do.

Neither did I.

Did I mention that I'd never had dogs of my own?

After I pulled Betsy off Billy for the umpteenth time, she enthusiastically humped a tall, hand-carved, wooden figure that David and Sally had hand carried from Bali. It fell over during the act, and the arm broke off. Then, Betsy humped the arm.

Moments later, I noticed a stray dog sitting outside the back door. Every once in a while, he'd howl. When I went to shoo him away, he didn't budge, so I made a lot of bellowing noises, but that didn't seem to faze him and only hurt my throat. I finally pushed him away with a broom.

And then…

I noticed three red dots of blood on the living room floor and a dark spot on the rug.

Did I mention that I tend to faint at the sight of blood?

This was fast becoming a predicament, to say the least. Fainting dead away with seven animals in someone else's house could only end badly — for me.

I sat down for a moment to compose myself. When the room was no longer spinning, I ran to the bedroom's full-length mirror to see if I'd cut myself recently.

It didn't appear so.

It was only when I returned to the living room and watched Betsy walking away that I realized what was happening: Betsy was in heat.

Wait… what?

That was never mentioned as a possibility.

I had no idea what to do.

I couldn't call David and Sally. They were happily biking in France according to their itinerary—with no cellphones. And, in the mid-'90s, the Internet wasn't really a thing yet.

Since I took my job as dog sitter seriously, I fetched a notebook and wrote down things I could do.

Number one: Don't faint.

That's when Betsy started humping my leg, interrupting my thoughts.

I figured I should call for help, so I put Betsy in the bathroom. She wasn't happy, but then neither was I. But, for the first time, Billy looked relieved.

With Betsy tucked away in the bathroom, I started calling friends and family who had dogs, used to have dogs or who'd ever come in close contact with a dog. I quickly discovered that most of them found my situation hilarious and were of no help at all.

Could things get more embarrassing?

When I'd exhausted the names in my address book and couldn't bear being laughed at one more time, I grabbed a clean kitchen towel and a couple of safety pins and wrestled with Betsy on the cold bathroom floor until I got her into a makeshift diaper.

Did I mention that this was turning into the worst beach vacation ever?

Then I had a terrifying thought: What if Betsy got pregnant on my watch?

The last of the seventeen people that I called suggested that I talk to a veterinarian. I looked at the emergency numbers that were pinned to the fridge and dialed the number for the local veterinarian.

I told her what had happened. She knew all the five cats but hadn't yet met Betsy and Billy.

"Is Billy fixed?" she asked.

"Um, I don't know," I stuttered. I'd never thought of that. "How would I know?"

"Turn him upside down and tell me what you see," she said.

I reported back what I saw or, rather, what I didn't see.

"Just leave the diaper on Betsy when she's inside and watch out for dogs when you're walking her. It will only last seven to ten days."

Seven to ten days?

My relaxing beach vacation had turned into an anxiety-ridden nightmare.

Finally, David and Sally returned, refreshed and rested. They wondered why I had dark circles under my eyes. I told them what had happened while they were biking their way through Europe, and they had a good chuckle. David glued the arm back on the antique statue. Sally bought new kitchen towels. Then they made an appointment to get Betsy fixed.

I went back to my tiny apartment and slept for two days.

I'll never forget my vacation by the beach — chasing after horny dogs, changing doggie diapers, doing load after load of laundry, scrubbing floors, and spot-cleaning rugs and pillows.

But mostly I'll remember because my friends and family will never let me forget.

— Meredith Besser —

90

Mental Health Hijacking

Animals are such agreeable friends — they ask no
questions, they pass no criticisms.
~George Eliot

Twenty minutes into André's session, a small girl appeared behind him, holding a betta fish by its tail. "FISH!" I yelled, which, in retrospect, was not the best reaction from a mental-health therapist. I should have said, "Excuse me, André. I'm sorry for interrupting you, but your daughter has taken the fish out of its tank." Instead, I panicked.

André swung around and, with impressive agility, picked up his six-year-old daughter, dipped her over the fish tank as if they were dancing, and calmly said, "Let Slippers go." She dropped Slippers into the tank. He gently placed her on the ground and said, "Pappi is in his meeting, and when he's in meetings, you have to stay upstairs. Remember?" She laughed and ran out of the camera's view.

"I'm sorry," André said as he sat in front of his laptop. "She just wanted to show you her fish."

"Slippers is a beautiful fish," I said. "And you never told me about your Olympian Dad Moves."

"That's what my wife says," he laughed.

When the pandemic hit, mental-health clinicians like me were forced to learn how to provide therapy over computer screens. We created makeshift offices in our homes as we sat in our bedrooms, living rooms, basements, and any place we could find that was private. I loved it.

Telehealth allowed me to see my clients in their natural environments, and the flexibility made it possible for more people to participate in therapy. A bonus was the many pets who made guest appearances.

I gazed upon a bearded dragon named Ferguson, who sat on my client's shoulder during every session and rarely moved. He'd angle his head to the side as if to say, "Look at me. I'm handsome." I made friends with a turtle named Daisy, who would walk across the keyboard and occasionally press a button that abruptly ended the telehealth connection. Her human would call back, stating, "She did it again." Yet, nothing compared to the time when I was utterly outwitted.

Jada, my sixteen-year-old client, closed her eyes and became absorbed in a virtualization exercise.

"Notice the sounds around you," I said softly. "Some sounds are obvious while others are in the background. Try to notice the background sounds."

The tip of a white tail appeared in the corner of the screen.

"Listen to those sounds," I whispered as I watched the tail grow slowly into a massive fluff that ascended higher and higher behind Jada's left shoulder. It was as long as Jada's head and neck and perfectly still.

"Notice what you see," I continued, as I am a professional and not easily distracted by fluffy tails. Slowly, a pair of erect ears appeared directly in front of Jada and her camera.

"Notice these details," I said as a giant, white head appeared, and two dark eyes stared directly at the camera. This dog, which looked like a mixed German Shepherd and Samoyed, was not looking at my image on the screen as humans do but slightly upward at the camera. I looked directly into my camera to meet the beast's gaze. That was my mistake. I shouldn't have made eye contact. Its ancestors, wolves, considered eye contact threatening and just plain rude. The challenge was officially accepted.

A mouth came in my direction, and there was a flashing of images of teeth and a tongue.

"Boris, no!" Jada screamed as I watched the ceiling in sporadic bursts of movement. "Bring me back my therapist!"

I realized Boris had taken her iPad into his mouth and was running through the house. I was hijacked by the family dog.

"Amanda, are you still there?" she yelled.

"Yes, still here!" I said as I listened to the sounds of a wild chase. "Save me!"

"I'll rescue you!" Jada laughed, out of breath. Then, there was darkness.

"Boris, you are so bad," she said as she picked up the iPad, and her face came into view. "Sorry, that's Boris. He likes to steal things."

"Thank you for saving me. I thought I was a goner."

Jada laughed, and we agreed that Boris could join all therapy sessions in the future if he agreed not to steal the therapist.

It wasn't only my clients' pets who engaged in hijinks. My small black cat, Mr. Bojangles, habitually showed his butt to my clients. Cat owners began calling this phenomenon Accidental Cat Butt. This occurs when a cat moves into the camera's view to get its human's attention. When they circle to face the human, their tail raises to signal that they are either interested or simply enjoying the affection provided. As the tail raises, the butt in all its glory is exposed to the camera and whoever is watching.

"I get so angry at her. I just can't…" Accidental Cat Butt.

"Wow, there it is," observed Alejandro.

"I don't want to quit, but I can't work all these hours for much longer. I tried to…" Accidental Cat Butt. "Aww, look at him. He's so cute. Can I see his face this time?" asked Dorothy.

"It's been stressful. My parents want me to visit, and I want…" Accidental Cat Butt. "Hey, nice butt, Bo!" complimented Ruth.

It's been three years since the pandemic broke out, and Mr. Bojangles and the many pets of my clients still either attend teletherapy or make guest appearances. These animals have always been a vital part of the fabric of mental health and therapeutic healing. Telehealth has given them a platform to connect with healthcare providers, and I hope we can continue to be open to these connections. And if you should ever find yourself in a telehealth session with me, please excuse the Accidental Cat Butt.

— Amanda Ann Gregory —

91

The Ben Test

The average dog is a nicer person
than the average person.
~Andy Rooney

A black-and-tan fur ball exploded into the living room. The puppy sprang into my lap and scrambled toward my face. After three slurps, including one directly on my mouth, he headed for his next victim. Samson had formally greeted me.

The dog belonged to a friend who had adopted him from a shelter after he was found along an interstate highway in a brown paper bag. The animal's bright brown eyes and relentless tongue proved irresistible.

A year later, our friend called with an unexpected question. "Samson needs a new home. Will you take him?" The dog languished in his pen while our friend worked, and he thought Samson would be happier with a family instead of an unmarried man.

We agreed. But my husband, Dale, insisted on one change. "A name suggests how you want a pet to behave. Do you want a wild dog with uncontrollable strength?" I could see his point.

Weighing fifty pounds with a broad chest and huge paws, Samson's dominant feature — a luxurious, long coat — indicated he was predominantly Spaniel. I researched Spanish names, and we chose "Bendito," which means "little blessing." Soon, we simply called him Ben.

Our biggest challenge was Ben's exuberance with visitors. Greeting our dog was a full-body contact sport. Whenever the doorbell rang, he raced toward the door with ear-splitting barks. Toenail grooves marked where he scratched impatiently to meet whatever new friend stood outside. I always grabbed his collar before opening the door to guests, who were often wide-eyed and wary of the wriggling maniac.

When guests stepped into our foyer, Ben greeted them like long-lost friends whether he had met them or not. I kept a roll of paper towels nearby in case little droplets of happiness wet unsuspecting shoes.

My cousin Andrew visited on college breaks, and it was hard to tell who was more excited to meet again, him or the dog. I relocated the greeting spot to the carport and allowed him to fend for himself.

One spring day, Andrew rang the doorbell and waited. I released the latch, and Ben burst out, yipping with joy. To my dismay, Andrew was accompanied by a petite, young lady.

Scrambling for Ben's collar, I watched in horror as Ben trampled her dainty, sandaled feet while nearly toppling her into the greasy spot on the cement floor. When she bent forward to wipe paw prints from her immaculate linen shorts, Ben sneaked a taste of her flavored lipstick. Strawberry was his favorite. Don't ask how I knew.

"Eww! Get him away from me!" The girl scrubbed the back of her arm against her mouth. Her shrieks continued even after I managed to send Ben on a lap around the yard to run off steam.

"I'm so sorry," I apologized. A red stain circled her mouth. If I gave her a matching foam nose, she could have passed for a clown. "Let's get you cleaned up."

Andrew chuckled, and I glared my displeasure at him for being amused by the girl's distress. I escorted her to the bathroom, and she eventually got clean enough to calm down. She sniffed, barely acknowledging my pleas for forgiveness while she reapplied her make-up. She remained mute during the entire visit, and we never saw her again.

Next time, Andrew had a different young woman in tow. I pinned Ben against the wall with my knee and grasped his collar firmly before I cracked the door. He still escaped, planting both feet on Andrew's chest while bestowing a doggie kiss. He headed straight for the girl, and my cousin made no attempt to stop him.

Ben and the girl danced a disjointed tango for dominance. Ben asserted the lead and backed her up against the car before managing to leap high enough to lick her face. A stream of spicy words followed, and her eyes narrowed. She clouted Ben on the nose. When he retreated, she jumped in the car and slammed the door just before the dog started lapping the window.

I tugged Ben's collar and glared at my cousin. "Call me next time, and I'll pen the dog!"

Andrew grinned. "What fun would that be?" After a brief visit, during which the young lady never got out of the car, the couple left behind a disheartened dog as they disappeared down the drive.

Six months later, Andrew arrived again. This time, I was in luck—Dale was home. "Let's go, big boy!" Dale trotted after the dog before I could warn him there might be a female friend. Ben erupted through the door, slurped Andrew's knee, and bounded for the girl. He leaned against her, and she stroked his ears while she knelt for a canine facial.

"This is Kara," Andrew announced. "Kara, this is my cousin Rhonda and her husband Dale. I guess you've already met Ben."

Kara stuck out one hand to greet Dale, still smiling, and ignored the dog while he slobbered all over her bare legs. Why did Andrew always bring guests in the summertime? I apologized profusely as I offered the paper towels I had snatched on my way out the door.

"Don't worry," Kara replied. "It's no big deal." She dabbed herself mostly dry and followed us inside for a visit around my kitchen table. Ben sat between the couple and showered them with affection by giving their legs a spit polish, whether they needed it or not.

When they left, Dale said, "Isn't Kara nice?"

"Yes, she is," I answered, "but why didn't you keep Ben away from her? You were no help at all!" I griped, but Dale just listened. Our "little blessing" sat on the carpet nearby with his tongue hanging out. I could swear he smirked.

A few seasons passed, and Andrew phoned. Dale answered, and his face lit with a huge smile. "That's great news, man! Congratulations!" He handed the phone to me, and I rejoiced with Andrew over the announcement that he and Kara were engaged.

The couple married and moved away, so our visits were few. Soon, they had a son and daughter, and we only saw them at our annual family reunion. One year, while Kara played with the horde of children that included their two, we stood with Andrew and watched.

Dale remarked, "Kara's a keeper. How did you choose a bride so well?"

"It was easy," Andrew said, "but one sure sign was when she faced The Ben Test. Before I got serious with any girl, I always brought her to meet your dog. I had to know how she would react before I decided to pursue the relationship."

"What?" Eyes wide and jaw slack, I needed more explanation.

"You remember the first two girls I brought?" Andrew's eyes sparkled.

"How could I forget?"

"They flunked. I didn't want a prissy girly girl who couldn't handle a little thing like a too-friendly dog. When Kara kept her cool, I knew she might be the one for me."

"The Ben Test?" I squeaked out the unfamiliar term.

"Yep." Andrew cast an adoring glance toward his wife and children as they laughed and played. "Kara passed."

— Rhonda Dragomir —

92

Do You Feel Lucky?

Some call it chaos; we call it family.
~Author Unknown

Many years ago, before we were married, my future wife's parents invited me to their home for a visit. Amanda and I had been dating for a while. I suppose her mom and dad realized they were not going to get rid of me, so they invited me to stay for a couple of days.

When I arrived, Amanda's mom said, "We want you to feel welcome." I said, "Thank you."

She said, "No. You don't understand. We really want you to feel welcome. We want you to feel like you are part of the family."

I smiled and said, "I really appreciate your hospitality."

I stayed in the bedroom of their youngest daughter, Amy, who bunked with Amanda. Staying in the room of a thirteen-year-old girl was a little awkward. The bed was very small, and my feet hung over the end. Stuffed animals covered the bed. The blankets were pink. It was not very manly, but I didn't mind. I looked forward to relaxing. My plan was to sleep in the next morning.

I was awakened early by a knock. I opened my eyes and looked at the red digital clock. It was 4:45.

It was Amanda's dad who knocked at the door. He said, "Today is Spirit Day at school, and Amy needs her red shirt."

I said, "Come on in."

He came in with Amy. They turned on the light and started digging through the closet.

It was 4:45 in the morning.

Amanda's parents had a dog. His name was Lucky. Lucky was not a small dog. He was a giant gray Weimaraner. He must have weighed a hundred pounds. Lucky ran through the open door, jumped onto the bed, and attempted to get under the covers. He grabbed the pink blankets with his teeth and started to pull them off me.

Still 4:45.

Amanda's dad and sister were still searching for the red shirt. They paid no attention to the dog. After a minute, Lucky let go of the blankets, but he started to lick my face and nibble my ear. All the while, Amanda's dad and her sister continued to look for the shirt.

It was 4:46 in the morning.

Amanda came in and started helping them. Three people were in the room looking for a red shirt. The lights were on, and the dog was trying to rip off my ear.

It was 4:47.

Amanda's mom walked into the room. The entire family was there: Amanda, her sister, her mom, and her dad. They all searched for the red shirt. Lucky the dog chewed on my ear. Nobody paid attention to Lucky. I thought I should jump up and scream, "Let me help you all find that red shirt!"

It was 4:48 in the morning.

Twenty minutes went by. They destroyed the bedroom… but they never found the red shirt.

They walked out, turned out the light, closed the door, and left Lucky on the bed with me. My hair and face were wet from dog slobber. Lucky had his teeth clenched on my ear.

After a minute, Amanda's mom opened the door and called the dog. As she slammed the door, I heard her scream, "You left the dog in there. You are going to wake up James if you're not careful. We want him to feel welcome!"

Looking back, I don't know if I felt welcome, but I sure felt Lucky.

— James Collins —

Chapter
11

Senior Moments

93

It Was a Magical Day After All

Sometimes it takes a wrong turn to get
you to the right place.
~Mandy Hale, The Single Woman

It was 1972, and my family had taken a summer vacation from Kansas to Florida, with an exciting day planned at Disney World. My mother, stepfather and two younger stepsisters, along with my sixty-seven-year-old Grandma Betty and myself, finally arrived at the holy grail of all amusement parks, and we girls were beside ourselves with anticipation.

To be honest, I think my grandma was, too. She hadn't traveled much in her life and certainly had never been anywhere as exciting as Disney World! Since we had been there before, my mother had many things she wanted to show her mother, so off we went to get the day started.

After the second ride, we all got off and got ready to stroll to the next one when one of us looked around and noticed that Grandma Betty wasn't with us. This was alarming for many reasons, the most important being that Grandma Betty had limited vision and couldn't read signs well. She had also started to show some signs of confusion. She could easily find herself lost in her own hometown, not to mention "The Most Magical Place on Earth"!

We all turned in circles, calling out her name, "GRANDMA BETTY, GRANDMA BETTY! GRANDMA!!" My mom was yelling, "MOM... MOM... MOM!" to no avail. We couldn't see her, and obviously she could not see or hear us. Cellphones didn't exist at that time, so there was no help there. Anyone who has been to Disney knows how crowded and busy the park is. It's pretty easy for a child to get lost in the shuffle, but we didn't think it would be that easy to misplace a grandma! The only thing we could figure was that she had exited off the last ride and started walking, looking for us, not knowing that we were still in other cars behind her waiting to get off.

My mother told us stay in that spot while she went to the "Missing Children" booth to report her lost mother. We impatiently waited until she came back and said that she had given them a description, so we might as well move to the next destination.

The rest of the day had a dark cloud hanging over it. Everything we saw or did was prefaced by, "I wish Grandma could see this," or "I wish Grandma Betty could ride this ride." We were worried, hot, disappointed and stressed, with my mother being the worst of all. With every step we took, we craned our necks, looking for my grandma, but we still couldn't find her. My mom would stop at every "Missing Children" booth to inquire whether there had been any reports of finding Grandma Betty, but there never were any.

As the day came to an end, we trudged to Disney's town square, hoping we might find her there while watching the Electrical Parade, the beautiful parade of neon lights, music and Disney characters. If not, we thought, she would surely stop at the gate or report herself to someone as being lost. With the crowds leaving the park, we figured we'd find her.

I was sitting on the curb, and I have to admit that I was in awe of the lights, music and floats covered in sparkling light. Along came Mickey Mouse! And then Minnie Mouse! And then Daffy Duck and Cinderella! And then along came Grandma Bett... GRANDMA BETTY? There she was, smack dab in the middle of the Disney parade, literally marching in all her glory, keeping beat with the band led by Pluto. She was swinging her white pocketbook in the crook of her arm, nodding and waving at the crowd, looking as pleased as Punch with herself!

I called out to my mom and pointed toward Grandma. "There she is! Grab her!" My mom stepped into the middle of the parade group and grabbed my grandma's arm. Grandma looked over, somewhat startled to see a familiar face, and stepped out of the line of Disney characters.

Breathing sighs of relief that we had finally found our MIA grandma, we asked her what had happened and why she was in the parade. "A parade?" she exclaimed. "I didn't know that I was in a parade! All I knew was that I had been lost most of the day, and when I saw this crowd of people all headed in one direction, I figured that they knew where they were going, and if I walked with them, I'd get somewhere that I could possibly find all of you! Everyone was waving at me, so I waved back. These people at Disney World are certainly friendly!"

I don't know that my grandma really minded that she missed a lot of the rides, and she got a good walking tour of the place on her own. And she's one of the rare few who got to participate in that world-famous Disney parade, perhaps having the most magical time of us all!

— Kathy Tharp Thompson —

Please Take the Ticket

Those who are quick in talking
are not always quick in listening.
~G.K. Chesterton

By the time we reached the airport, my mother was in a huff. "We're going to be late," she said as she pulled into the newly renovated parking area.

My husband David and I had come to pick up my oldest son, who had flown in to spend Christmas with the family. As always, Mom had insisted on driving us to the airport since my husband and I were from out of state and didn't know our way around.

We picked a lane that didn't look too busy. When our turn came, Mom rolled down her window to grab the parking ticket from the machine. We watched and waited for the gate to lift so we could drive through. Instead, we heard a voice. "Please take the ticket."

"Give me a minute," Mom answered.

It's a well-known fact that I often talk to myself. So does my sister, so I didn't think anything of my mother's words.

The machine sounded again. "Please take the ticket."

"I'm trying. I can't reach it," she said.

This time, my husband and I glanced at each other with our eyebrows raised. Certainly, Mom knew the voice was automated and not a real person speaking to her.

"Please take the ticket."

"I'm trying. I'm trying. It's too far away. Give me a minute."

In fairness to my mother, automated machines had recently arrived in the world, and there weren't many around yet. We had never run into one at the airport before. In the old days, the machine spit out a parking ticket, and if you couldn't reach the ticket, you simply opened your door and grabbed it. Now, the new metal safety railings on either side of the car made it impossible to open the door.

"Please take the ticket."

"It's too far. I'm trying. I'm trying."

The traffic behind us grew impatient. Horns honked. In the rearview mirror, I saw people trying to back up so they could find another lane. All the while, the machine continued, "Please take the ticket. Please take the ticket. Please take the ticket."

Mom was frustrated, but David and I found our situation hilarious, especially since before taking off for the airport, we had argued with Mom when she insisted on squeezing the three of us into the front seat since the backseat heater was broken. We had wrenched our body parts in an effort to get our seat belts buckled. And now, here we were, dressed in heavy, cumbersome coats, smashed against each other so tight that we couldn't move. Once David and I started laughing, we couldn't stop, which only hindered our efforts to find a solution.

Meanwhile, the machine and my mother continued their dueling duet.

It took forever to breach the bulky wall of coats and body matter that belonged to me and my mother and unbuckle my belt. All the time, "Please take the ticket," and Mom's "I'm trying" rang through the air.

Free from my shackles, I scooted forward in my seat, searched for my mother's belt and tried to unfasten it. The entire time I worked, she and the machine continued to fight it out.

By this time, I was laughing so hard that I could hardly speak. "Mom, I unbuckled your belt. Try to scoot closer to the window."

"Please take the ticket. Please take the ticket."

"I'm trying. I'm trying. I need to scoot over."

As I leaned forward into the dashboard, I finally had a grand view of my mother. Between her bulky coat and short arms, I held my breath as I watched her struggle to reach the ticket, all the while talking to that blasted machine. It was close, but she finally managed to get ahold of the ticket. The gate opened, and we drove through.

Although Mom seemed harried, within minutes she erupted into laughter along with us and continued laughing each time we told the story to someone new during our visit.

For the record, my husband and I never asked Mom if she actually thought there was a person talking to her through the machine. Some things are better left unknown.

—Jill Burns—

Lips All Sugary

Dementia was like a truth serum.
~Amy Tan

My grandmother Mimi was at the point in her dementia when putting names with faces—even family names and faces—was pretty hit or miss. For the most part, she knew who I was. She knew her daughters, and a couple of other grandchildren, but in-laws and greats were fuzzy acquaintances at best. She was ninety-five years old, for God's sake! And we loved her greatly, whether she knew us or not.

But we had a task to do: Mimi needed to be moved from her assisted-living apartment to a single room in the memory unit. But how to move her without upsetting her?

We needed a distraction: a man.

I should mention that my grandmother was a huge flirt. HUGE! She had been one her whole life. She'd flirt with her doctors and lie about her ailments. She'd flirt with waiters, orderlies, and any other attractive man she met. And we knew the perfect tall, dark and handsome man to bring with us to help with the move—not for his muscle but for his charm.

The young man happened to be her grandson... a.k.a. my son. But she'd never piece that together.

It was foolproof.

My son joined my aunts, mother and me for the move. We arrived at Mimi's door with boxes, bags and a small dolly that we set outside

The young man happened to be her grandson... a.k.a. my son. But she'd never piece that together.

It was foolproof.

as we ushered my son Mac inside.

As soon as she saw him, she was enchanted. Dressed in black with a killer smile (thanks to years of braces), Mac turned heads everywhere he went. A retirement village was no different. Mimi politely said hello to us, but she only had eyes for Mac.

"Mac, why don't you sit down with Mimi and show her pictures from your trip to Washington, D.C.?"

While Mac chattered away with Mimi in the other room, we women went through Mimi's closet and dresser, picking and choosing which clothes were too ragged to move again, which trinkets to keep and which to throw away, and what sentimental value each thing had.

We chose special things to give each grandchild, but my mother and aunts did the hard task of choosing what would be best for their mother now that she couldn't decide those things for herself.

Finally, we rose from the floor with creaking knees and returned to the living room.

"Let's have some of that ice cream we brought," my aunt Nancy suggested. "Mother, do you want some ice cream?" she asked as she held up a carton of Cherry Cordial ice cream we'd brought.

"Oh, yes! Please!" my grandmother piped up from her chair near the heating vent. She was an ice-cream junkie. She'd eat nothing but ice cream if we let her.

While my aunt started dishing up ice cream, my mom and I started dragging bags and boxes into the hallway. Minutes later, we were huffing and puffing with the exertion, but we'd done it. Mission accomplished.

Mom and I grabbed our bowls of ice cream and pulled out the two folding chairs that were tucked away for company.

It was then that we heard what was going on ten feet away from us.

Mimi giggled and held her spoon to her mouth. "Mmmm…" she hummed in ecstasy as she devoured the melting pink ice cream.

She smiled at Mac coyly and licked her lips. "Here I am with my lips all sugary and no one to kiss."

Mac's spoon clattered hard against his bowl as her flirty words registered.

My spoon clattered, too. She'd said the same thing to my husband the week before! We stopped by with ice cream, and she tried to dazzle my husband with her sugary lips!

Mimi giggled again.

"How often do you use that line?" I asked her.

Mimi shrugged and took another lick from her spoon.

I couldn't believe my grandmother had a pick-up line! How many men had heard this come-on?

I laughed but also thought maybe I'd better step in before she made another move on my son.

"We have to go," I said. I carried our bowls into the kitchen and washed them up quickly. She ignored me and kept "mmm-ing" over her ice cream with Mac.

He rose from his chair. "Well, Mimi, we've got to get going." We each gave her a hug goodbye and made our way out of the apartment.

"Bye, man in black! You were the best boyfriend I ever had." She waved goodbye and blew him a kiss as we closed the door.

"I feel like I need a shower," Mac said as he grabbed one of the boxes we'd piled by the door.

"She'll forget all about it in an hour," I assured him.

"Yeah, but I won't."

Neither would we, I laughed to myself. Our ruse had worked exactly as we'd planned — although we'd probably have to recruit a new man to sit down and have ice cream with her next time.

Maybe my brother?

—Juliann Wetz—

He Stuck It to Me

I don't have awkward moments. I have an awkward
life, occasionally interrupted by normalcy.
~Robert Pattinson

"Honey, my school is having a fundraiser, a gala event. Wouldn't it be fun to dress up and attend?"

My husband replied, "Not only can't I hear well in a crowded room anymore, but I can't remember names. I don't see this as being a fun event for me."

"I'll be the brains and ears of our outfit if you go with me. I'll help you recall names."

I told him that a memory expert had recently explained an easy way to remember a list. "You have to use visualization techniques to make the names of items stick to your own body. For example, if you need shampoo, eggs, bread, and milk, all you have to do is engage your five senses. Imagine shampoo oozing down your head. Visualize yourself rolling a dozen eggs up and down your forearms. Tie an imaginary gallon of milk to your knee and feel the heaviness. Shove a loaf of soft bread under your shirt near your squishy breadbasket."

My husband said, "What are you implying about my stomach? Listen, people would think I was strange dragging a leg, wiping my eyes, flapping my arms, and rubbing my gut. I admit it's a technique that could possibly work to remember a couple of things but not more."

"That's all you have to remember: a couple of names," I said and talked my dear hubby into dressing up and acting out. "When I introduce you to people, you just say their names aloud and touch a body part to make the name stick. I'll be right beside you."

Dressed in our finest, I introduced him to my co-workers and parents of my students. I smiled, watching my honey as he shrugged his shoulder, rubbed his chin, or patted his thigh. I winked my approval. He whispered, "I can't remember if it's your boss or her husband on my shoulder or my funny bone."

I assured him, "Don't panic. I'll stick close since the names aren't sticking."

A couple whose children had been in my class three years approached. I tried introducing them to my husband. I looked at Bill and said, "Honey, this is…" NOTHING! My mind went blank. I could not remember their names, but I could retrieve details about their jogging routes, the fact that she was a NICU nurse and he was a banker, but not one of their names. In an attempt to save my pride, I turned with a Vanna White, *Wheel of Fortune* flair to my husband and said, "This is my husband…" NOTHING! My memory bank was blank, totally and completely insufficient. My hands got sweaty. My mouth went dry, and my husband "what's his name" watched me fumble. He stepped up, patted my shoulder, elbowed me, extended his hand and said, "Bill, my name is Bill."

After a brief conversation with the parents (who also introduced themselves), my honey asked, "How did I do?" Then, he poked my arm, rubbed his belly and tousled my hair.

The next day, I made an appointment with my doctor, who administered a battery of memory tests and asked me to spell the word "world" backward. She ruled out dementia and Alzheimer's and said, "Welcome to the world of brief brain blips and memory slips called senior citizenship."

— Linda O'Connell —

97

Double Vision

You can't help getting older,
but you don't have to get old.
~George Burns

Our daughter and her young family were not home, so my husband and I went for a quick swim in their pool. Then we went back home. Just before arriving home I began looking for my sunglasses. They were not in the vehicle's cubby, on the floor, or in my purse. I patted the top of my head, twice. Not there. Had they slipped behind me and were tangled in my long hair? A thorough search and squeeze of hair did not reveal the glasses. We searched under and behind the car seat. I could not understand how "we" had left them behind.

Once in our driveway, my husband joined in the search. We searched under and behind the car's seat. He double-checked all the locations, and we still could not find them. They were officially invisible, leaving only one conclusion.

I lamented, "Oh, dear! They must be on the pool deck." I worried that our two-year-old grandchild would find them and break them while trying to put them on the dog or himself.

My chivalrous husband said, "You are tired. You go inside and I will drive back and get your glasses before the kids arrive home."

We walked up to the front door. I tried inserting the key but was having trouble seeing the key's slot. It was too dark. Why? Because I was wearing my sunglasses.

During our frantic search, neither my husband nor I had noticed the glasses, a pair as big as two black TV screens, sitting on my nose!

It is a good thing that I have not mentioned to my daughter about the "other thing." We have a landline, and of course cellphones too. One day I was on the phone with a friend, relentlessly searching for my cellphone to check something on the Internet. I couldn't find it anywhere... until I realized I was not talking on the landline.

— Mary Ellen Angelscribe —

98

The Mothership

Times when families laugh together are among
the most precious times a family can have.
~Fred Rogers

Ding! Ding! Ding! The sound of my mother's dinner bell rang out, calling me home. I plopped on my sled headfirst. I wanted just one more ride down the snowy hill. With the wind in my face, I whizzed to the bottom as the sun lowered. The forest flew by in a blur, and I landed in a snowbank with a thud. I wiped the snow from my eyes. I was alone. It was nearly dark. I heard a branch creak in the wind. Suddenly, I was afraid.

The previous night, I'd watched a show about the legendary Bigfoot. It was the 1970s, an era when unsolved mystery programs were popular. Weekly episodes covered topics like the Bermuda Triangle, the Loch Ness Monster, or UFOs. I grew up in New England hearing stories of ghosts and accused witches. We lived in a region where the famous UFO sightings at Exeter occurred. Alien abductees Betty and Barney Hill were local legends. I grew up on scary stories and I knew they weren't real. Mostly.

As I dragged my sled uphill, tall pines swayed in the wind. *Snap!* A branch broke. Maybe an animal was in the woods. I told myself it was just a raccoon. But... what if Bigfoot was watching me?

At dusk, mottled pine-tree bark can play tricks on the eyes. I strained to see between the trees. Then, something in the forest moved. I dropped my sled and tore home as fast as I could through a foot of snow. Trembling and sobbing, I burst through the kitchen door. Safe at last! Everyone was sitting at the dinner table waiting for me.

"What's wrong?" my mother asked, alarmed by my hysterics.

"I saw Bigfoot! He's out there! In the woods!"

For years to come, my family told and retold the story of the time I saw Bigfoot. It became the stuff of family legend. I laughed along with them. But even as an adult, I was embarrassed by my childhood foolishness. I wished they would forget the entire episode.

Decades later, in August 2013, I was fixing dinner with my teenage sons. My phone rang, displaying my mother's cellphone number. She rarely called from her cellphone, so I worried something was amiss.

"Hi, what's going on? Is everything okay?"

"I'm not sure. Dad and I were driving home from the store. We pulled over because there is something weird in the sky. Glowing objects are flying in the air. There must be forty or fifty of these things."

"Seriously? You must be having a close encounter," I joked.

My sons clambered closer to the phone to hear, their interest piqued by my end of the conversation. I put Mom on speakerphone.

"Where are you?"

"We are at the land trust by the river. Cars are parked along the road by Hilltop Farm. The flying things are oval-shaped. They are glowing an orange-y yellow. More are rising up from behind the hill. They are floating everywhere, filling the sky. One, two, three…" She started to count them.

"What does Dad think they are?"

"He's baffled, too. I know this is going to sound nuts," she said. "I think we're seeing UFOs. I've never seen anything like this in my life."

I looked at my eldest son. He shrugged and whispered something to his brother.

My parents were intelligent, practical folks. They rarely drank other than a glass of wine or beer during holidays. They both worked full-time well past the age most people retired. They tended to be skeptics, definitely not the type to jump to conclusions. So, I didn't doubt something was in the sky.

"They are flying in formation now!" Her voice was shrill.

"Mom, maybe I should call the authorities." This didn't seem funny anymore.

"The police are here. I saw a cruiser parked on the main road by the farm. What are they going to do anyway?"

"She's right," my son said.

"Oh, no! Now, a big, round, glowing disk is rising up over the hill."

"How fast is it rising?" I asked.

"It's barely moving, but it's bigger than the other things. It must be the mothership!"

At the sound of the words "mothership," my sons dashed out the door. Before I could say, "Hey, wait for me!" they were in the car zooming off to the land trust.

By now, I was having visions of my parents being abducted by aliens. Was I having a crazy dream? There had to be a logical explanation.

"Are you still there, Mom?" Silence.

A moment later, I heard Dad say, "That's not a mothership. It's the moon rising."

"Oh." Mom giggled. "Now, I am imagining things. But what are those balls in the sky? More keep coming and floating off to the west."

Minutes later, I heard car doors slam and my sons' voices in the background.

"Hey, what is going on? Hello? I'm still on the line." She'd set the phone down. The suspense was killing me.

I heard chatter followed by Dad's hearty laughter. I gave a sigh of relief. My parents weren't going to be whisked away to outer space like Wilford Brimley in the movie *Cocoon*.

Just when I thought I'd been forgotten, Mom said sheepishly, "Everything's fine. Talk to your son." She passed the phone off.

"Hi. It's just sky lanterns." He laughed.

"Huh? What are sky lanterns?"

"They are kind of like a small hot-air balloon. They are lit with a flame and glow as they float up. Someone is having a wedding at the farm and set them off. The police are directing traffic. Other drivers pulled over to see the lights, too."

"I'm relieved it's not a fleet of alien invaders." I laughed.

"Not me. I wanted to see the mothership!" he said.

So, no UFOs were flying in formation. No mothership had visited Earth. The UFOs were just ethereal floating lanterns, a full moon, and human imagination. The UFOs and the mothership became the stuff of family legend to be told and retold with a chuckle.

And, since then, no one has ever mentioned my Bigfoot sighting again.

— Caroline Kiberd —

The Haunted Remote

One of the things that binds us as a family
is a shared sense of humor.
~Ralph Fiennes

My husband Bob and I visited my grandparents on a perfect fall Saturday, not too hot and not too cold. Their windows were open to the sounds of neighborhood kids and the faint smell of ketchup wafting across town from the Heinz factory. As usual, Grandma and Grandpa were planted in their matching recliners, watching their massive television with the volume cranked to eleven. Grandpa never wore his hearing aids, and the remote control was his responsibility.

"Lookie who's here," Grandpa said when we walked into the living room.

"Orville," Grandma said with her voice raised, "TV's too loud. Turn it down."

He answered her with his usual reply. "What? I can't hear you. The TV's too loud." But he grabbed his remote off the end table and lowered the volume to a seven or eight.

I went to the kitchen for some iced tea, and their attention returned to the television. My grandparents adhered to a standard lineup of programs, which included *Wheel of Fortune*, *Lawrence Welk*, and *Days of Our Lives*. ("Like sands through the hourglass, so are the days of our lives.") But what they liked best was sports. Their favorite sport was basketball, and their favorite team was the Iowa Hawkeyes.

I sat on the "davenport" next to Bob and handed him a glass of tea poured from a large jug that was always in their "ice box."

Grandma and Grandpa were watching a nature show where a bug laboriously rolled some round object across a vast desert. Next, an identical insect arrived, and the two battled for possession of the ball, which was easily ten times their size.

"Are they fighting over a rock?" I asked.

"Dung," Grandpa said without looking away from the TV.

"They're dung beetles," Grandma confirmed. "The rolling kind."

Bob and I gave each other a look.

I said, "And you're watching this… why?"

Grandma said, "Nothing else on."

Grandpa glanced at the clock on the wall. "Hawks don't play until three."

It wasn't long before I, too, was mesmerized by the life-and-death struggle of dung beetles.

Then, soft, instrumental music floated through the air.

I turned my head and tried to pin down the location of the sound. It was coming from somewhere in the room but not from the television. The tinkling tune continued long enough that I was able to identify it as "Winchester Cathedral." My grandparents seemed oblivious to the noise. Bob nudged me with his elbow.

"Grandma, don't you hear that music?"

She looked at me and pointed in Grandpa's general direction. "He can't hear it. It's his remote control. I keep telling everybody it plays music. But they say I'm crazy, so there you have it."

"Is it a new remote?" I asked.

"Had it for years," Grandpa said. "It's the darndest thing. Just started playing music a couple of weeks ago — or so she says."

Bob squinted one eye. "I don't know how a remote control could play music, mechanically speaking."

"See," Grandma said. "Your husband thinks I'm crazy, too."

I got up and grabbed the remote off the table. And, yes, it was playing "Winchester Cathedral." Without pushing any buttons, the music stopped just as mysteriously as it had started.

"Hey, gimme that," Grandpa said. "It's almost time for the tipoff."

I smiled and held the remote out of his reach. "Do we have to watch the game? I'm seriously getting into this dung-beetle saga," I said.

Nowadays, people get antsy if their cellphone isn't within arm's reach. My grandfather was that way about his remote control. He lowered his voice to a growl and gestured toward me. "Give it."

Once the basketball game started, we might as well have been at Hawkeye Arena as my grandparents began their litany of cheers, jeers, and cursing.

The first quarter came on fast and furious with lots of movement up and down the court, turnovers, and wild shots. The two teams were tied when the referee charged the Hawks with a personal foul.

A lanky opponent, looking confident, stepped up to the free-throw line. He bounced the ball once. He bounced the ball twice. He went up for the shot....

And the television screen switched to dung beetles.

"Orville, what are you doing over there?"

"Nothing," he said, scrambling for the remote.

He flipped back to the game. The free throw had been successful, and the Hawkeyes were behind. But they had possession of the ball.

Missed shot.

Rebound.

Missed shot.

Rebound.

"Come on, you idiots," Grandma said.

Just as the point guard launched a ball from the three-point line... dung beetles again.

Grandma came unglued. "Orville!"

"I didn't touch the remote."

It went on this way until halftime, switching from basketball to dung beetles at every crucial moment.

During halftime, my Uncle Harold dropped in. "How's the game?"

"They're blowing it," Grandma said.

Grandpa told Harold about the television changing channels during the game. My uncle was a mechanic and could fix almost anything.

Harold shrugged and sat down in the corner chair. "Sounds like your remote is haunted."

"You're a big help," Grandma said.

There were no channel-changing ghosts during the second half of the game. The Hawkeyes pulled it out at the last minute with the assist of my grandparents' persistent badgering.

A week later, with several family members gathered around, Harold related the story of how he drove my grandparents nuts by changing their television channels during the basketball game. As it turned out, he had been standing in the yard outside their living room with his own remote control aimed through the window screen.

"Smart aleck," Grandma said (or perhaps she called him something a little saltier).

So, the mystery of the changing channels was solved. But Harold denied any knowledge of "Winchester Cathedral" and said he didn't know how a remote control could play music.

Grandma said, "Shelley heard it, too."

"Don't drag me into this," I said.

Back then, the Internet didn't exist, but even with the current enlightenment of Google, I haven't figured out the musical remote. Maybe it really was haunted.

Now, many years later, following the Covid pandemic, Bob and I have gotten in the habit of watching too much television. One evening, we found ourselves engrossed in a Netflix documentary about hummingbirds. I smiled to myself, remembering the day of the dung beetles. It hit me that many years of sand had passed through our hourglass since that perfect fall Saturday. And I realized that we had become my grandparents.

When I think of Grandma and Grandpa now, I like to imagine them in Heaven watching some celestial basketball game. I'm not sure if cussing is allowed there, but quite likely the remote control plays "Winchester Cathedral."

— Shelley Jones Clark —

100

Romance

We're all a little weird… And when we find someone
whose weirdness is compatible with ours, we join
up with them and fall into mutually satisfying
weirdness — and call it love.
~Robert Fulghum

About twenty years ago, I was in Newport visiting my folks, who had been together since 1938. We had just returned from a dinner at the Atlantic Beach Club (formerly Johnny's House of Seafood). Mom and Dad were sitting in the living room on their leather loveseat, and I walked into the kitchen to make them a pot of tea.

This is what I overheard from the kitchen:

Mom turned to Dad and said, "The proof is in the pudding, Old Boy, and you don't tell me that you love me very much anymore."

Dad replied, "You know I love you."

"Uh-huh, and I remember how you used to hold my hand." There was a long, silent pause, and I was picturing Dad holding her hand.

She then said, "And, you know, you used to kiss me a lot more than you do now."

There was an even longer pause, and I could picture them kissing.

A moment later, Mom said, "I really loved it when you used to nibble the back of my ears and neck."

Dad instantly got up and started walking away.

"What is it?" asked Mom.

"I'll be right back," Dad replied with a laugh. "I just have to get my teeth from the bathroom."

—John Chapman Elliott—

101

The Last Laugh

A good laugh is sunshine in the house.
~William Thackeray

Family and friends stood in small groups throughout the room. We had come together to honor Uncle John, the family patriarch, and to comfort each other as we mourned his passing. Quiet conversations seemed appropriate out of respect for the deceased.

But Uncle John had a larger-than-life personality. The words "subdued" and "conventional" never applied to him. So, the conversations about him did not remain subdued for long. Discreet chuckles quickly erupted into louder laughter punctuating stories of John's legendary antics. He was someone who could never be described as politically correct. And he frequently manifested his down-to-earth sense of humor when least expected.

A small cluster of people stood with my husband's cousin, Tom, as he shared memories of his dad. We joined Tom just as another round of laughter emanated from the group. He continued to fondly recount his father's exploits and favorite sayings. Then, he began to wonder aloud at what his dad's response might be, looking down from heaven at the roomful of loved ones.

But as Tom spoke, he stopped abruptly in mid-sentence. "What was that?"

The rest of us looked around the room. "What was what?"

"That. Do you hear it?" Tom's brow furrowed as he tried to identify the sound. "It's laughter."

Of course, we all heard laughter. Almost everyone in the room was chuckling at recalled memories. But Tom remained unconvinced it was one of us.

"Someone's laughing, but… it doesn't sound right." His attention was drawn to his father's body. "It's coming from… it sounds like it's coming from the casket… from Pop!"

We looked at each other, eyes wide in disbelief, and followed Tom as he strode to the front of the room. We all could hear the laughter now, a muted but rather odd, almost mechanical, "Ha ha ha. Ha ha ha. Ha ha ha." The repetition was unsettling. And, yes, it was, indeed, coming from the casket. It didn't seem possible, yet we could not deny what we were hearing.

A moment later, we had our answer. Tom bent over his father's body and then turned back to us. The strange laughter had stopped, but a grin stretched across Tom's face as he held up his father's wristwatch. "Pop bought this a few weeks ago."

I still didn't understand. What did a watch have to do with the strange laughter?

Tom smiled broadly. "He bought it because he liked the laughter alarm function. No one thought to turn it off after he died. The joke's on us. Guess Pop had the last laugh after all!"

— Ava Pennington —

Meet Our Contributors

Sharon E. Albritton studied journalism at Fullerton College in California. She and her husband are currently enjoying retired life in the Lakelands of South Carolina. Sharon is an active member of her church and leads a prayer ministry known as "Standin in the Need of Prayer."

Barbara Alpert lives in Florida with her hubby Dave. She's written books for children and adults. Her most recent, *Weight A Minute: God Cares About Your Body, Soul & Spirit*, was released in January 2020. She loves working from home turning writers' manuscripts into published masterpieces. E-mail her at comlish@aol.com.

Monica A. Andermann's writing has been included in such publications as *Woman's World*, *Guideposts*, and *Sasee* as well as many other titles in the *Chicken Soup for the Soul* series. When she is not writing, she can most frequently be found puttering in her garden, binge-reading magazines or taking long walks through her neighborhood.

Donna Anderson is a mom of three and grandmother of four who lives in Texas with her husband Tom and their toy-obsessed Golden Retriever, Ohbe. When she's not writing or researching the genealogies of family and friends, she can be found at the local history museum where she volunteers as a historian and exhibit curator.

Mary Ellen Angelscribe is author of *Expect Miracles* and *A Christmas filled with Miracles*. Read her miraculous and funny pet newspaper column which has run for two decades on Facebook at www.facebook.com/PetTipsandTales and www.facebook.com/AngelScribe1111/. Her swimming cats were featured on *Animal Planet*! E-mail her at angelscribe@msn.com.

Tom Armstrong is a retired engineer living in a suburb of Worcester, MA with his new wife and old dog. Tom credits any writing ability attributed to him to his late wife and talented writer Louise for whom he was a dedicated soulmate and proofreader.

Lynn Assimacopoulos began writing at five and continues throughout her lifetime. As a nurse she wrote for professional nursing journals. She also enjoys writing prose and poetry and has written two nonfiction books. Now retired, she continues to write while her other hobbies have been genealogy and rock collecting.

Kimberly Avery is a writer, speaker, blogger, and self-described underachieving wife, mother of four, and grandmother of two perfect grandchildren. From Atlanta, GA, she spends her days reheating her coffee, reading Erma Bombeck, and writing humorous tales of everyday life. Learn more at KimberlyAvery.com.

Dave Bachmann is a retired teacher who taught language arts to special needs students for thirty-nine years. He now lives in California with his wife Jay and their fifteen-year-old Lab, where he writes poems and stories for children and grown-ups.

Anne Bardsley barely survived raising five children. She is now a gigi to five munchkins who light up her life. She's the author of *How I Earned My Wrinkles*, *Angel Bumps: Hello from Heaven*, and newly released *Heartstrings from Heaven*, book two in the *Angel Bumps* series. Anne lives in St. Pete, FL with her tan husband.

Fran Baxter-Guigli grew up in Seattle, WA and graduated from the University of Washington. She received a master's degree from the University of California, Berkeley, where she worked for more than twenty years. She lives near Sacramento, CA with her husband, who also writes.

Jillian Bell is a Toronto-based writer. She loves fitness, dogs, and vintage shopping.

Katie Bergen is a wife and mom of two living in Canada. She loves spending her time hiking in the mountains, paddleboarding and running. She hopes to write inspiring words to motivate others to deepen their faith and live confidently in who they are.

Meredith Besser is an essayist, fiction writer and playwright. Her work has appeared in *New Monologues for Women by Women*, *Literature: The Human Experience* and the *Los Angeles Times*, among others. When not dog-sitting she's busy working on her collection of humorous essays.

Melanie Brening is a Minneapolis, MN–based freelance writer whose work has appeared in a handful of anthologies, a few online and print magazines as well as countless to-do lists. She lives with her husband, two children and a bad caffeine habit.

Merry Broughal is the founder and president of Olalo of Hope - Kenya, a nonprofit charity working in Kenya. She enjoys reading, writing, spending time with her grandkids, and trips to Kenya. (She also despises spiders!) E-mail her atmerrybroughal@gmail.com.

Jill Burns lives in the mountains of West Virginia with her wonderful family. She's a retired piano teacher and performer. She enjoys writing, music, gardening, nature, and spending time with her grandchildren.

C. Allan Butkus has a Master's in Communication from the University of Hawaii. He spent fourteen years in the U.S. Air Force, is president of Twin Lakes Writers in Mountain Home, AR, and winner of 158 awards for writing. C. Allan has authored six adventure-thrillers and one nonfiction book. He has been married for fifty years and has three daughters. Learn more at callanbutkus.com.

Eva Carter is a freelance writer and photographer. She lives in Dallas, TX with her husband Larry and their two cats.

Shelley Jones Clark has an MFA from Hamline University in creative writing for children and an MD from the University of Iowa. She mostly writes middle-grade novels but dabbles in adult essays and short stories. Shelley lives with her husband Bob and a shy, ninety-pound Pit Bull named Webster. She has three adult kiddos.

James R. Coffey's work appears regularly in numerous journals and magazines including *Aboriginal Science Fiction*, *Journal of Compressed Creative Arts*, *Close to the Bone*, *AntipodeanSF*, Red Cape Publishing anthology: *O is for Outbreak*, and *History Defined*.

Rachael M. Colby has a heart for reconciliation and a passion to uplift those who serve in tough places. This Jamaican-born multi-genre award-winning writer, wife, mom, beach bum, and artist writes to inspire faith and motivate. She resides in Cape Cod, MA, runs on coffee and chocolate, and blogs at TattooItOnYourHeart.com.

James Collins is a pastor and teacher. He is a retired U.S. Army chaplain with multiple combat tours. He and his wife share their home with their three extraordinary children, three dogs, and a lifetime collection of books.

Ginny Huff Conahan taught in Los Angeles, CA and in Fort Collins, CO for a total of thirty-four years. Four of her stories have been published in the *Chicken Soup for the Soul* series. She has a doctorate from the University of Southern California. She enjoys spending time with her kids and grandkids. E-mail her at gcona@comcast.net.

Mackenzie Conley, a freshman at a STEM school, has been writing stories since she could string words together. Mackenzie's goal for the future includes going to college and finally publishing one of her novels. Her first story published by Chicken Soup for the Soul was written when she was thirteen.

Valli Cowan is a retired elementary school teacher. She has lived most of her life in the Northern Virginia area and raised her children there. She now lives in Southern California, where she continues her adventures with her husband and family, always keeping an eye out for the humorous aspects of her life.

John Crawford is a writer and editor living in the Boston area. He can be found on Twitter @crawfordwriter where he writes missives about climate change. This is his second story to appear in the *Chicken Soup for the Soul* series.

Writer, humorist, and photographer **Ann Cunningham** is a frequent contributor to the *Chicken Soup for the Soul* series. (This book contains her nineteenth contribution.) She resides in the Black Hills of South Dakota with her two dogs and two cats. Learn more about Ann's writing and photography at AnnCunninghamWriter.com.

Elton A. Dean is an Associate Faculty Lead and Computer Information Systems instructor at Post University. He retired from the Massachusetts Army National Guard in 2016 and lives in North Carolina with his wife and son.

Sergio Del Bianco has a background in fine arts and psychology. He is an artist and writer, interested in the intersection of art, psychology, and the humanities. He resides in Europe with his spouse and growing family of rescue animals. E-mail him at sergiodelbianco@yahoo.com or through Twitter @DelBianco97.

Kathy Diamontopoulos enjoys spending time with her husband Lou along with her Australian Shepherd, Miss Marlee. When she's not on the trails photographing wildlife, she enjoys quiet time in her various gardens.

Rhonda Dragomir is a multimedia creative who treasures her fairy-tale life in Central Kentucky, insisting her home is her castle even if her prince refuses to dig a moat. She has published works in several anthologies and periodicals, and her first novel, a historical romance, will be released in 2024.

John Chapman Elliott worked for the CIA's special operations group for forty-four years, was the senior advisor to the former director of the CIA, and has worked and lived in countless countries. Fluent in six languages, he holds a Bachelor of Science in Business, an MBA, a Juris Doctorate law degree, and is a published author.

Amanda Ann Gregory, LCPC, is a trauma psychotherapist, national speaker, and author. She has provided trauma therapy for more than fifteen years in outpatient and residential settings and is currently in private practice. She lives in Chicago, IL with her partner and is raising a sassy black cat named Mr. Bojangles.

Terry Hans, a retired dental hygienist, is compiling a collection of hilarious stories as told to her by patients in the exam room. A previous contributor to the *Chicken Soup for the Soul* series, Terry enjoys time with her family, writing, and cheering for her grandsons at their sporting events. She and her husband are enjoying retirement in North Carolina.

Susan M. Heim is an author, editor, and library marketer. She is a longtime editor for the *Chicken Soup for the Soul* series and has authored several parenting and *Chicken Soup for the Soul* books, including the *Devotional Stories* series. Her articles have appeared in many magazines and websites.

A Los Angeles native, **Karyn Hirsch** has welcomed cultures from around the world to shape her outlook and culinary tastes. Through her blog, she shares her love of food that brings people together. She has recently completed an entertaining collection of short stories for children. E-mail her at karynskitchen2020@gmail.com.

Crystal Hodge believes in the value of remembering who we come from and is currently putting a collection of family memories and stories together for her daughters and granddaughter in the hope that future generations will share them at their own dinner tables. E-mail Crystal at crystalhodge1202@gmail.com.

Teresa B. Hovatter is a single mother of three, and a grandmother to five boys. She has had a successful career in real estate since 1994. Her passion for writing has grown over the last several years and she is finally on her path to fulfilling her heart's desire. Faith and family are her priorities; travel, her pleasure.

Kaitlyn Jain is an optimist who tries to find humor in everyday life. She wrote *Passports and Pacifiers* about traveling with her husband and four young kids. Jain graduated from Davidson College as a four-year starter in volleyball and earned her MBA from New York University. Learn more at kaitlynjain.com or follow her on Instagram @KaitlynJain.

Tanya Janke has worked in three schools, two shopping malls, a theatre, a market research company, and a berry patch. She now spends her days writing. Her first play, an adaptation of *The Little Prince*, was produced in Toronto.

Susan Jensen M.D. graduated from SUNY Upstate Medical Center and did her rehabilitation medicine residency at the VA Wadsworth/UCLA program. Now retired from clinical practice, she enjoys writing, travel, discovering new hobbies and making new friends.

Mary Kay is a recently retired IT Systems Engineer who writes stories for the entertainment and embarrassment of her family and friends. Her published work can be found at marykaywrites.com. Mary's pride and joy are her six nieces and nephews, for whom she serves as a cautionary tale.

Ellen Edwards Kennedy is the author of a four-book cozy mystery series and is about to publish a Bible-based picture book, *Walk With a Stranger*. She is the founder and mentor of NC Scribes, a weekly Zoom group of writers who have had many Chicken Soup for the Soul stories published.

Caroline Kiberd writes for children's publications and on her blog "Sprouts". She has four grown children and a houseful of pets. Caroline enjoys nature, gardening, history, and genealogy.

Kathleen Kohler writes about faith and family for numerous magazines and anthologies. She and her husband own a Certified Organic farm in the Pacific Northwest and have three children and seven grandchildren. Visit www.kathleenkohler.com or www.sultanfresh.com where she writes about her family and Silver Maple Farm.

Sharon Landeen is a mother of four, grandmother of two and great-grandmother of five. She is a former elementary school teacher and 4-H leader. She lives in Tucson, Arizona with her dog, Archie. Sharon enjoys University of Arizona basketball, traveling, and spending time with her family.

Mary Elizabeth Laufer graduated Phi Beta Kappa from SUNY Albany with a degree in English education. Her stories and poems have appeared in magazines, newspapers, and several anthologies. She especially enjoys writing for children, and recently finished her first middle-grade novel, *Katelyn's Crow*.

A court reporter by day, **Jody Lebel** writes romantic suspense novels and short stories, which have sold to *Woman's World*, the *Chicken Soup for the Soul* series, and dozens of others. She was raised in charming New England and now lives with her two cats in sunny Florida.

Arlene Lassiter Ledbetter earned a Bachelor of Arts in English from Dalton College in Georgia. She has written adult Sunday school curriculum and been published in numerous magazines. Arlene's byline has appeared in eight *Chicken Soup for the Soul* books. Her favorite moments are shared with her grandchildren.

Lynne Leichtfuss has stories published in rock climbing books, *California Climber* and *Decision* magazines. Her life took a 180-degree turn when her adventure husband of thirty-nine years died. She chose to return to their outdoor roots of rock climbing, kayaking, backpacking, working in the High Sierra. She blogs at lynneslifeclimb.wordpress.com.

Barbara LoMonaco is the Senior Editor for the *Chicken Soup for the Soul* series and has had stories published in many titles. She graduated from USC and has a teaching credential. She lives in Southern California where she is surrounded by boys: her husband, her three grown sons and her two grandsons. Thankfully, her three lovely daughters-in-law have diluted the mix somewhat, but the boys are still in the majority.

Marie Loper-Maxwell is the mom of many, lover of learning and devourer of books. She spends most of her time with her husband, parents, siblings, and seven children reading, writing, and making memories.

Adrienne Matthews is a previous contributor to the *Chicken Soup for the Soul* series and has also been published in both *Mysterious Ways* and *Guideposts*. She is enjoying retirement alongside her husband Greg and is proud mom to Eric. She feels led by God to share her stories of blessings and to offer joy and hope to others.

Debbi Mavity lives in the beautiful state of West Virginia with her Labrador Retriever, Otis. She enjoys hiking, writing, and giving new life to old, broken things. Debbi has previously been published in three *Chicken Soup for the Soul* books. Follow her on social media @MavsMutthouse.

Janell Michael is a retired elementary school teacher. She has two children and two grandchildren. She published her first book, *Fairytales Redeemed*, in 2018. She has some of her short stories published in various books, including the *Chicken Soup for the Soul* series. She is working on a new book of short stories based on Jer. 29:11.

Marya Morin is a freelance writer. Her stories and poems have appeared in publications such as *Woman's World* and Hallmark. Marya also penned a weekly humorous column for an online newsletter and writes custom poetry on request. She lives in the country with her husband. E-mail her at Akushla514@hotmail.com.

Loretta Morris is a retired special education teacher. She has been a member of the Naperville Writers Group since 2013 and has been published several times in their yearly anthology, *Rivulets*. Her story, "When Change Blew In," was published in *Chicken Soup for the Soul: Miracles & Divine Intervention*.

Alice Muschany's publications have appeared in numerous *Chicken Soup for the Soul* books, *Guideposts*, *Sasee*, Gloria Gaynor's *We Will Survive* and Erma Bombeck Writer's Workshop collection, *Laugh Out Loud*. She enjoys hiking, swimming, and gardening. Above all, she absolutely adores spending time with her precious grandchildren.

Linda O'Connell, a seasoned early childhood teacher from St. Louis, MO, is an accomplished freelance writer. She finds humor and inspiration in everyday situations and writes from her heart. Linda is a frequent contributor to the *Chicken Soup for the Soul* series. She blogs at https://lindaoconnell.blogspot.com.

Rachel Ollivant lives in Vancouver, WA with her husband David and their four children. When she's not writing, she enjoys reading, gardening, knitting, taking care of twenty-four houseplants, and leading a young-adult ministry at her church.

January Gordon Ornellas's work has been published in the *Los Angeles Times* and several *Chicken Soup for the Soul* books. Her most recent story is about a bear encounter in Alaska. Although the bear never consented to being written about, January feels he would enjoy the story. January writes a blog, "Midlife Bloomer", and is completing a book, *My Above Average Colon*.

Mary Oves is a Jersey native, adjunct English professor, and freelance writer. A widow with three grown sons, she was recently named the 2022 Grand Prize winner of the Humorist-in-Residence Erma Bombeck Writer's Residency. When not writing or teaching, Mary is satisfying her wanderlust through adventure travel.

Marie T. Palecek loves discovering profound insights in simple, everyday things. She shares these nuggets in her transformational devotional book, *Listen for His Voice*. Visit www.marietpalecek.com for information or a sneak peek inside. Marie lives in Minnesota and enjoys all four seasons outdoors with her family and dogs.

Sandi Parsons lives and breathes stories as a reader, writer, and storyteller. She lives with her favorite husband and two problem puppies.

Ree Pashley is an American ex-pat residing in Tanzania, East Africa. She holds degrees in criminal justice and social work and has a strange love for reading or editing legal documents. Ree is a freelance writer, a hiking enthusiast, and a mother to eight wonderful (but very loud) children.

Jenny Pavlovic, Ph.D. lives in Wisconsin with her dogs Herbie, Audrey, and Brighty, her cat Junipurr and pony Keanna. She loves walking dogs and ponies, gardening, swimming, and kayaking. Her books include *Pal the Pig's Best Day*, *8 State Hurricane Kate*, and *the Not Without My Dog Resource and Record Book*. She's training to be an equine assisted coach.

Ava Pennington is a freelance writer and speaker. She writes for nationally circulated magazines and is published in thirty-five anthologies, including twenty-seven *Chicken Soup for the Soul* books. Ava also authored *Reflections on the Names of God: A Devotional*, endorsed by Kay Arthur. Learn more at www.AvaPennington.com.

Sherm Perkins is a retired teacher from Ohio. In 2007, *Chicken Soup for the Child's Soul* published his short story "The Hill." Sherm is in the final draft phase of his first novel *Another Second Chance*. His Parkinson's disease progression is being slowed down by active exercise for the body and by writing for the mind.

As a writer and editor, **Sheri Radford** spends her days wrestling with commas, taming adjectives, and banishing adverbs. As the author of five silly books for kids, she spends her evenings playing, imagining, and creating. She lives in Vancouver with her husband and Chairman Meow, the world's most photogenic feline.

Mark Rickerby is a screenwriter and co-owner of Temple Gate Films. This is his thirtieth story published in the *Chicken Soup for the Soul* series. He is also a singer and voice actor. His greatest joys in life are his wife Claudia and daughters Emma and Marli. E-mail him at markrickerbyauthor@gmail.com.

Bill Rouhana is the CEO of Chicken Soup for the Soul. He is married to Amy Newmark, the Publisher and Editor-in-Chief of Chicken Soup for the Soul. They like to tell stories about each other. Their four children and five grandchildren just shake their heads.

Maureen Rubin is an Emeritus Professor of Journalism at California State University, Northridge. She worked in the Carter White House and Congress. She has a JD from Catholic University Law School, an

M.A. in Public Relations from University of Southern California and a B.S. in Journalism from Boston University.

Laurel L. Shannon is the pseudonym of a NW Ohio–based author who lives with her rescued Australian Terrier, along with three cats who staged a bloodless coup and now rule their portion of the world.

Since retiring from a career in adult education, **Marilyn Cohen Shapiro** is now writing down her family stories as well as the accounts of ordinary people with extraordinary lives. Read her blog at theregoesmyheart.me.

Christine M. Smith is retired and lives with her husband James in Oklahoma. She loves sharing stories about her friends, family, and sometimes even strangers, if she has an audience! Writing them for others to read is a perfect hobby! E-mail her at iluvmyfamilyxxx000@yahoo.com.

Reverend James L. Snyder is an award-winning author whose writings have appeared in over eighty periodicals and thirty books. He is recognized as an authority on the life and ministry of A. W. Tozer. His first book, *The Life of A. W. Tozer: In Pursuit of God*, won the Reader's Choice Award in 1992. Learn more at jamessnyderministries.com.

Gary Sprague lives in Maine with his family. His novels, including the *Joe Walker* series and the humorous *Lettahs From Maine* series, are available at amazon.com/author/garysprague. Connect with Gary on Facebook @garyspraguewriter.

Mary J. Staller is a member of the Florida Writers Association and co-founder of a critique group. Published in short stories, she is currently working on a novel. A volunteer judge of writing contests, Mary advocates for writers helping writers. For fun she'll grab her ukulele and head to the beach. Learn more at www.marystaller.com.

For decades, **Judy Stengel's** passion for writing has ignited her soul and brought joy to her and others. A retired reading teacher with a master's degree, Judy has led writing groups up north and now in Florida, where she can also be found on nature trails with her husband, expanding her spirituality and creativity.

Kathy Tharp Thompson is from Wichita, KS. A 1983 graduate of Wichita State University, Kathy enjoys traveling, reading, music, adventures and laughter and loves to write about the humorous side of life. Kathy and her husband Donald have a twenty-year-old son, Trenton.

Pat Wahler is a Missouri native and proud contributor to twenty previous titles in the *Chicken Soup for the Soul* series. She is the author of five novels written under the supervision of one bossy cat and a lively Pekingese-mix. Connect with Pat at www.PatWahler.com.

Dorann Weber is a freelance photographer who has a love for writing—especially writing for the *Chicken Soup for the Soul* series. She is a contributor for Getty Images and worked as a photojournalist. Her photos and verses have appeared on Hallmark cards. Dorann enjoys reading, hiking and spending time with her family.

Juliann Wetz is grateful for the wacky escapades of her family; it gives her lots of material to write about. Her work has previously appeared in *Highlights for Children*, *Child Life*, *German Life*, *Reading Today*, *Dog Fancy*, *Daughters Newsletter* and a host of others. Follow her at browsingtheatlas.com.

Lori Zenker is very grateful to the *Chicken Soup for the Soul* series for including another one of her stories—making this one her eleventh! She lives and writes about her life in small town Ontario. She lives in an old house that is almost an empty nest—because it's never really an empty nest until the kids take all their stuff!

Meet Amy Newmark

Amy Newmark is the bestselling author, editor-in-chief, and publisher of the *Chicken Soup for the Soul* book series. Since 2008, she has published 190 new books, most of them national bestsellers in the U.S. and Canada, more than doubling the number of Chicken Soup for the Soul titles in print today. She is also the author of *Simply Happy*, a crash course in Chicken Soup for the Soul advice and wisdom that is filled with easy-to-implement, practical tips for enjoying a better life.

Amy is credited with revitalizing the Chicken Soup for the Soul brand, which has been a publishing industry phenomenon since the first book came out in 1993. By compiling inspirational and aspirational true stories curated from ordinary people who have had extraordinary experiences, Amy has kept the thirty-year-old Chicken Soup for the Soul brand fresh and relevant.

Amy graduated *magna cum laude* from Harvard University where she majored in Portuguese and minored in French. She then embarked on a three-decade career as a Wall Street analyst, a hedge fund manager, and a corporate executive in the technology field. She is a Chartered Financial Analyst.

Her return to literary pursuits was inevitable, as her honors thesis in college involved traveling throughout Brazil's impoverished northeast region, collecting stories from regular people. She is delighted to have come full circle in her writing career — from collecting stories "from the people" in Brazil as a twenty-year-old to, three decades later, collecting stories "from the people" for Chicken Soup for the Soul.

When Amy and her husband Bill, the CEO of Chicken Soup for the Soul, are not working, they are visiting their four grown children and their spouses, and their five grandchildren.

Follow Amy on Twitter @amynewmark. Listen to her free podcast — Chicken Soup for the Soul with Amy Newmark — on Apple, Google, or by using your favorite podcast app on your phone.

Thank You

We owe huge thanks to all our contributors and fans. We received thousands of submissions for this popular topic, and we spent months reading all of them. Laura Dean, Maureen Peltier, and D'ette Corona read all of them and narrowed down the selection for Associate Publisher D'ette Corona and Publisher and Editor-in-Chief Amy Newmark. Susan Heim did the first round of editing, and then D'ette chose the perfect quotations to put at the beginning of each story and Amy edited the stories and shaped the final manuscript.

As we finished our work, D'ette continued to be Amy's right-hand woman in working with all our wonderful writers. Barbara LoMonaco, Kristiana Pastir and Elaine Kimbler jumped in to proof, proof, proof. And yes, there will always be typos anyway, so please feel free to let us know about them at webmaster@chickensoupforthesoul.com, and we will correct them in future printings.

The whole publishing team deserves a hand, including our Vice President of Marketing Maureen Peltier, our Vice President of Production Victor Cataldo, and our graphic designer Daniel Zaccari, who turned our manuscript into this beautiful, entertaining book.

Sharing Happiness, Inspiration, and Hope

Real people sharing real stories, every day, all over the world. In 2007, *USA Today* named *Chicken Soup for the Soul* one of the five most memorable books in the last quarter-century. With over 110 million books sold to date in the U.S. and Canada alone, more than 300 titles in print, and translations into nearly fifty languages, "chicken soup for the soul®" is one of the world's best-known phrases.

Today, thirty years after we first began sharing happiness, inspiration and hope through our books, we continue to delight our readers with new titles, but have also evolved beyond the bookshelves with super premium pet food, television shows, a podcast, video journalism from aplus.com, licensed products, and free movies and TV shows on our Crackle, Redbox, Popcornflix and Chicken Soup for the Soul streaming apps. We are busy "changing your life one story at a time®." Thanks for reading!

Share with Us

We all have had Chicken Soup for the Soul moments in our lives. If you would like to share your story or poem with millions of people around the world, go to chickensoup. com and click on Submit Your Story. You may be able to help another reader and become a published author at the same time. Some of our past contributors have launched writing and speaking careers from the publication of their stories in our books!

We only accept story submissions via our website. They are no longer accepted via mail or fax. Visit our website, www.chickensoup. com, and click on Submit Your Story for our writing guidelines and a list of topics we are working on.

To contact us regarding other matters, please send us an email through webmaster@chickensoupforthesoul.com, or write us at:

Chicken Soup for the Soul
P.O. Box 700
Cos Cob, CT 06807-0700

One more note from your friends at Chicken Soup for the Soul: Occasionally, we receive an unsolicited book manuscript from one of our readers, and we would like to respectfully inform you that we do not accept unsolicited manuscripts, and we must discard the ones that appear.

Paperback: 978-1-61159-089-0
eBook: 978-1-61159-327-3

More laughs and fun

Chicken Soup for the Soul

Read, Laugh, Repeat

101 Laugh-Out-Loud Stories

Amy Newmark

Paperback: 978-1-61159-075-3
eBook: 978-1-61159-315-0

to entertain the whole family

Chicken Soup for the Soul

My Wonderful, Wacky Family

101 Loving Stories about Our Crazy, Quirky Families

Amy Newmark

Paperback: 978-1-61159-097- 5
eBook: 978-1-61159-334-1

Fun and family

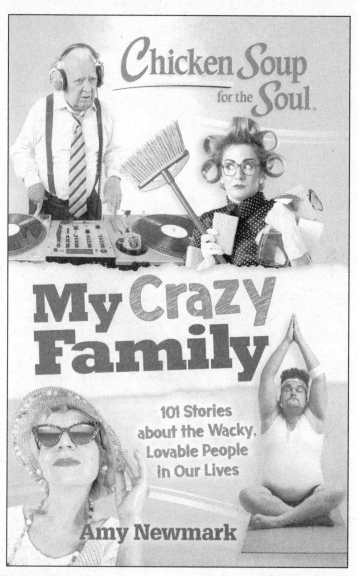

Paperback: 978-1-61159-997-0
eBook: 978-1-61159-277-1

to entertain you and yours

Changing your life one story at a time®
www.chickensoup.com